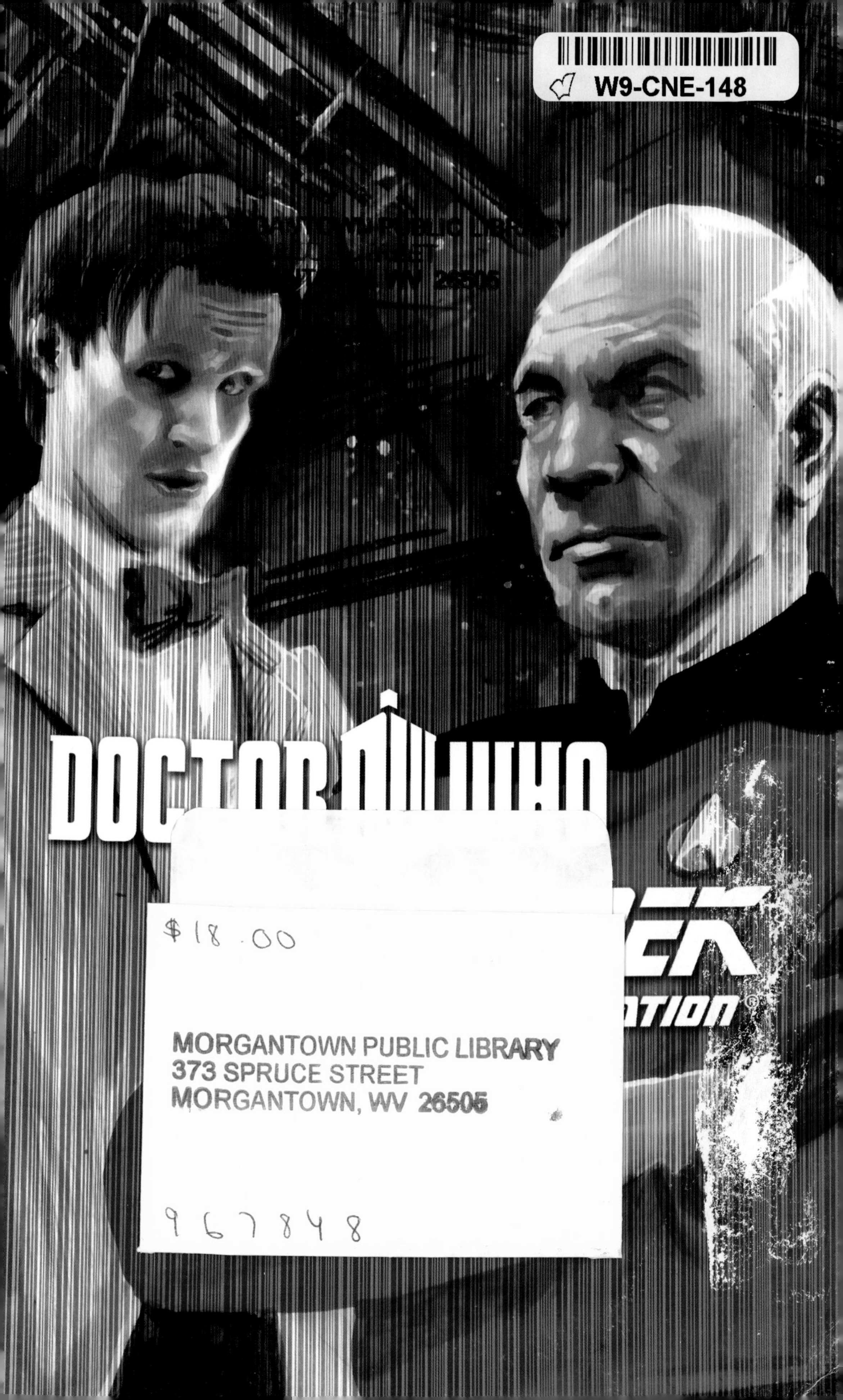
DOCTOR WHO

Written by **Scott & David Tipton** with **Tony Lee**

Art by **J.K. Woodward**

Additional Art by **The Sharp Bros.** (Issue #3) and
Gordon Purcell (Issue #4)

Letters by **Shawn Lee** and **Robbie Robbins**

Series Edits by **Denton J. Tipton**

Cover by **J.K. Woodward**

Collection Edits by **Justin Eisinger** and **Alonzo Simon**

Collection Design by **Robbie Robbins**

Special thanks to Risa Kessler and John Van Citters of CBS Consumer Products, and Kate Bush, Georgie Britton, Caroline Skinner, Denise Paul, and Ed Casey at BBC Worldwide for their invaluable assistance.

IDW founded by Ted Adams, Alex Garner, Kris Oprisko, and Robbie Robbins

ISBN: 978-1-61377-403-8

15 14 13 12   1 2 3 4

IDW®

Ted Adams, CEO & Publisher
Greg Goldstein, President & COO
Robbie Robbins, EVP/Sr. Graphic Artist
Chris Ryall, Chief Creative Officer/Editor-in-Chief
Matthew Ruzicka, CPA, Chief Financial Officer
Alan Payne, VP of Sales
Dirk Wood, VP of Marketing
Lorelei Bunjes, VP of Digital Services

Become our fan on Facebook **facebook.com/idwpublishing**
Follow us on Twitter **@idwpublishing**
Check us out on YouTube **youtube.com/idwpublishing**
www.IDWPUBLISHING.com

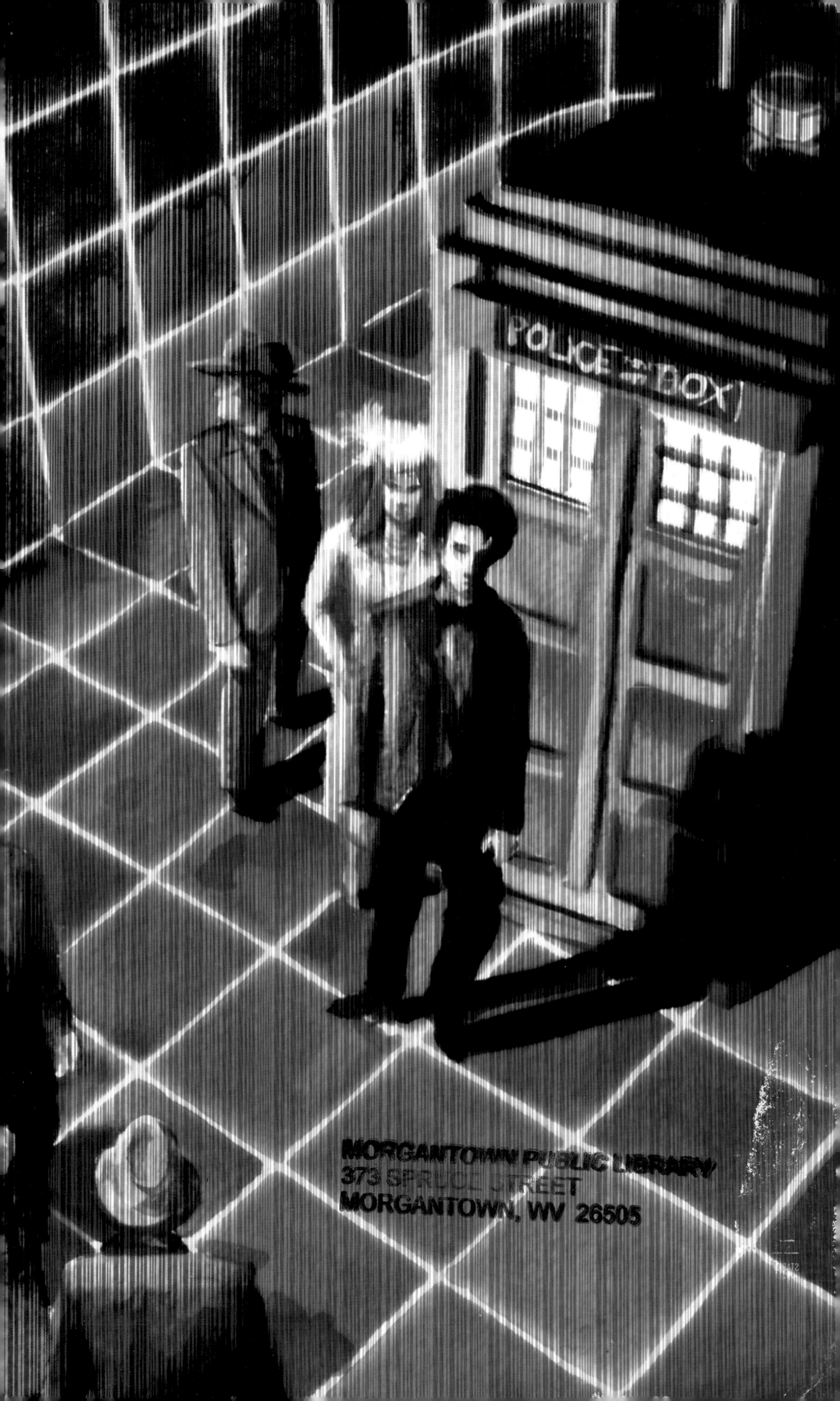
POLICE BOX

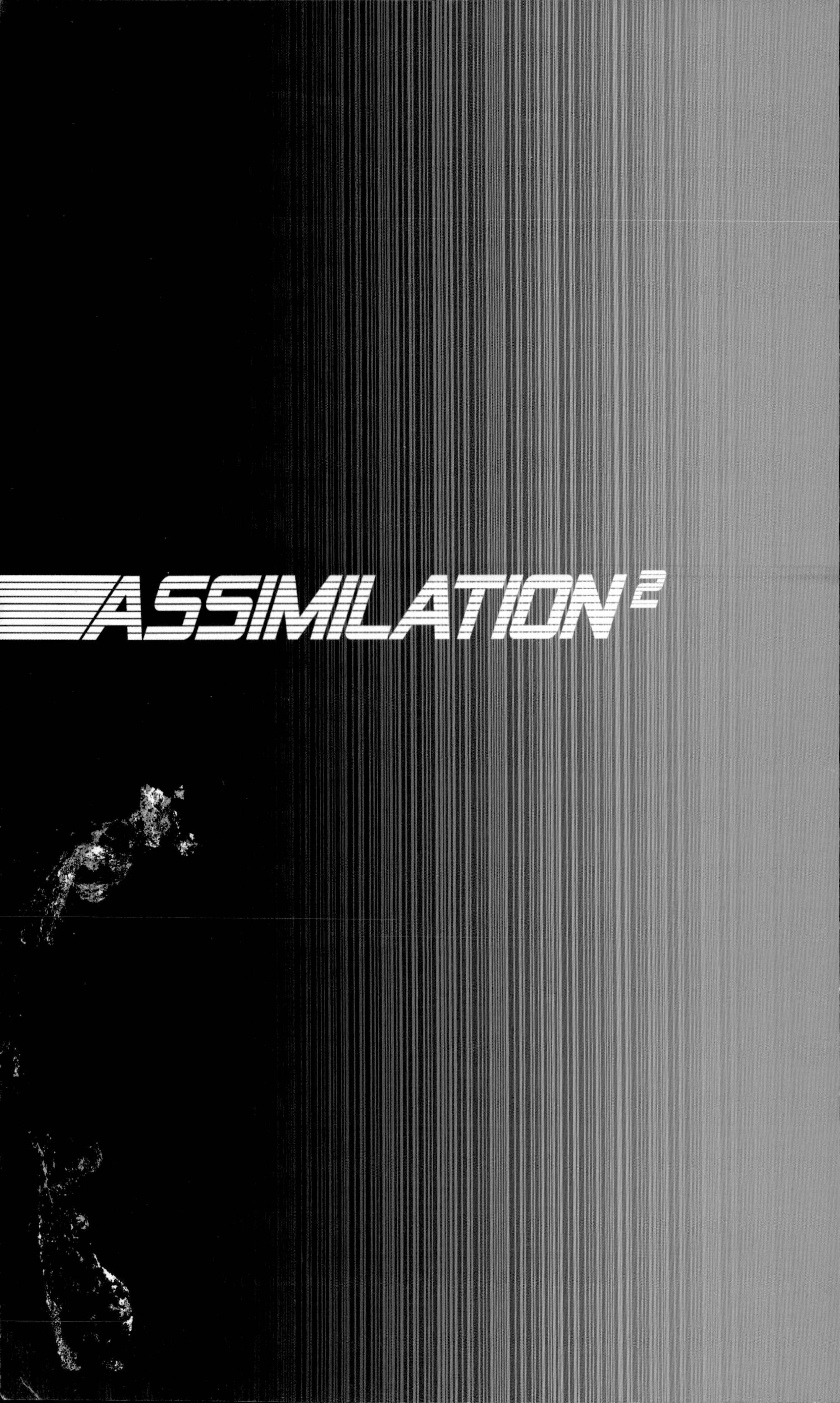
ASSIMILATION²

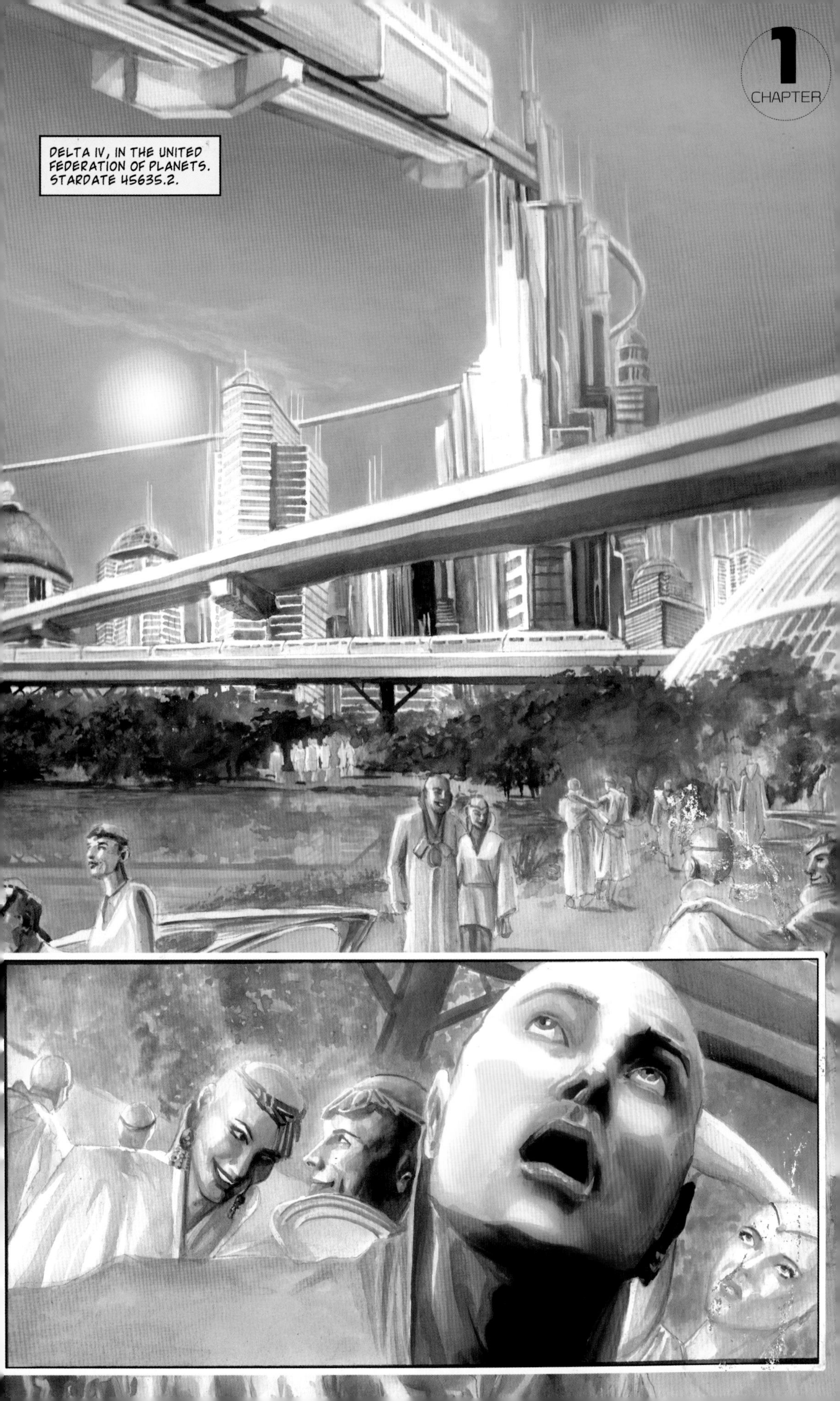
1
CHAPTER
DELTA IV, IN THE UNITED FEDERATION OF PLANETS. STARDATE 45635.2.

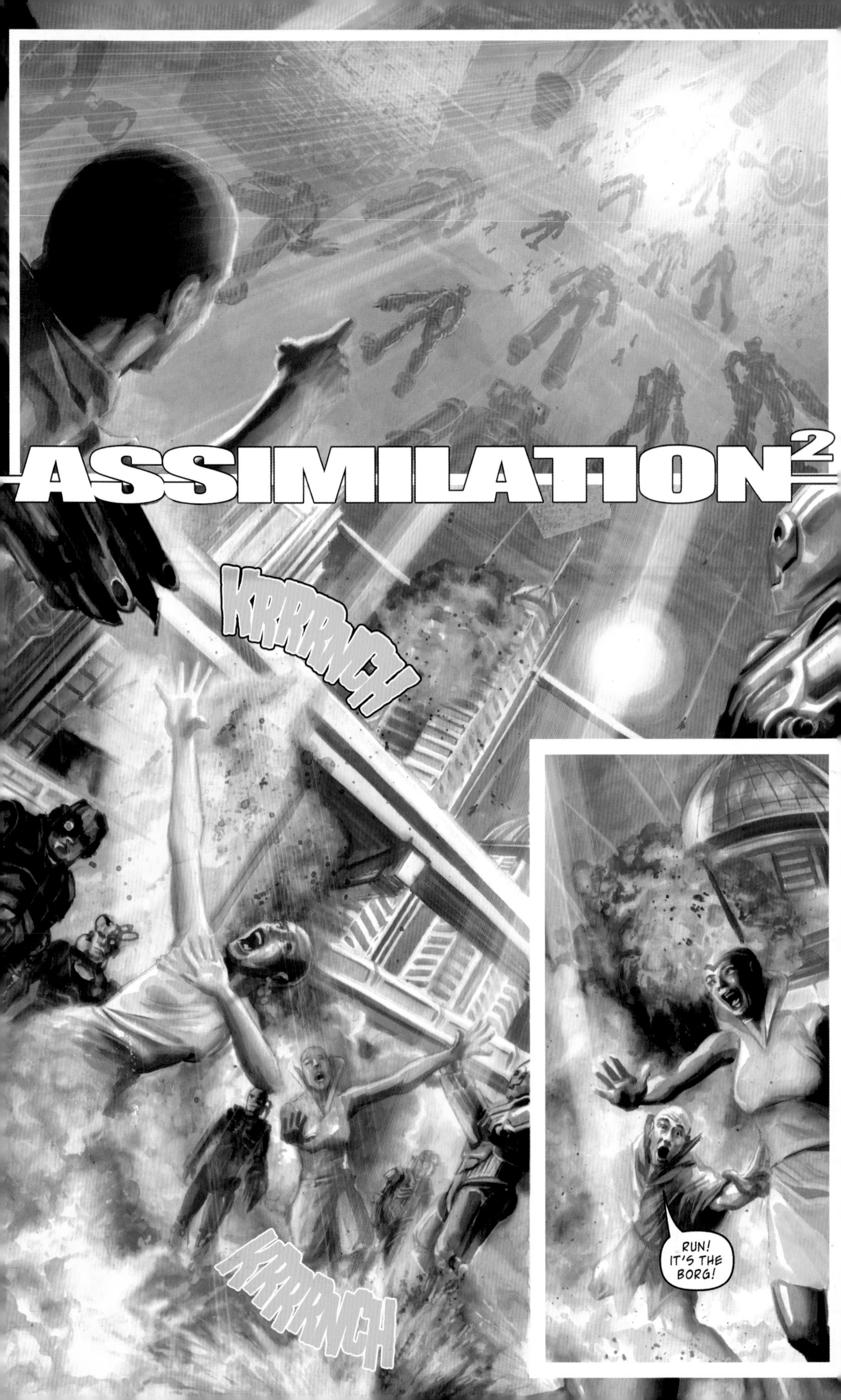
ASSIMILATION²
KRRRNCH
KRRRNCH
RUN! IT'S THE BORG!

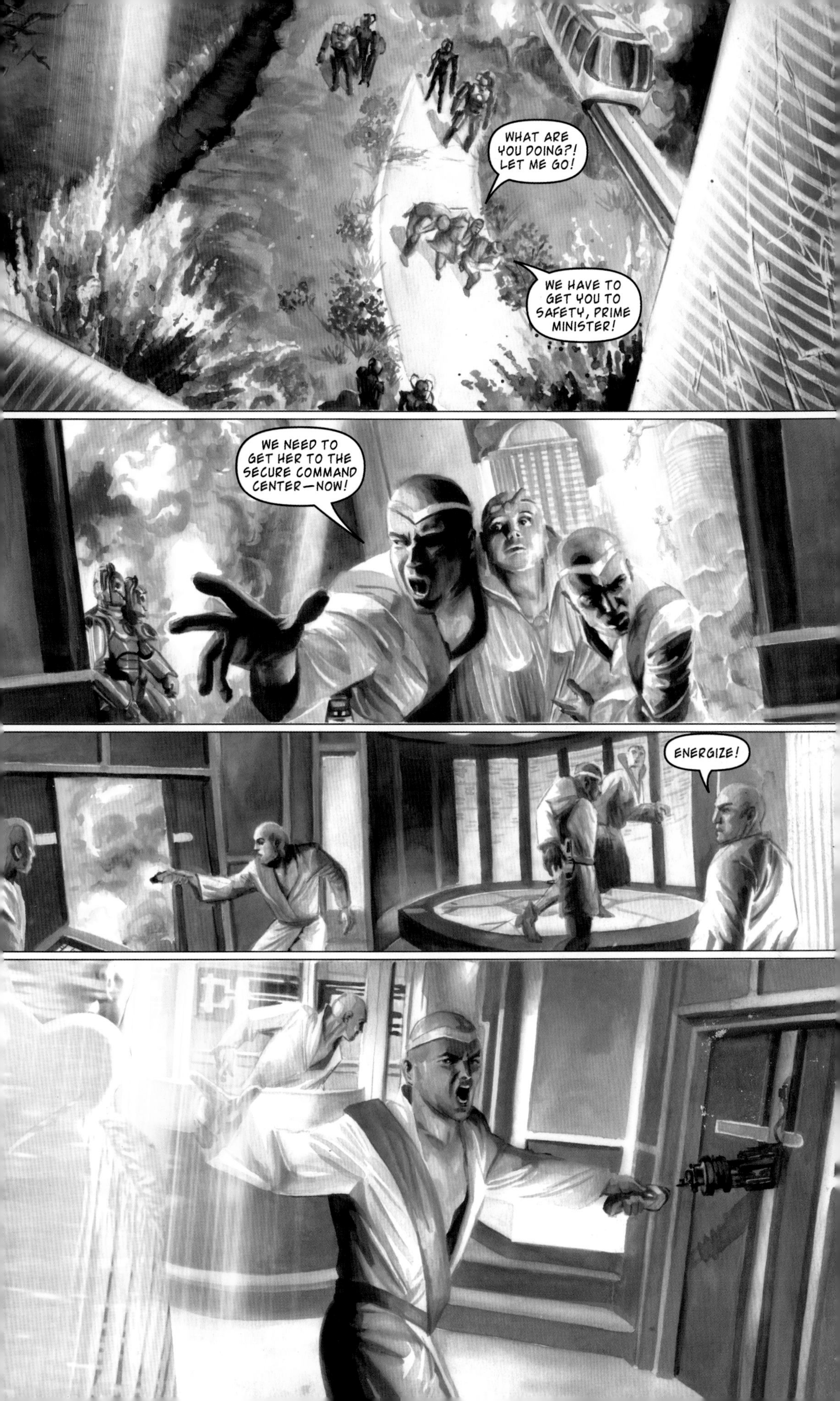
WHAT ARE YOU DOING?! LET ME GO!
WE HAVE TO GET YOU TO SAFETY, PRIME MINISTER!
WE NEED TO GET HER TO THE SECURE COMMAND CENTER—NOW!
ENERGIZE!

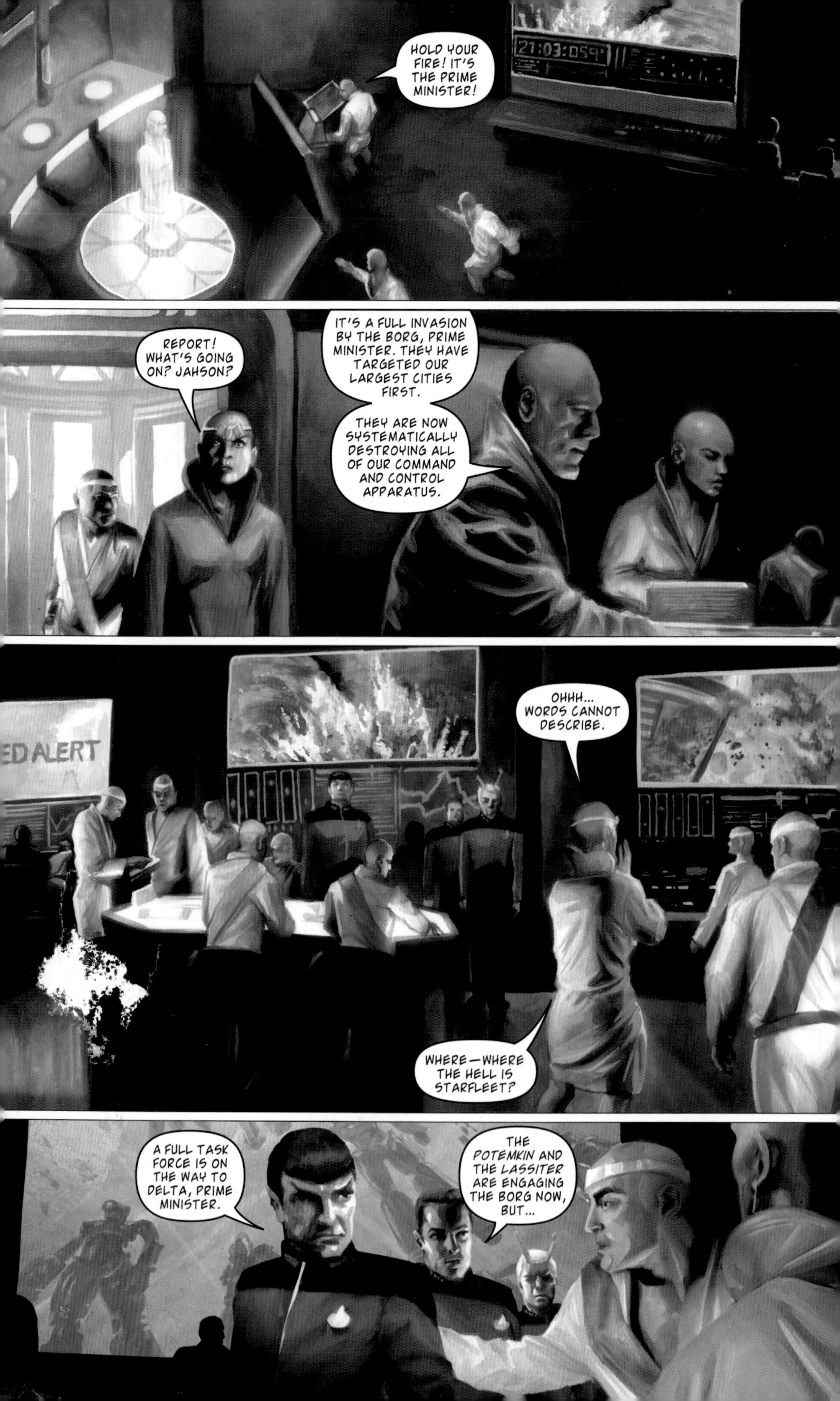
21:03:059
HOLD YOUR FIRE! IT'S THE PRIME MINISTER!
REPORT! WHAT'S GOING ON? JAHSON?
IT'S A FULL INVASION BY THE BORG, PRIME MINISTER. THEY HAVE TARGETED OUR LARGEST CITIES FIRST.
THEY ARE NOW SYSTEMATICALLY DESTROYING ALL OF OUR COMMAND AND CONTROL APPARATUS.
ED ALERT
OHHH... WORDS CANNOT DESCRIBE.
WHERE—WHERE THE HELL IS STARFLEET?
A FULL TASK FORCE IS ON THE WAY TO DELTA, PRIME MINISTER.
THE *POTEMKIN* AND THE *LASSITER* ARE ENGAGING THE BORG NOW, BUT...

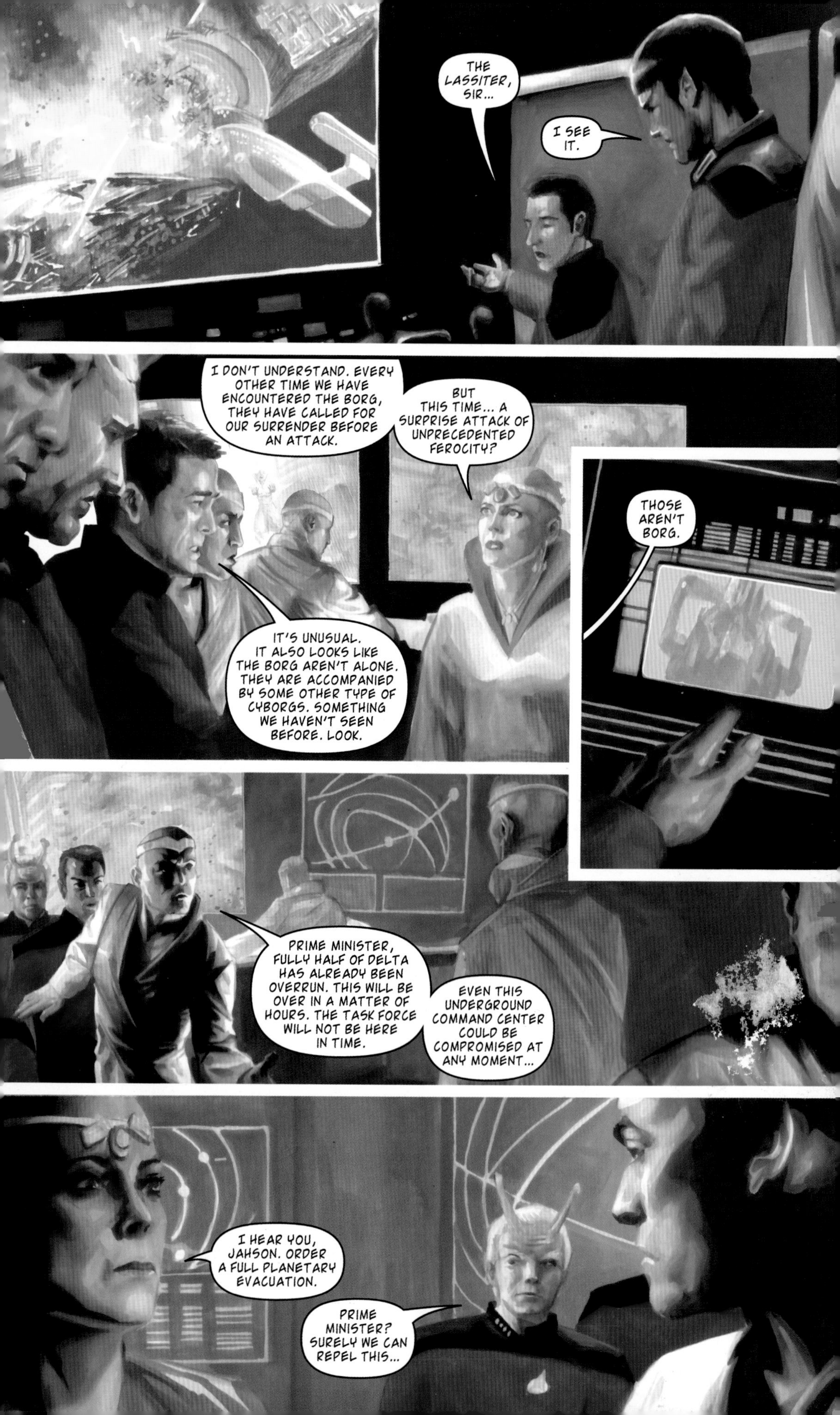
THE LASSITER, SIR...
I SEE IT.
I DON'T UNDERSTAND. EVERY OTHER TIME WE HAVE ENCOUNTERED THE BORG, THEY HAVE CALLED FOR OUR SURRENDER BEFORE AN ATTACK.
BUT THIS TIME... A SURPRISE ATTACK OF UNPRECEDENTED FEROCITY?
IT'S UNUSUAL. IT ALSO LOOKS LIKE THE BORG AREN'T ALONE. THEY ARE ACCOMPANIED BY SOME OTHER TYPE OF CYBORGS. SOMETHING WE HAVEN'T SEEN BEFORE. LOOK.
THOSE AREN'T BORG.
PRIME MINISTER, FULLY HALF OF DELTA HAS ALREADY BEEN OVERRUN. THIS WILL BE OVER IN A MATTER OF HOURS. THE TASK FORCE WILL NOT BE HERE IN TIME.
EVEN THIS UNDERGROUND COMMAND CENTER COULD BE COMPROMISED AT ANY MOMENT...
I HEAR YOU, JAHSON. ORDER A FULL PLANETARY EVACUATION.
PRIME MINISTER? SURELY WE CAN REPEL THIS...

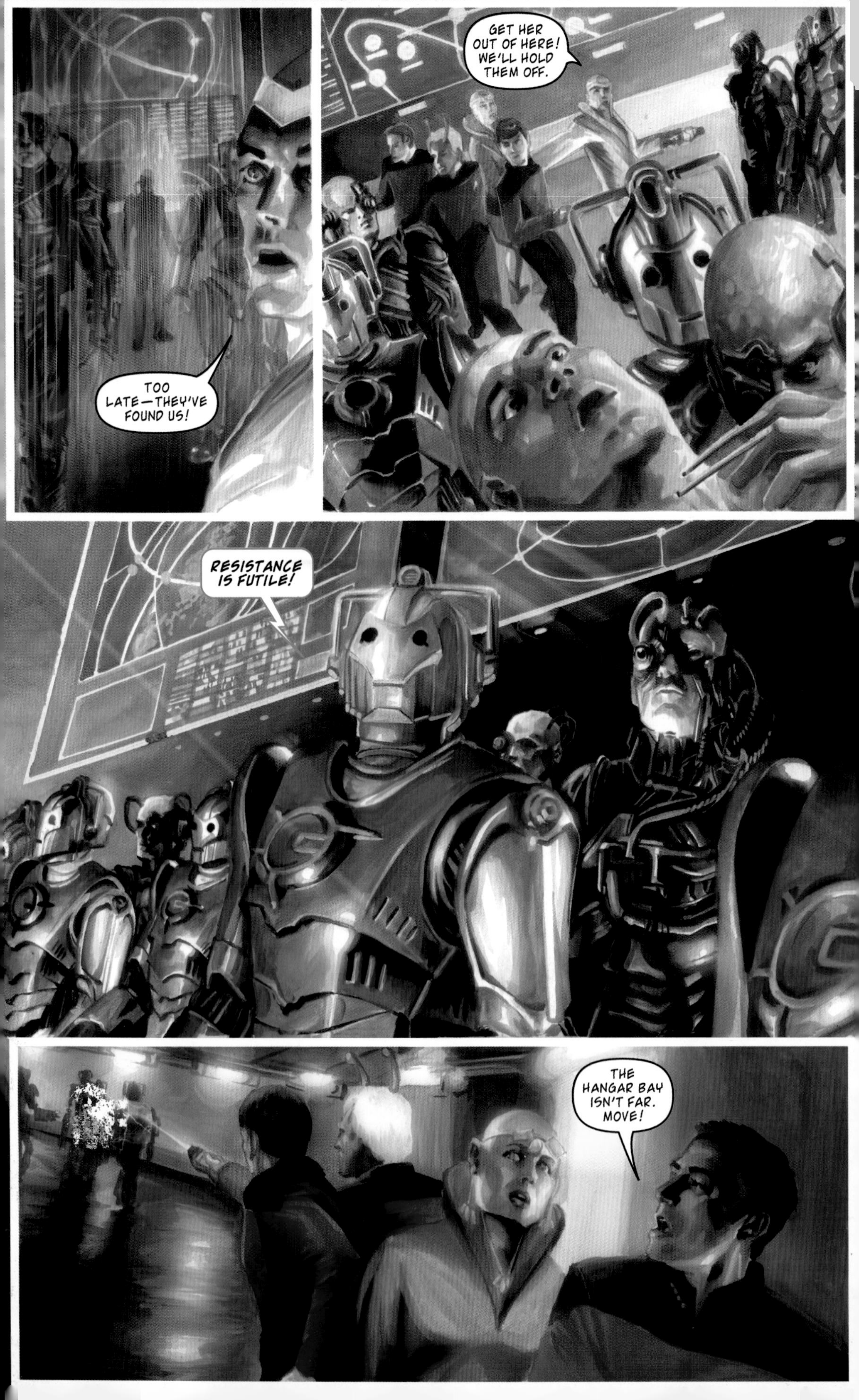
TOO LATE—THEY'VE FOUND US!
GET HER OUT OF HERE! WE'LL HOLD THEM OFF.
RESISTANCE IS FUTILE!
THE HANGAR BAY ISN'T FAR. MOVE!

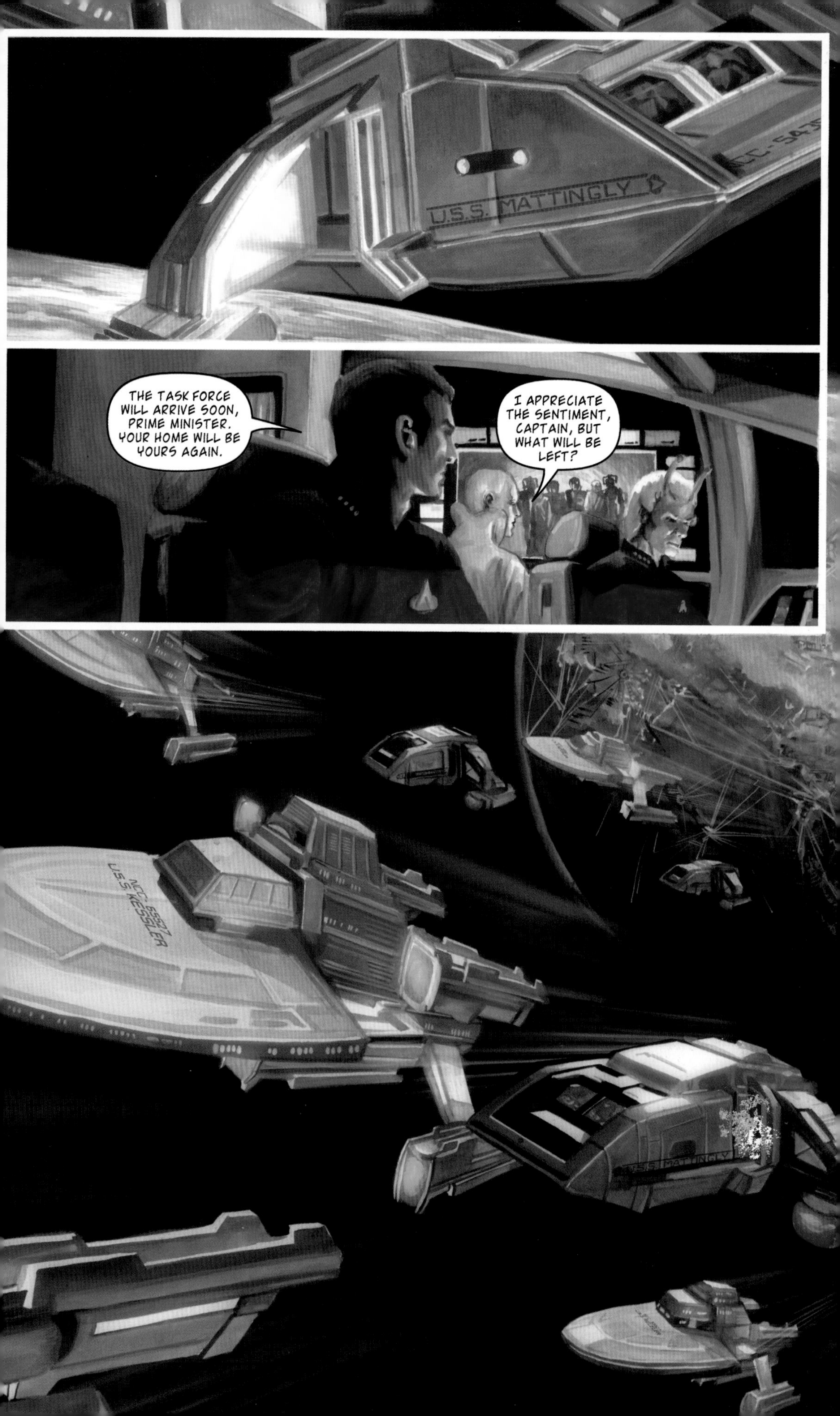
U.S.S. MATTINGLY
THE TASK FORCE WILL ARRIVE SOON, PRIME MINISTER. YOUR HOME WILL BE YOURS AGAIN.
I APPRECIATE THE SENTIMENT, CAPTAIN, BUT WHAT WILL BE LEFT?
NCC-65537 U.S.S. KESSLER
U.S.S. MATTINGLY

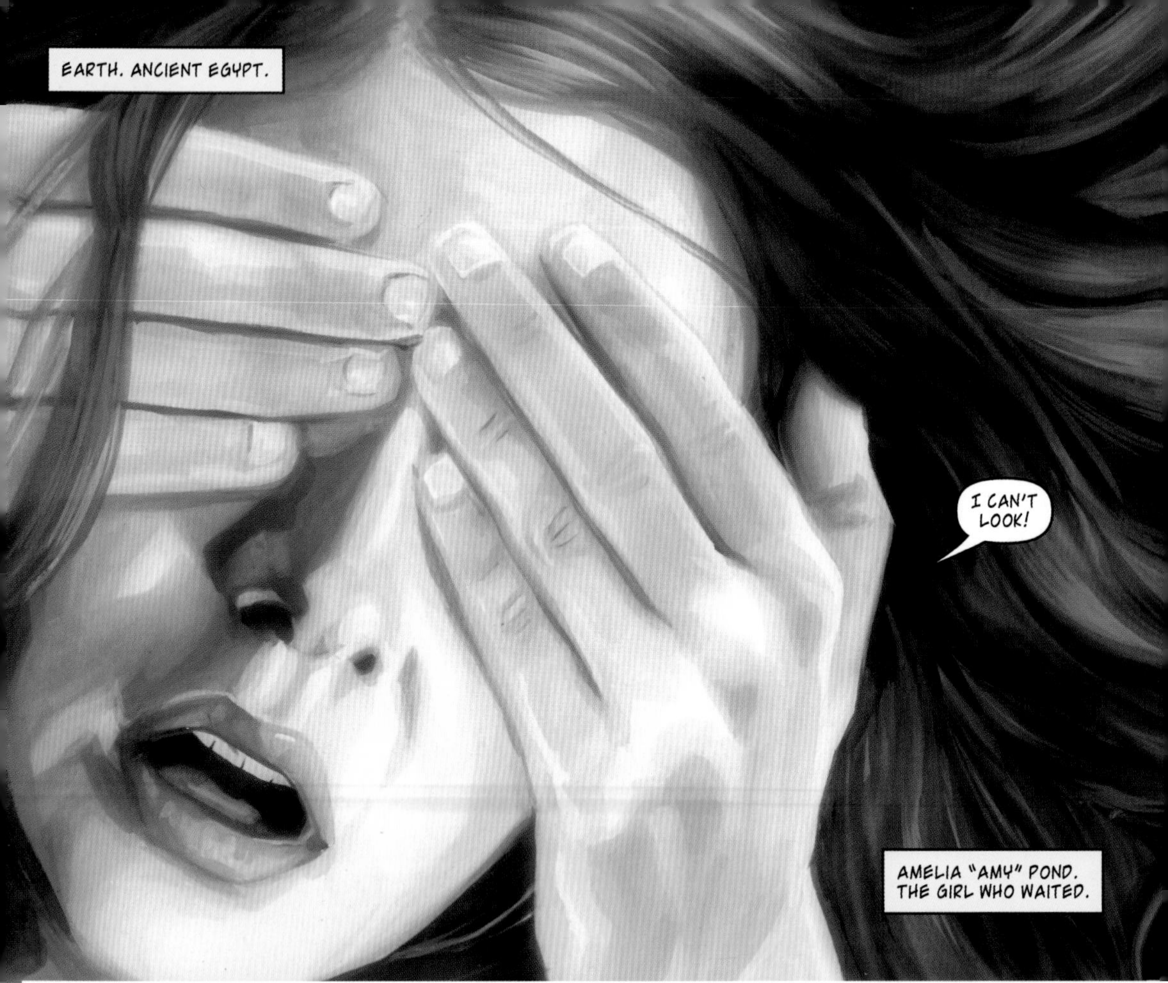
EARTH. ANCIENT EGYPT.
I CAN'T LOOK!
AMELIA "AMY" POND. THE GIRL WHO WAITED.
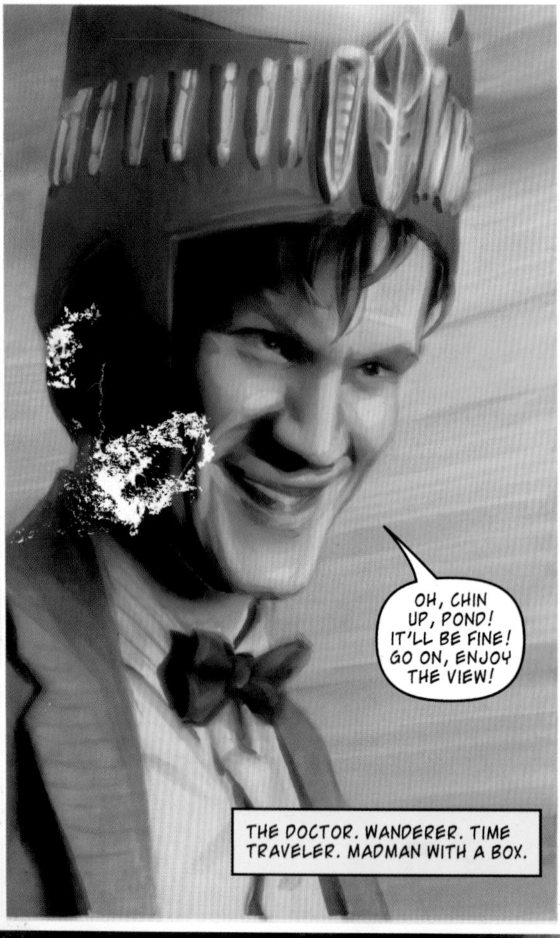
OH, CHIN UP, POND! IT'LL BE FINE! GO ON, ENJOY THE VIEW!
THE DOCTOR. WANDERER. TIME TRAVELER. MADMAN WITH A BOX.
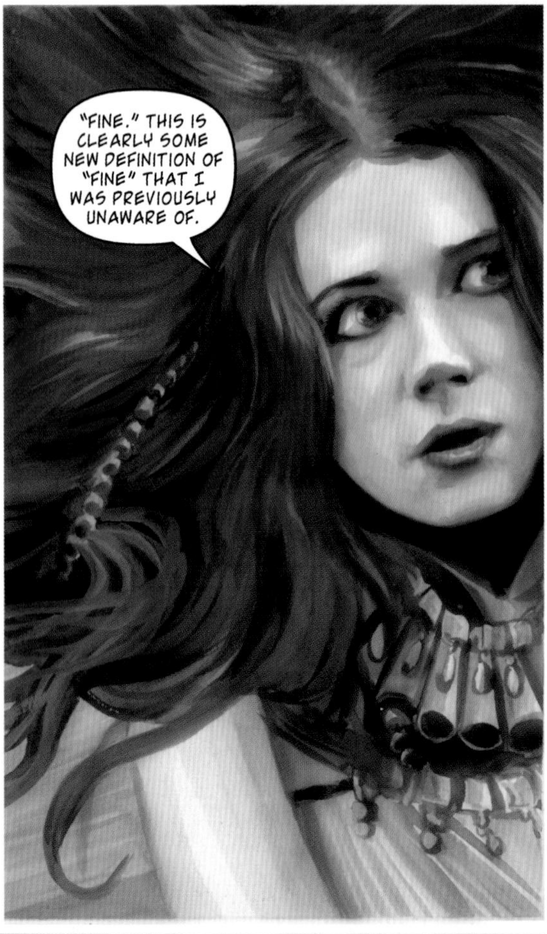
"FINE." THIS IS CLEARLY SOME NEW DEFINITION OF "FINE" THAT I WAS PREVIOUSLY UNAWARE OF.

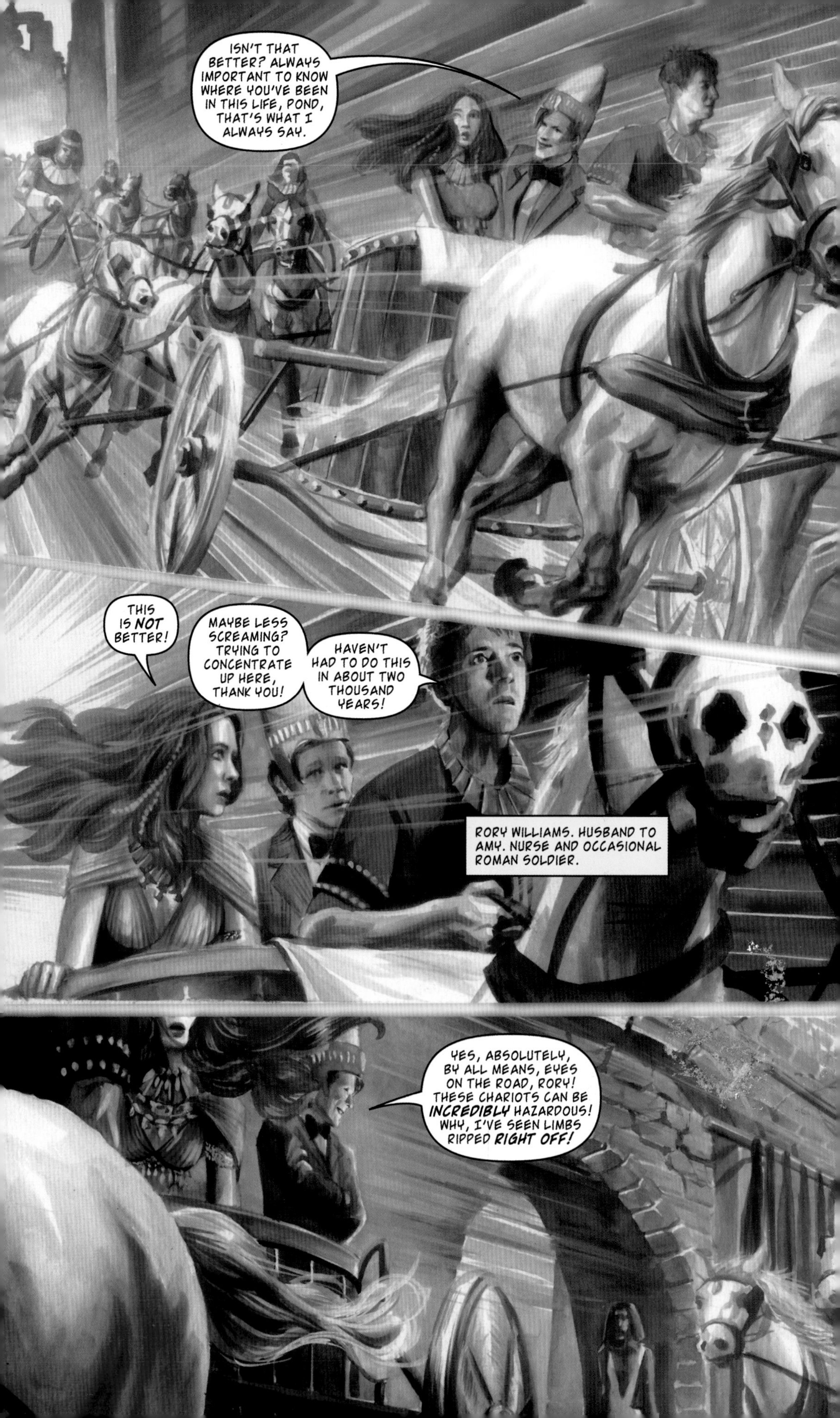
ISN'T THAT BETTER? ALWAYS IMPORTANT TO KNOW WHERE YOU'VE BEEN IN THIS LIFE, POND, THAT'S WHAT I ALWAYS SAY.
THIS IS **NOT** BETTER!
MAYBE LESS SCREAMING? TRYING TO CONCENTRATE UP HERE, THANK YOU!
HAVEN'T HAD TO DO THIS IN ABOUT TWO THOUSAND YEARS!
RORY WILLIAMS. HUSBAND TO AMY. NURSE AND OCCASIONAL ROMAN SOLDIER.
YES, ABSOLUTELY, BY ALL MEANS, EYES ON THE ROAD, RORY! THESE CHARIOTS CAN BE ***INCREDIBLY*** HAZARDOUS! WHY, I'VE SEEN LIMBS RIPPED ***RIGHT OFF!***

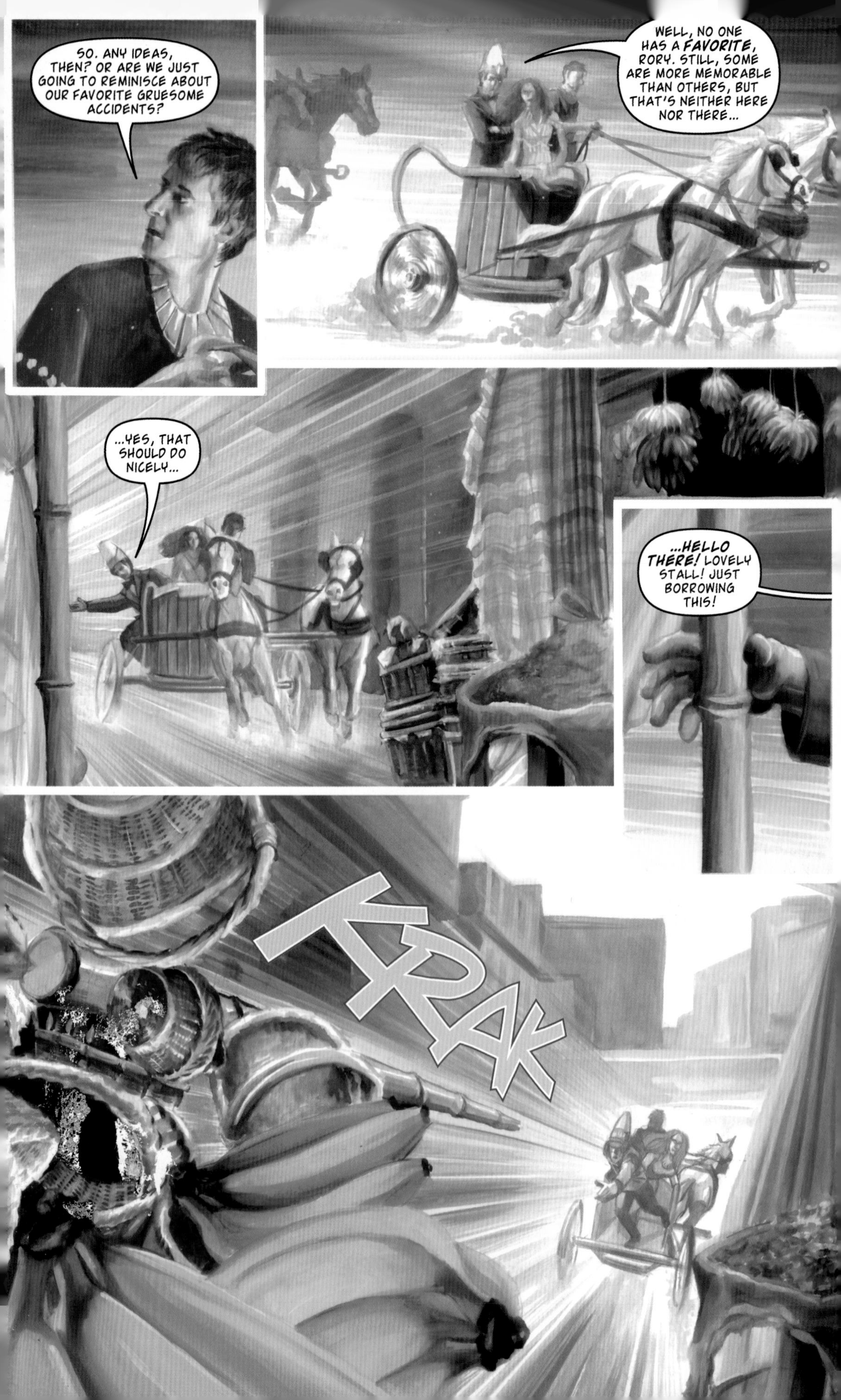
SO. ANY IDEAS, THEN? OR ARE WE JUST GOING TO REMINISCE ABOUT OUR FAVORITE GRUESOME ACCIDENTS?
WELL, NO ONE HAS A FAVORITE, RORY. STILL, SOME ARE MORE MEMORABLE THAN OTHERS, BUT THAT'S NEITHER HERE NOR THERE...
...YES, THAT SHOULD DO NICELY...
...HELLO THERE! LOVELY STALL! JUST BORROWING THIS!
KRAK

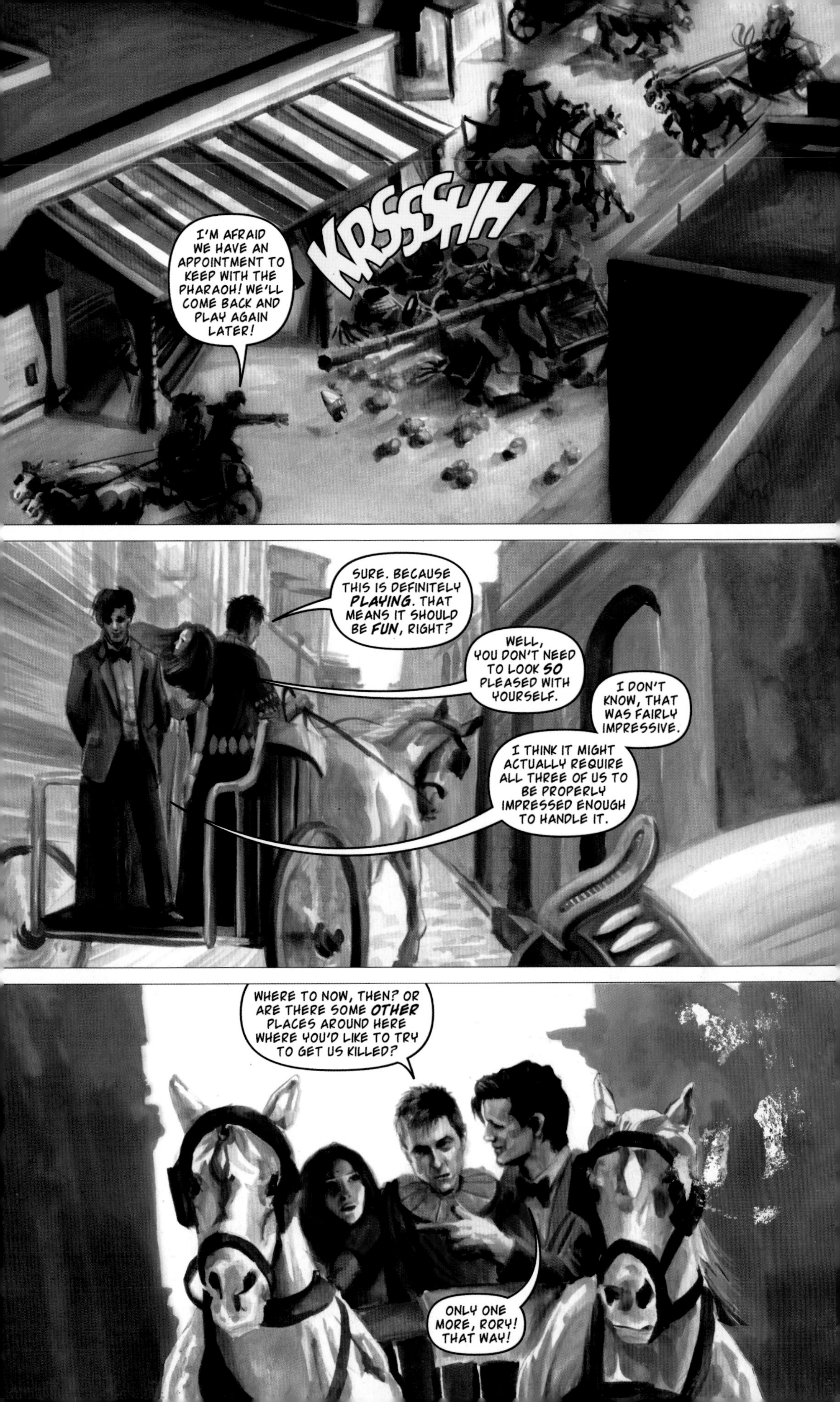
KRSSSHH
I'M AFRAID WE HAVE AN APPOINTMENT TO KEEP WITH THE PHARAOH! WE'LL COME BACK AND PLAY AGAIN LATER!
SURE. BECAUSE THIS IS DEFINITELY PLAYING. THAT MEANS IT SHOULD BE FUN, RIGHT?
WELL, YOU DON'T NEED TO LOOK SO PLEASED WITH YOURSELF.
I DON'T KNOW, THAT WAS FAIRLY IMPRESSIVE.
I THINK IT MIGHT ACTUALLY REQUIRE ALL THREE OF US TO BE PROPERLY IMPRESSED ENOUGH TO HANDLE IT.
WHERE TO NOW, THEN? OR ARE THERE SOME OTHER PLACES AROUND HERE WHERE YOU'D LIKE TO TRY TO GET US KILLED?
ONLY ONE MORE, RORY! THAT WAY!

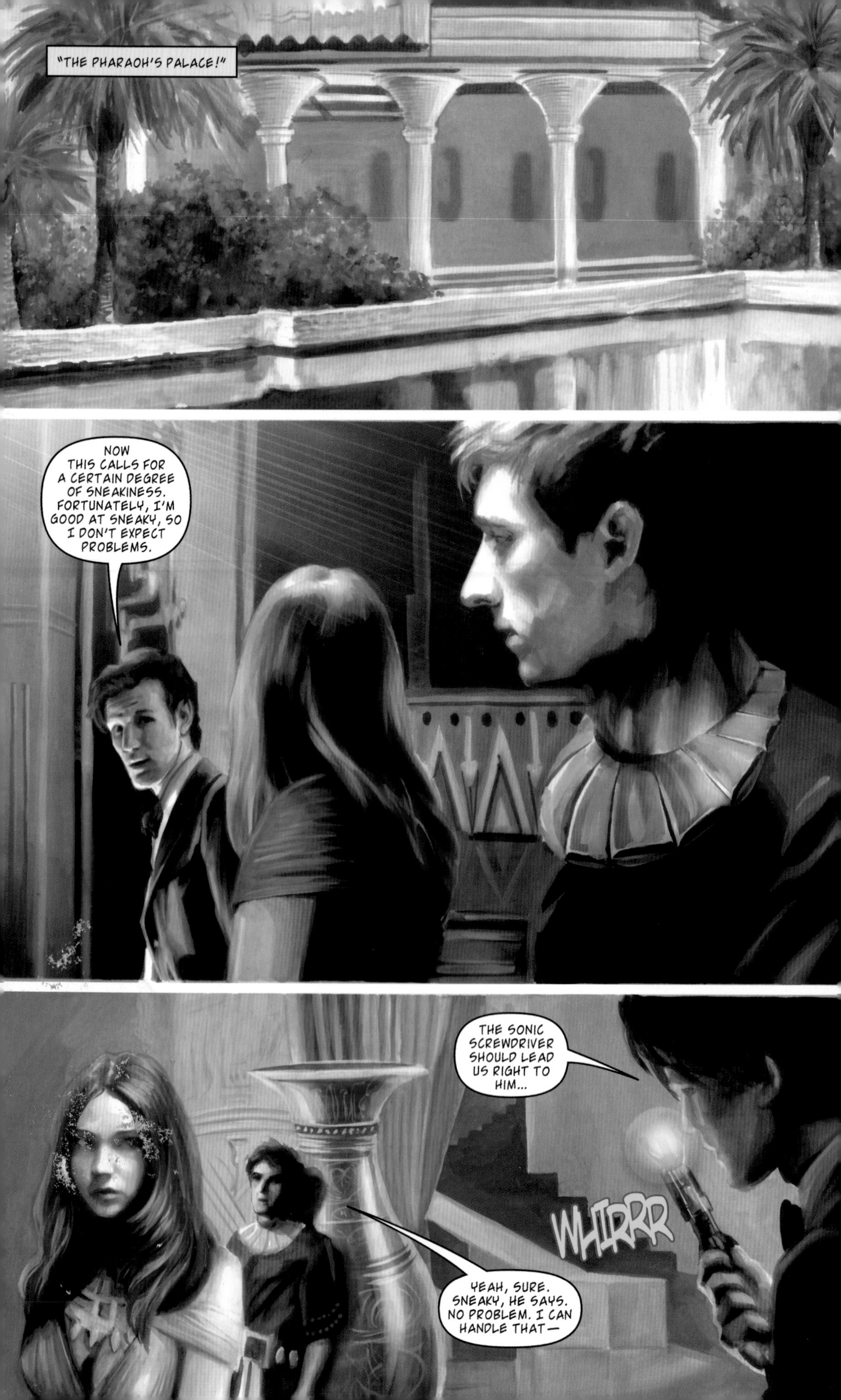
"THE PHARAOH'S PALACE!"
NOW THIS CALLS FOR A CERTAIN DEGREE OF SNEAKINESS. FORTUNATELY, I'M GOOD AT SNEAKY, SO I DON'T EXPECT PROBLEMS.
THE SONIC SCREWDRIVER SHOULD LEAD US RIGHT TO HIM...
WHIRRR
YEAH, SURE. SNEAKY, HE SAYS. NO PROBLEM. I CAN HANDLE THAT—

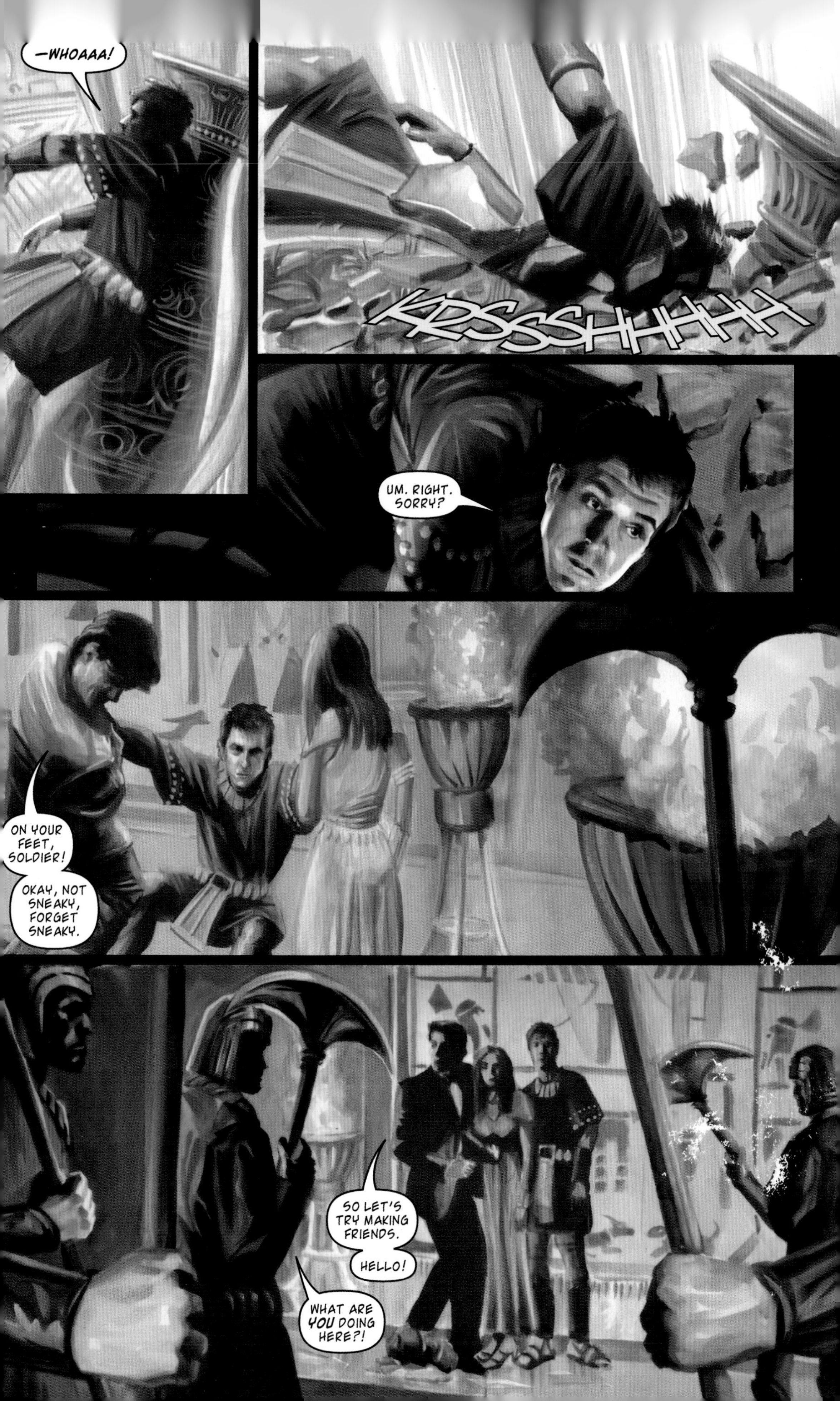
—WHOAAA!
KRSSSHHHHH
UM. RIGHT. SORRY?
ON YOUR FEET, SOLDIER!
OKAY, NOT SNEAKY, FORGET SNEAKY.
SO LET'S TRY MAKING FRIENDS.
HELLO!
WHAT ARE YOU DOING HERE?!

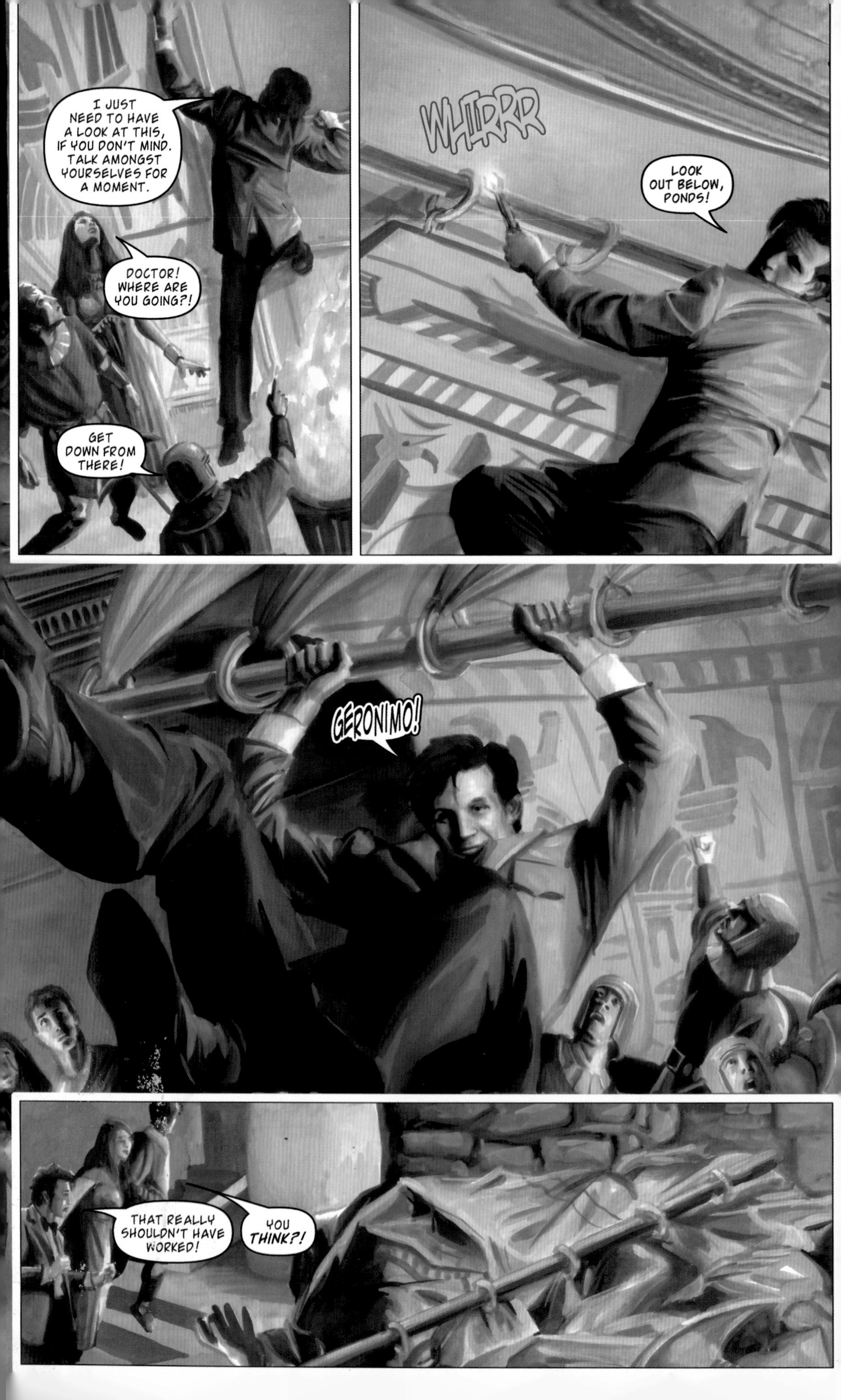
I JUST NEED TO HAVE A LOOK AT THIS, IF YOU DON'T MIND. TALK AMONGST YOURSELVES FOR A MOMENT.
DOCTOR! WHERE ARE YOU GOING?!
GET DOWN FROM THERE!
WHIRR
LOOK OUT BELOW, PONDS!
GERONIMO!
THAT REALLY SHOULDN'T HAVE WORKED!
YOU *THINK?!*

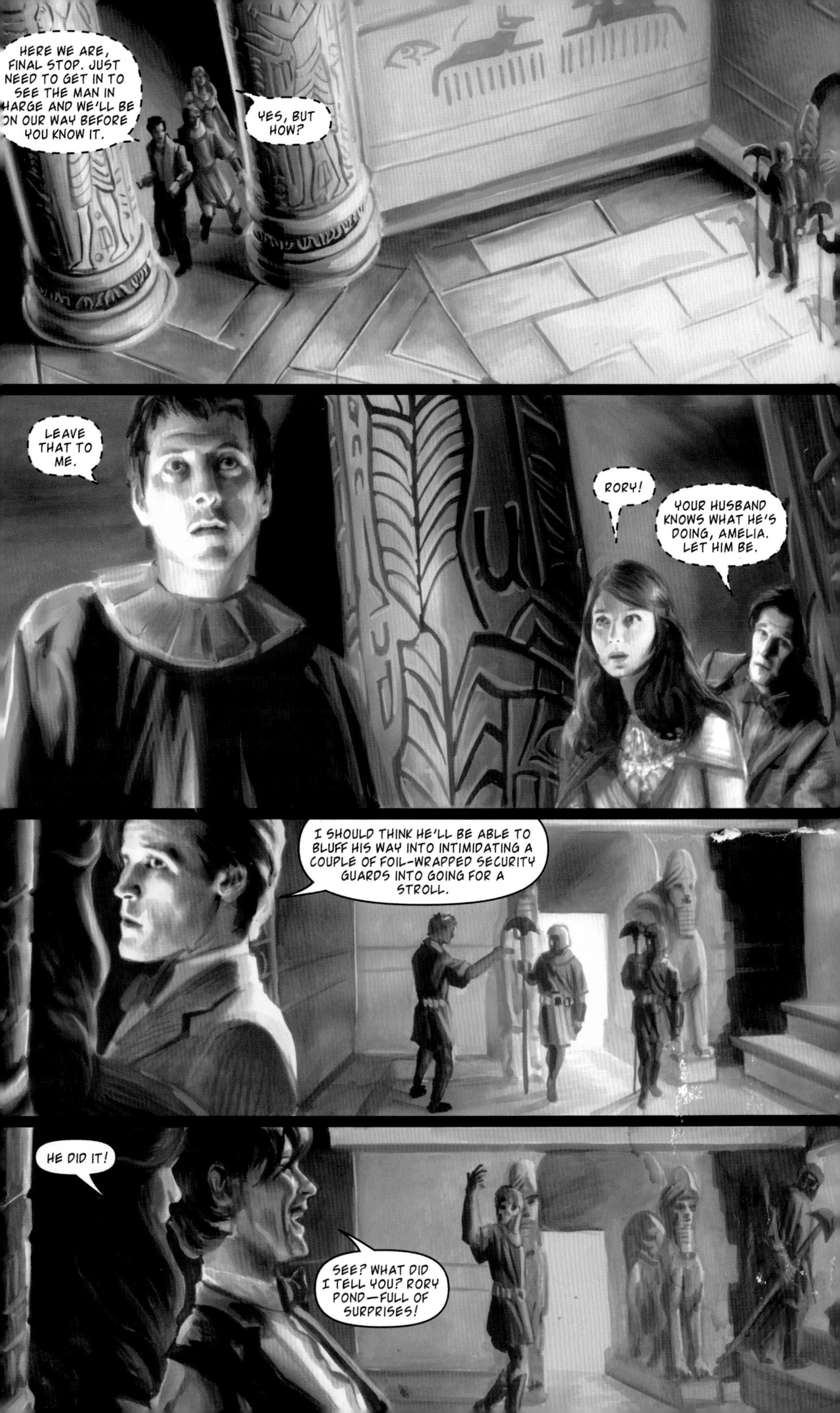

HERE WE ARE, FINAL STOP. JUST NEED TO GET IN TO SEE THE MAN IN CHARGE AND WE'LL BE ON OUR WAY BEFORE YOU KNOW IT.
YES, BUT HOW?
LEAVE THAT TO ME.
RORY!
YOUR HUSBAND KNOWS WHAT HE'S DOING, AMELIA. LET HIM BE.
I SHOULD THINK HE'LL BE ABLE TO BLUFF HIS WAY INTO INTIMIDATING A COUPLE OF FOIL-WRAPPED SECURITY GUARDS INTO GOING FOR A STROLL.
HE DID IT!
SEE? WHAT DID I TELL YOU? RORY POND—FULL OF SURPRISES!

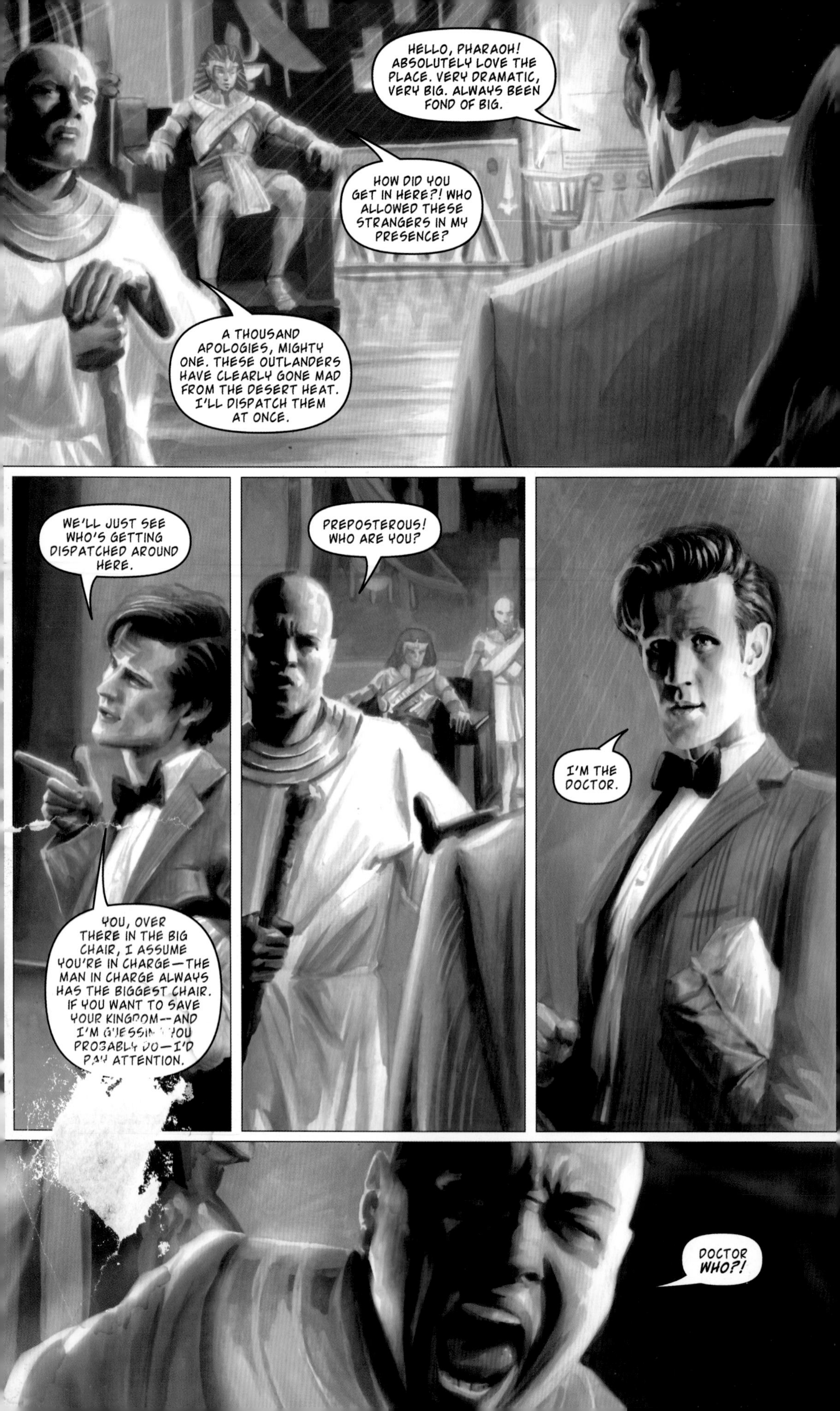

HELLO, PHARAOH! ABSOLUTELY LOVE THE PLACE. VERY DRAMATIC, VERY BIG. ALWAYS BEEN FOND OF BIG.
HOW DID YOU GET IN HERE?! WHO ALLOWED THESE STRANGERS IN MY PRESENCE?
A THOUSAND APOLOGIES, MIGHTY ONE. THESE OUTLANDERS HAVE CLEARLY GONE MAD FROM THE DESERT HEAT. I'LL DISPATCH THEM AT ONCE.
WE'LL JUST SEE WHO'S GETTING DISPATCHED AROUND HERE.
YOU, OVER THERE IN THE BIG CHAIR, I ASSUME YOU'RE IN CHARGE—THE MAN IN CHARGE ALWAYS HAS THE BIGGEST CHAIR. IF YOU WANT TO SAVE YOUR KINGDOM--AND I'M GUESSIN' YOU PROBABLY DO—I'D PAY ATTENTION.
PREPOSTEROUS! WHO ARE YOU?
I'M THE DOCTOR.
DOCTOR **WHO?!**

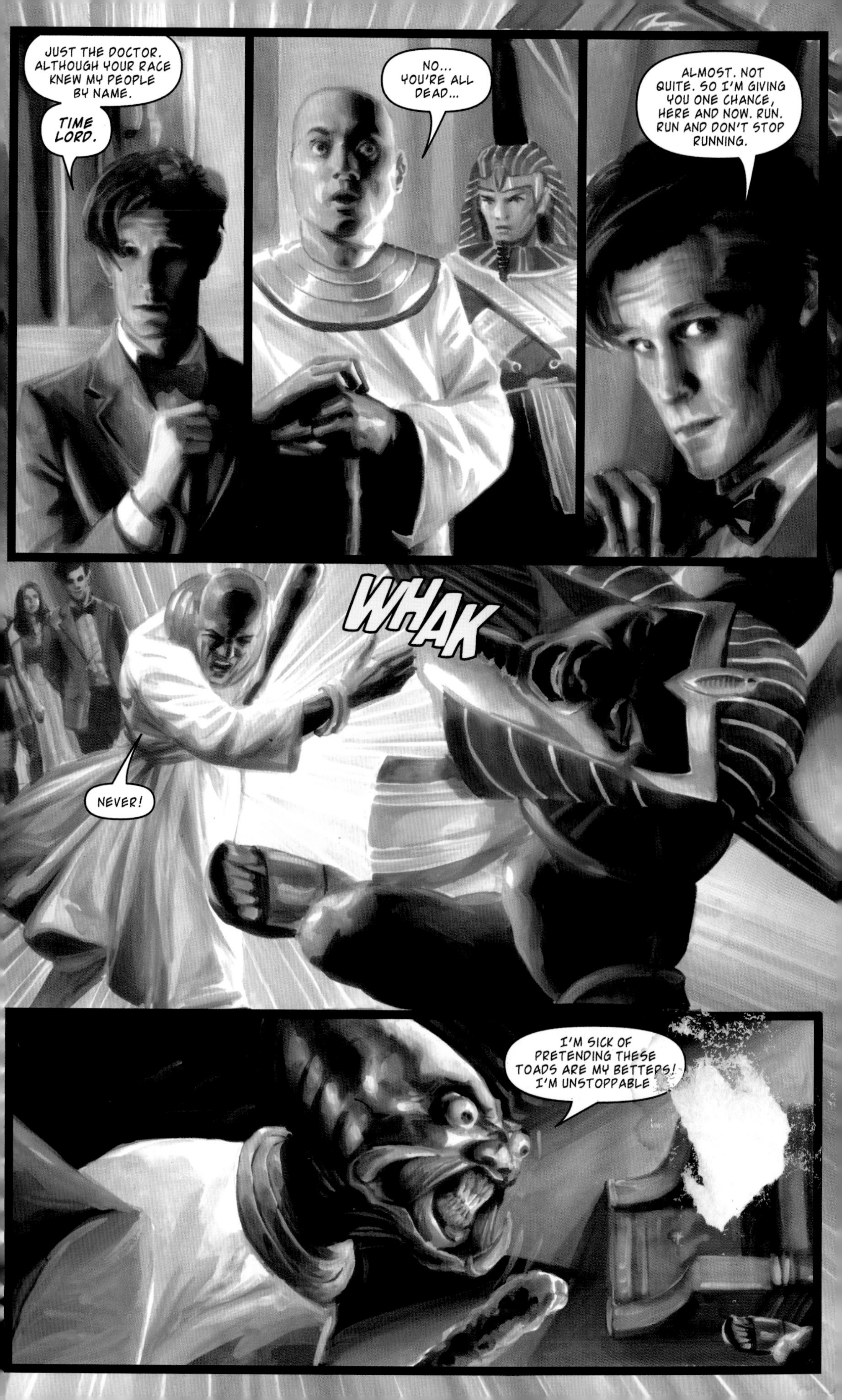
JUST THE DOCTOR. ALTHOUGH YOUR RACE KNEW MY PEOPLE BY NAME.
TIME LORD.
NO... YOU'RE ALL DEAD...
ALMOST. NOT QUITE. SO I'M GIVING YOU ONE CHANCE, HERE AND NOW. RUN. RUN AND DON'T STOP RUNNING.
WHAK
NEVER!
I'M SICK OF PRETENDING THESE TOADS ARE MY BETTERS! I'M UNSTOPPABLE

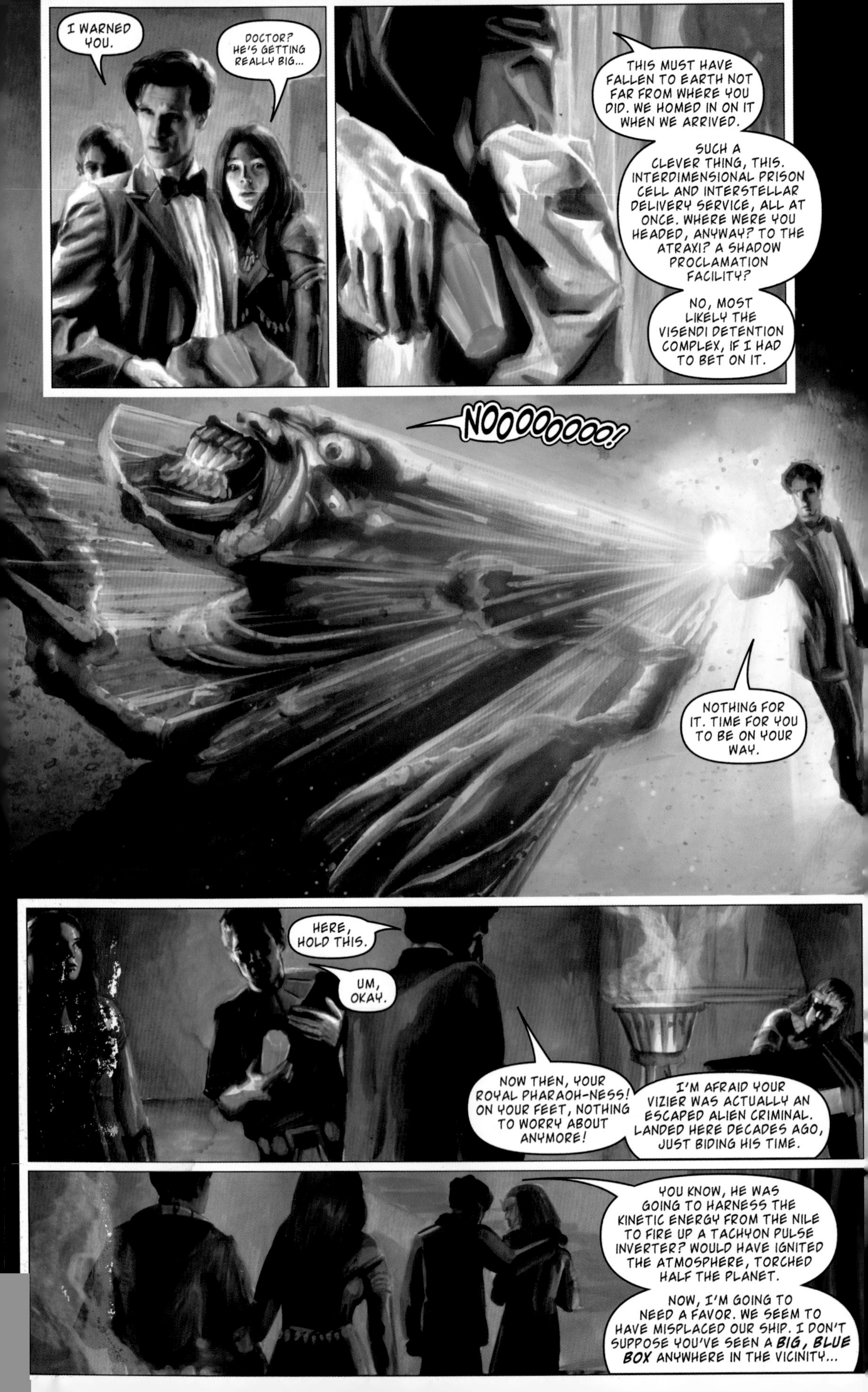

I WARNED YOU.
DOCTOR? HE'S GETTING REALLY BIG...
THIS MUST HAVE FALLEN TO EARTH NOT FAR FROM WHERE YOU DID. WE HOMED IN ON IT WHEN WE ARRIVED.
SUCH A CLEVER THING, THIS. INTERDIMENSIONAL PRISON CELL AND INTERSTELLAR DELIVERY SERVICE, ALL AT ONCE. WHERE WERE YOU HEADED, ANYWAY? TO THE ATRAXI? A SHADOW PROCLAMATION FACILITY?
NO, MOST LIKELY THE VISENDI DETENTION COMPLEX, IF I HAD TO BET ON IT.
NOOOOOOOO!
NOTHING FOR IT. TIME FOR YOU TO BE ON YOUR WAY.
HERE, HOLD THIS.
UM, OKAY.
NOW THEN, YOUR ROYAL PHARAOH-NESS! ON YOUR FEET, NOTHING TO WORRY ABOUT ANYMORE!
I'M AFRAID YOUR VIZIER WAS ACTUALLY AN ESCAPED ALIEN CRIMINAL. LANDED HERE DECADES AGO, JUST BIDING HIS TIME.
YOU KNOW, HE WAS GOING TO HARNESS THE KINETIC ENERGY FROM THE NILE TO FIRE UP A TACHYON PULSE INVERTER? WOULD HAVE IGNITED THE ATMOSPHERE, TORCHED HALF THE PLANET.
NOW, I'M GOING TO NEED A FAVOR. WE SEEM TO HAVE MISPLACED OUR SHIP. I DON'T SUPPOSE YOU'VE SEEN A ***BIG, BLUE BOX*** ANYWHERE IN THE VICINITY...

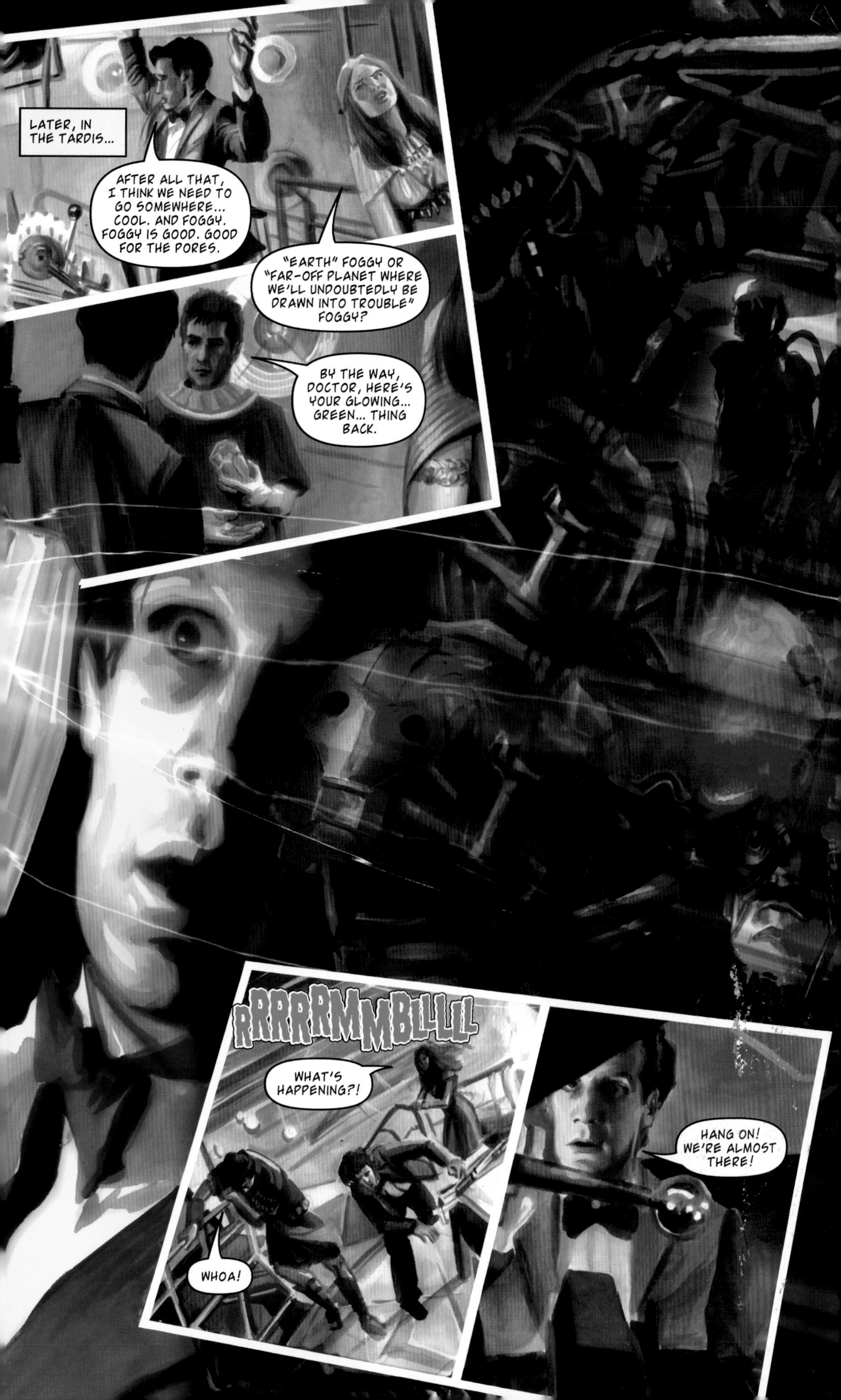
LATER, IN THE TARDIS...
AFTER ALL THAT, I THINK WE NEED TO GO SOMEWHERE... COOL. AND FOGGY. FOGGY IS GOOD. GOOD FOR THE PORES.
"EARTH" FOGGY OR "FAR-OFF PLANET WHERE WE'LL UNDOUBTEDLY BE DRAWN INTO TROUBLE" FOGGY?
BY THE WAY, DOCTOR, HERE'S YOUR GLOWING... GREEN... THING BACK.
RRRRRMMBLLLL
WHAT'S HAPPENING?!
WHOA!
HANG ON! WE'RE ALMOST THERE!

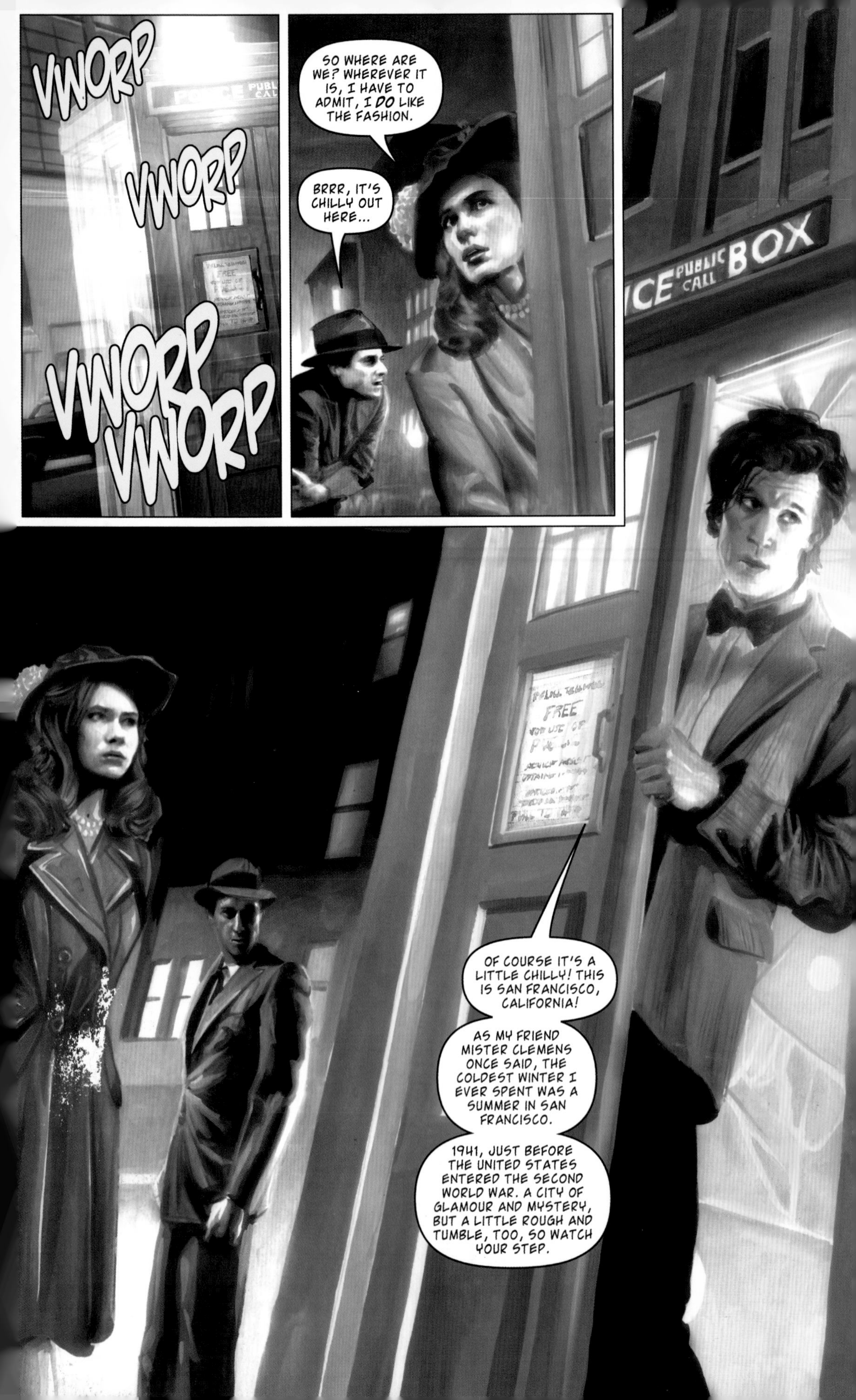
VWORP
VWORP
VWORP
VWORP
POLICE PUBLIC CALL
SO WHERE ARE WE? WHEREVER IT IS, I HAVE TO ADMIT, I DO LIKE THE FASHION.
BRRR, IT'S CHILLY OUT HERE...
POLICE PUBLIC CALL BOX
FREE
OF COURSE IT'S A LITTLE CHILLY! THIS IS SAN FRANCISCO, CALIFORNIA!
AS MY FRIEND MISTER CLEMENS ONCE SAID, THE COLDEST WINTER I EVER SPENT WAS A SUMMER IN SAN FRANCISCO.
1941, JUST BEFORE THE UNITED STATES ENTERED THE SECOND WORLD WAR. A CITY OF GLAMOUR AND MYSTERY, BUT A LITTLE ROUGH AND TUMBLE, TOO, SO WATCH YOUR STEP.

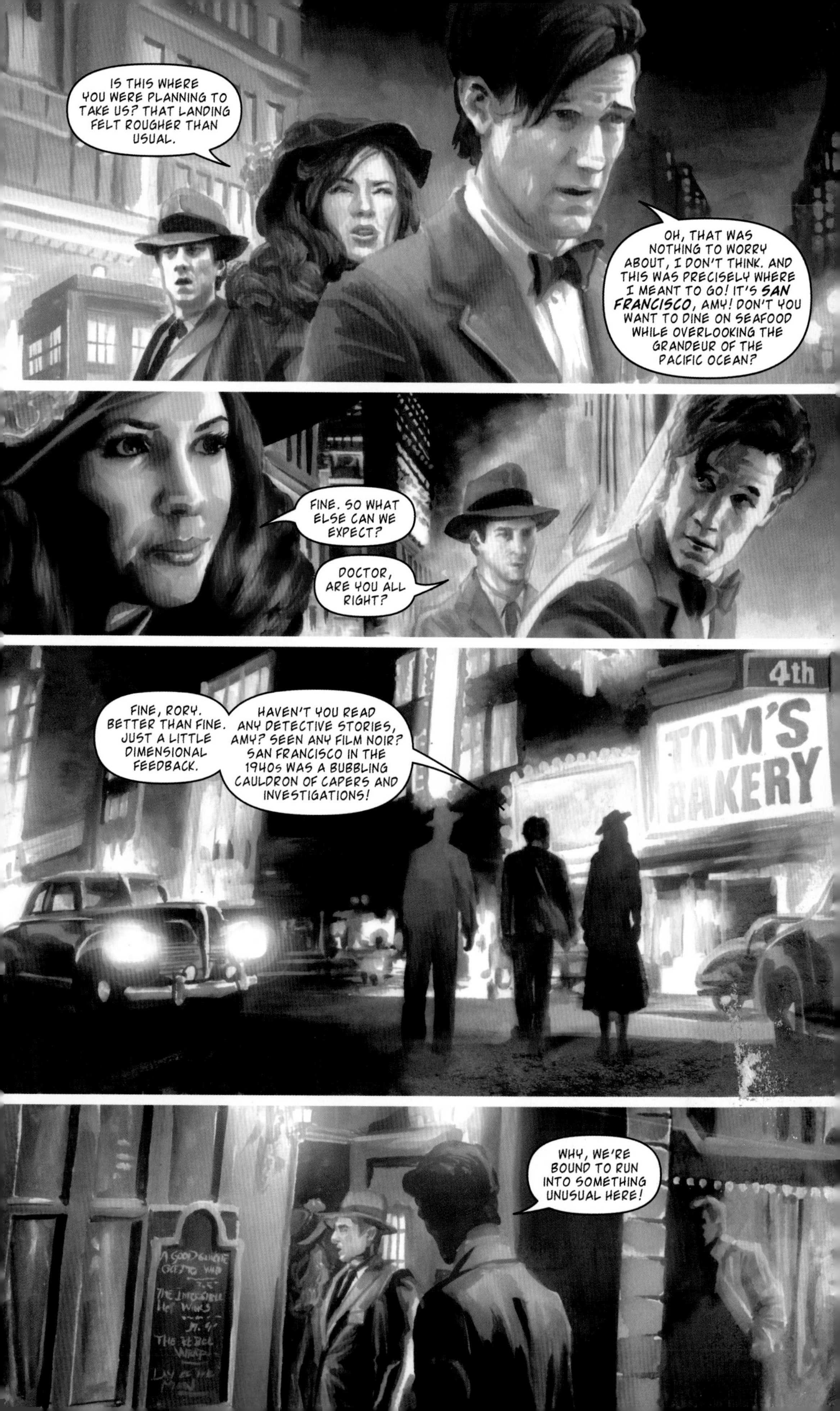
IS THIS WHERE YOU WERE PLANNING TO TAKE US? THAT LANDING FELT ROUGHER THAN USUAL.
OH, THAT WAS NOTHING TO WORRY ABOUT, I DON'T THINK. AND THIS WAS PRECISELY WHERE I MEANT TO GO! IT'S SAN FRANCISCO, AMY! DON'T YOU WANT TO DINE ON SEAFOOD WHILE OVERLOOKING THE GRANDEUR OF THE PACIFIC OCEAN?
FINE. SO WHAT ELSE CAN WE EXPECT?
DOCTOR, ARE YOU ALL RIGHT?
4th
TOM'S BAKERY
FINE, RORY. BETTER THAN FINE. JUST A LITTLE DIMENSIONAL FEEDBACK.
HAVEN'T YOU READ ANY DETECTIVE STORIES, AMY? SEEN ANY FILM NOIR? SAN FRANCISCO IN THE 1940s WAS A BUBBLING CAULDRON OF CAPERS AND INVESTIGATIONS!
WHY, WE'RE BOUND TO RUN INTO SOMETHING UNUSUAL HERE!

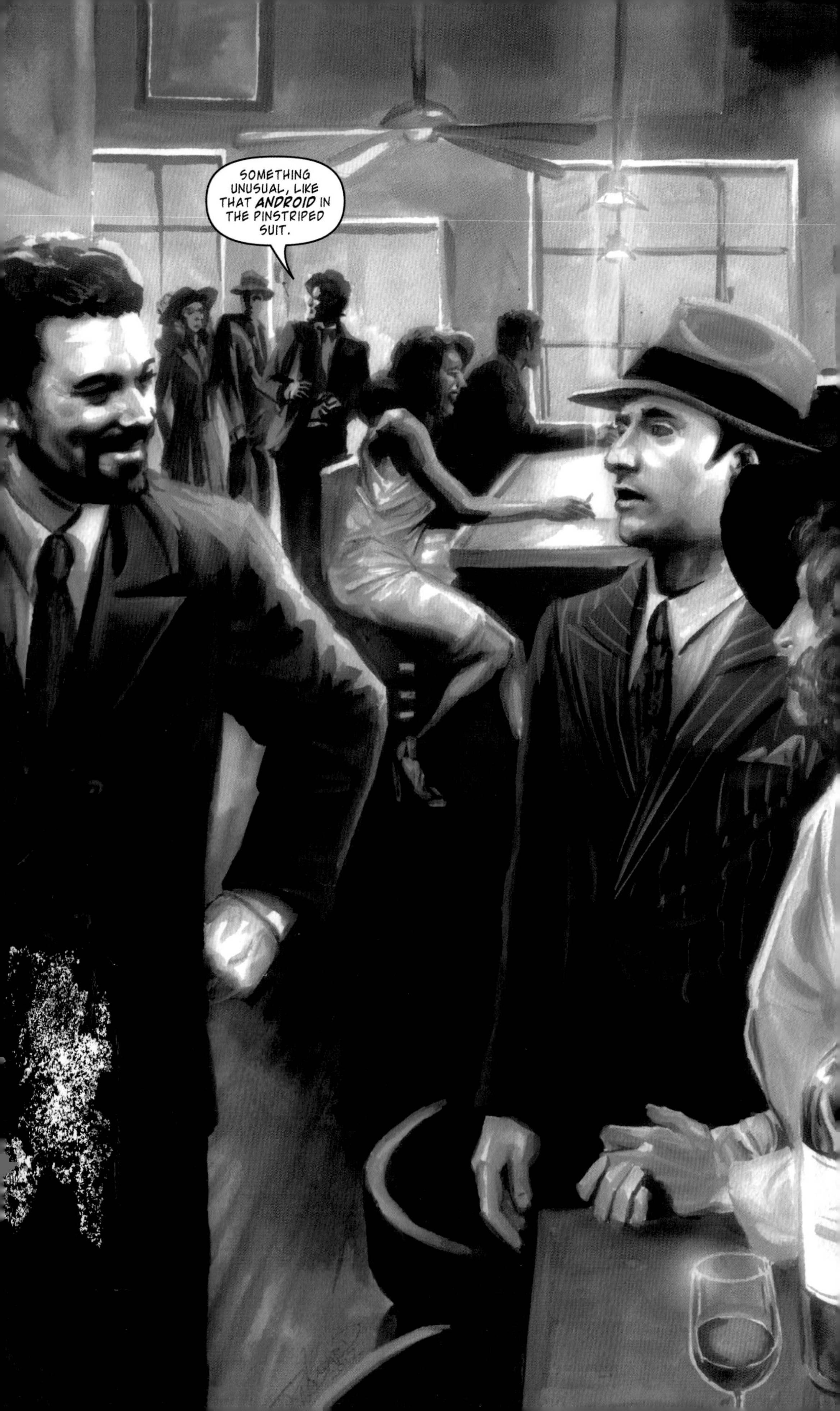
SOMETHING UNUSUAL, LIKE THAT ANDROID IN THE PINSTRIPED SUIT.

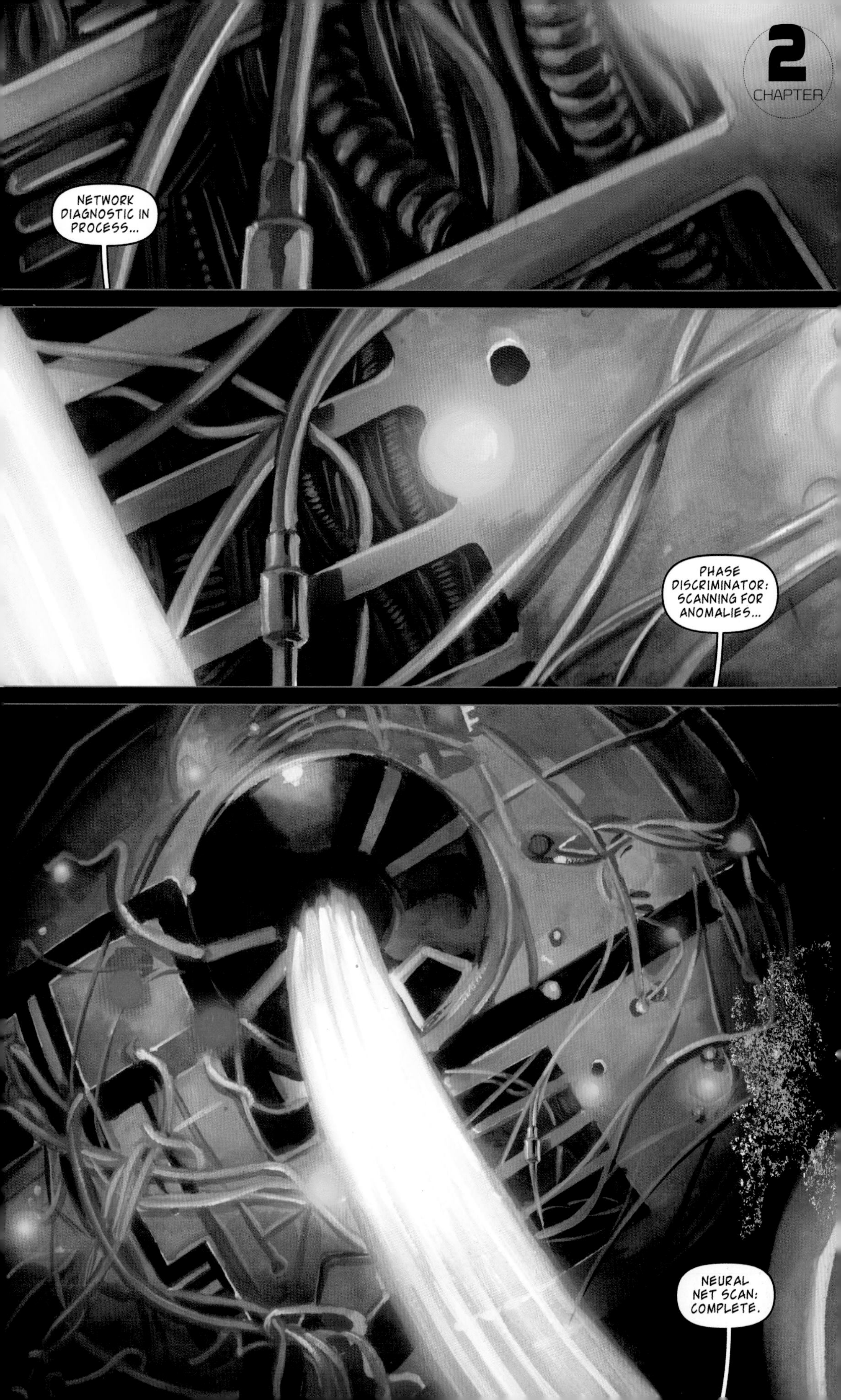
2
CHAPTER
NETWORK DIAGNOSTIC IN PROCESS...
PHASE DISCRIMINATOR: SCANNING FOR ANOMALIES...
NEURAL NET SCAN: COMPLETE.

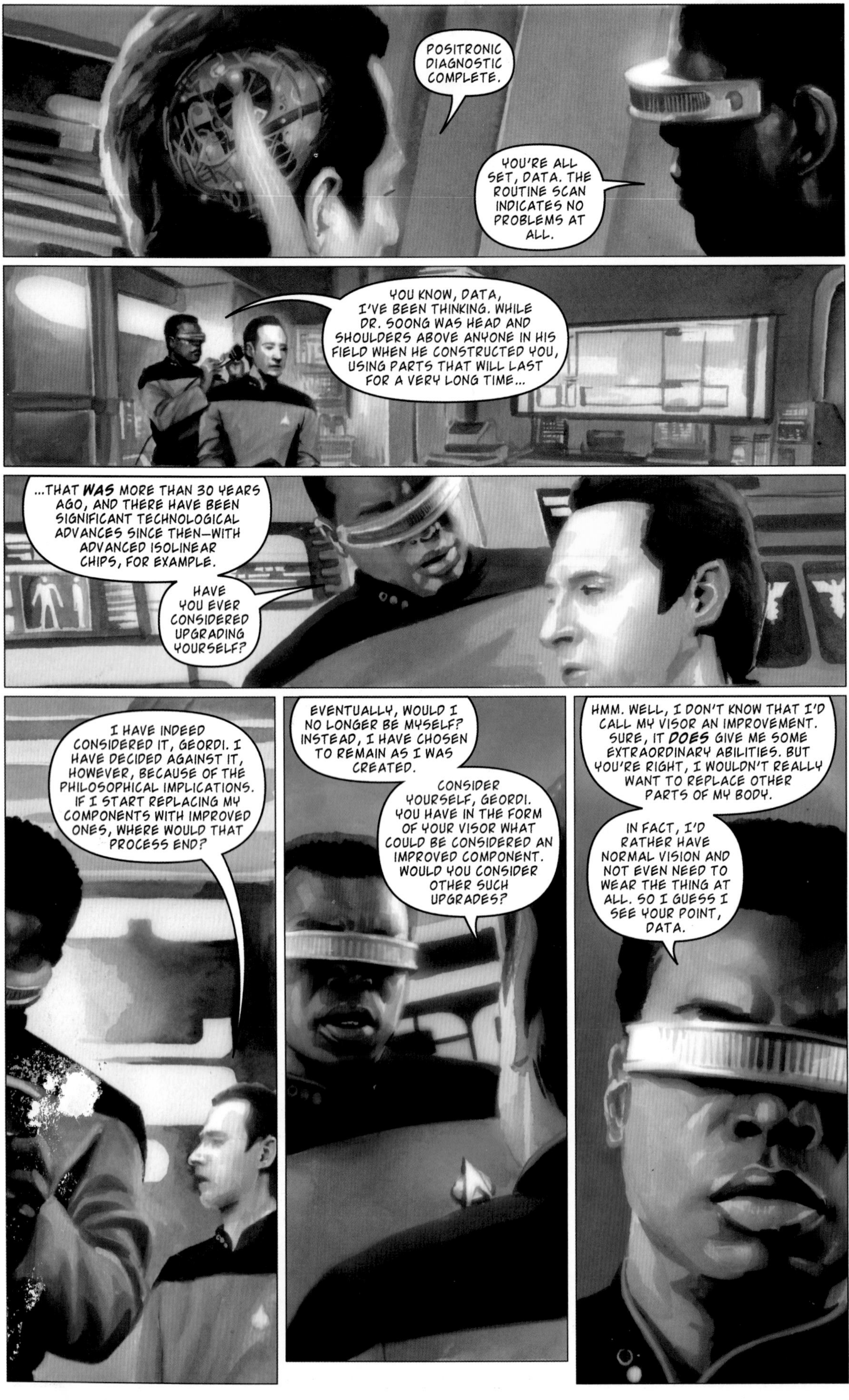
POSITRONIC DIAGNOSTIC COMPLETE.
YOU'RE ALL SET, DATA. THE ROUTINE SCAN INDICATES NO PROBLEMS AT ALL.
YOU KNOW, DATA, I'VE BEEN THINKING. WHILE DR. SOONG WAS HEAD AND SHOULDERS ABOVE ANYONE IN HIS FIELD WHEN HE CONSTRUCTED YOU, USING PARTS THAT WILL LAST FOR A VERY LONG TIME...
...THAT ***WAS*** MORE THAN 30 YEARS AGO, AND THERE HAVE BEEN SIGNIFICANT TECHNOLOGICAL ADVANCES SINCE THEN—WITH ADVANCED ISOLINEAR CHIPS, FOR EXAMPLE.
HAVE YOU EVER CONSIDERED UPGRADING YOURSELF?
I HAVE INDEED CONSIDERED IT, GEORDI. I HAVE DECIDED AGAINST IT, HOWEVER, BECAUSE OF THE PHILOSOPHICAL IMPLICATIONS. IF I START REPLACING MY COMPONENTS WITH IMPROVED ONES, WHERE WOULD THAT PROCESS END?
EVENTUALLY, WOULD I NO LONGER BE MYSELF? INSTEAD, I HAVE CHOSEN TO REMAIN AS I WAS CREATED.
CONSIDER YOURSELF, GEORDI. YOU HAVE IN THE FORM OF YOUR VISOR WHAT COULD BE CONSIDERED AN IMPROVED COMPONENT. WOULD YOU CONSIDER OTHER SUCH UPGRADES?
HMM. WELL, I DON'T KNOW THAT I'D CALL MY VISOR AN IMPROVEMENT. SURE, IT ***DOES*** GIVE ME SOME EXTRAORDINARY ABILITIES. BUT YOU'RE RIGHT, I WOULDN'T REALLY WANT TO REPLACE OTHER PARTS OF MY BODY.
IN FACT, I'D RATHER HAVE NORMAL VISION AND NOT EVEN NEED TO WEAR THE THING AT ALL. SO I GUESS I SEE YOUR POINT, DATA.

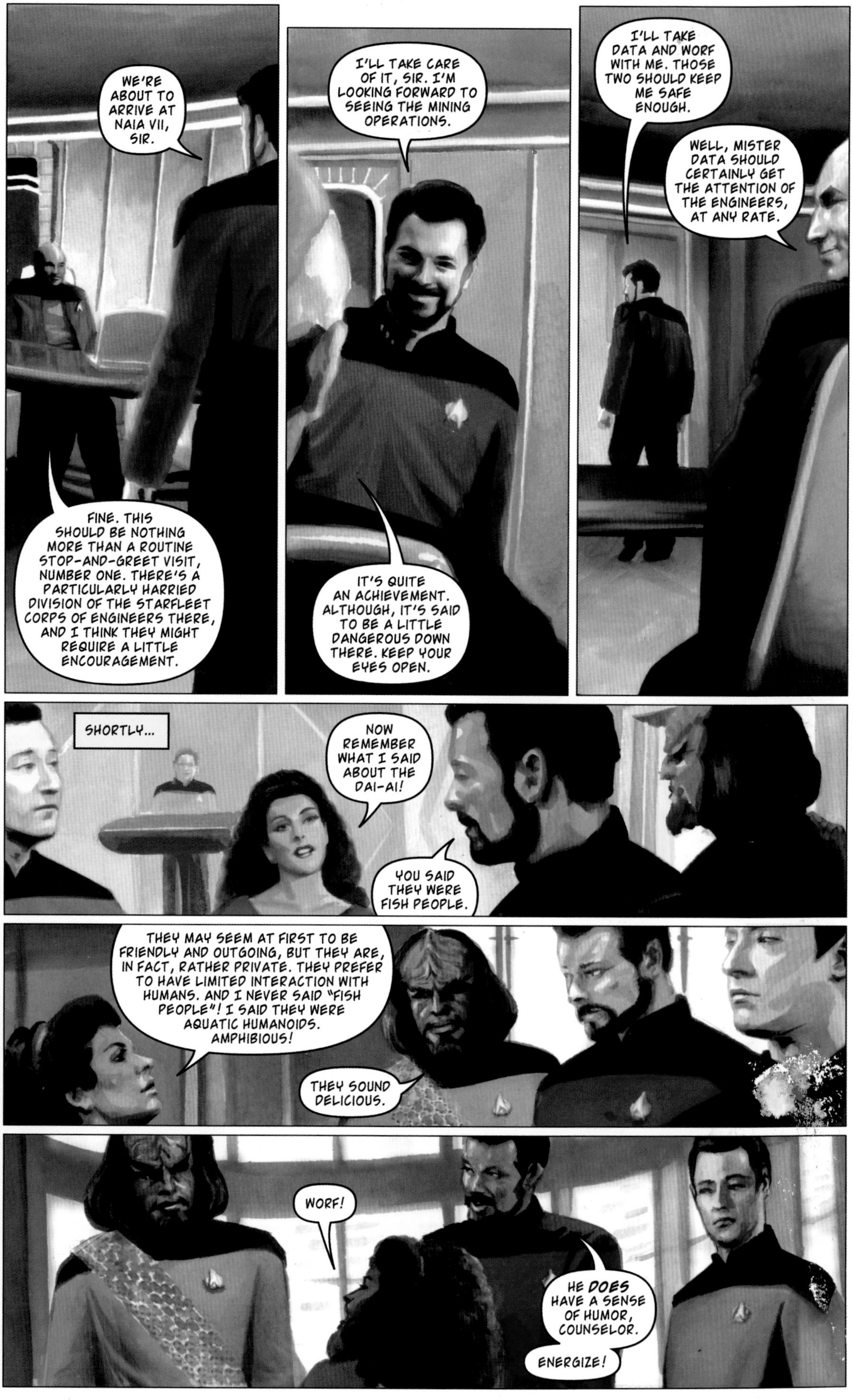
WE'RE ABOUT TO ARRIVE AT NAIA VII, SIR.
FINE. THIS SHOULD BE NOTHING MORE THAN A ROUTINE STOP-AND-GREET VISIT, NUMBER ONE. THERE'S A PARTICULARLY HARRIED DIVISION OF THE STARFLEET CORPS OF ENGINEERS THERE, AND I THINK THEY MIGHT REQUIRE A LITTLE ENCOURAGEMENT.
I'LL TAKE CARE OF IT, SIR. I'M LOOKING FORWARD TO SEEING THE MINING OPERATIONS.
IT'S QUITE AN ACHIEVEMENT. ALTHOUGH, IT'S SAID TO BE A LITTLE DANGEROUS DOWN THERE. KEEP YOUR EYES OPEN.
I'LL TAKE DATA AND WORF WITH ME. THOSE TWO SHOULD KEEP ME SAFE ENOUGH.
WELL, MISTER DATA SHOULD CERTAINLY GET THE ATTENTION OF THE ENGINEERS, AT ANY RATE.
SHORTLY...
NOW REMEMBER WHAT I SAID ABOUT THE DAI-AI!
YOU SAID THEY WERE FISH PEOPLE.
THEY MAY SEEM AT FIRST TO BE FRIENDLY AND OUTGOING, BUT THEY ARE, IN FACT, RATHER PRIVATE. THEY PREFER TO HAVE LIMITED INTERACTION WITH HUMANS. AND I NEVER SAID "FISH PEOPLE"! I SAID THEY WERE AQUATIC HUMANOIDS. AMPHIBIOUS!
THEY SOUND DELICIOUS.
WORF!
HE *DOES* HAVE A SENSE OF HUMOR, COUNSELOR.
ENERGIZE!

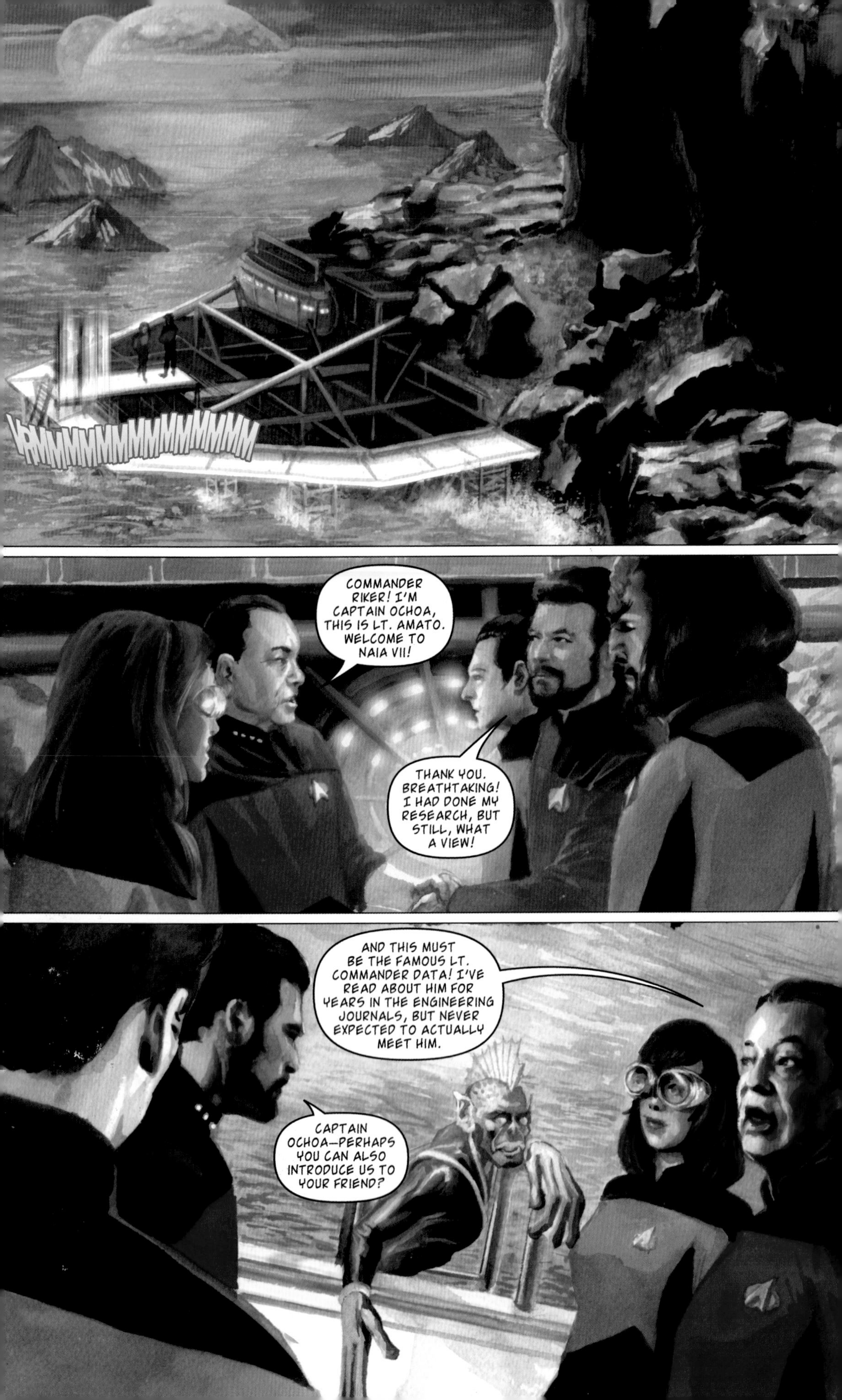
VRMMMMMMMMMMMMMM
COMMANDER RIKER! I'M CAPTAIN OCHOA, THIS IS LT. AMATO. WELCOME TO NAIA VII!
THANK YOU. BREATHTAKING! I HAD DONE MY RESEARCH, BUT STILL, WHAT A VIEW!
AND THIS MUST BE THE FAMOUS LT. COMMANDER DATA! I'VE READ ABOUT HIM FOR YEARS IN THE ENGINEERING JOURNALS, BUT NEVER EXPECTED TO ACTUALLY MEET HIM.
CAPTAIN OCHOA—PERHAPS YOU CAN ALSO INTRODUCE US TO YOUR FRIEND?

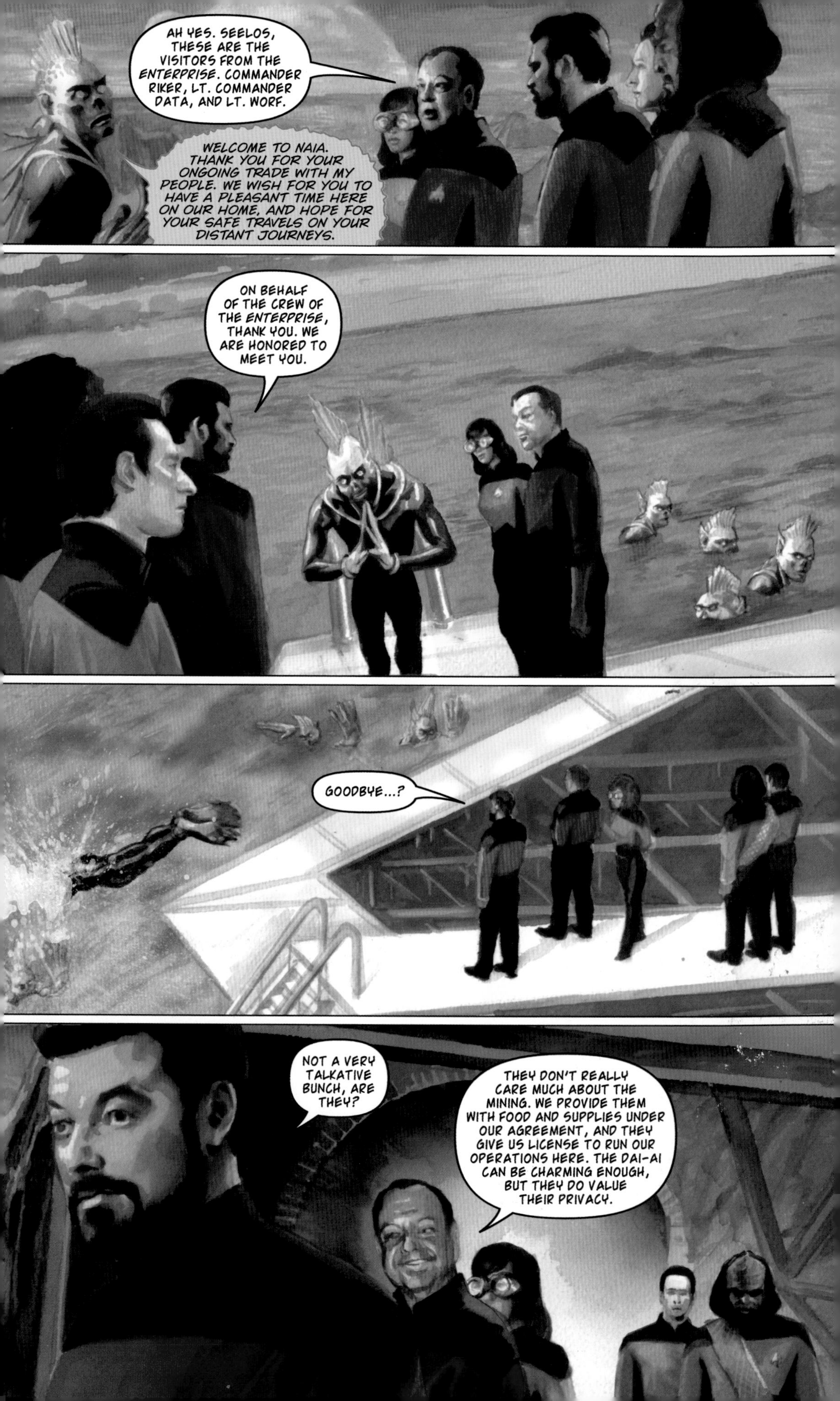
AH YES. SEELOS, THESE ARE THE VISITORS FROM THE *ENTERPRISE*. COMMANDER RIKER, LT. COMMANDER DATA, AND LT. WORF.
WELCOME TO NAIA. THANK YOU FOR YOUR ONGOING TRADE WITH MY PEOPLE. WE WISH FOR YOU TO HAVE A PLEASANT TIME HERE ON OUR HOME, AND HOPE FOR YOUR SAFE TRAVELS ON YOUR DISTANT JOURNEYS.
ON BEHALF OF THE CREW OF THE *ENTERPRISE*, THANK YOU. WE ARE HONORED TO MEET YOU.
GOODBYE...?
NOT A VERY TALKATIVE BUNCH, ARE THEY?
THEY DON'T REALLY CARE MUCH ABOUT THE MINING. WE PROVIDE THEM WITH FOOD AND SUPPLIES UNDER OUR AGREEMENT, AND THEY GIVE US LICENSE TO RUN OUR OPERATIONS HERE. THE DAI-AI CAN BE CHARMING ENOUGH, BUT THEY DO VALUE THEIR PRIVACY.

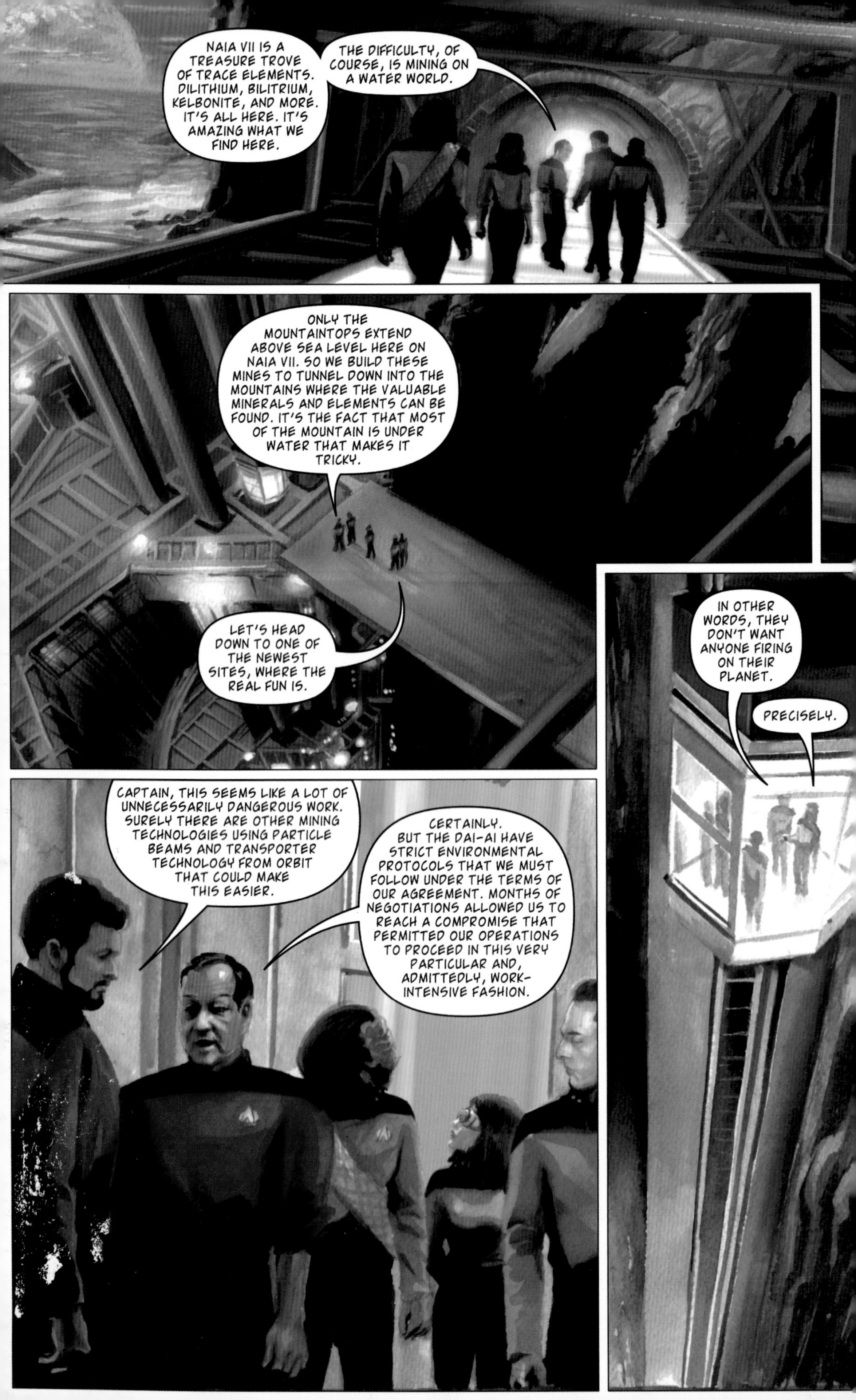
NAIA VII IS A TREASURE TROVE OF TRACE ELEMENTS. DILITHIUM, BILITRIUM, KELBONITE, AND MORE. IT'S ALL HERE. IT'S AMAZING WHAT WE FIND HERE.
THE DIFFICULTY, OF COURSE, IS MINING ON A WATER WORLD.
ONLY THE MOUNTAINTOPS EXTEND ABOVE SEA LEVEL HERE ON NAIA VII. SO WE BUILD THESE MINES TO TUNNEL DOWN INTO THE MOUNTAINS WHERE THE VALUABLE MINERALS AND ELEMENTS CAN BE FOUND. IT'S THE FACT THAT MOST OF THE MOUNTAIN IS UNDER WATER THAT MAKES IT TRICKY.
LET'S HEAD DOWN TO ONE OF THE NEWEST SITES, WHERE THE REAL FUN IS.
CAPTAIN, THIS SEEMS LIKE A LOT OF UNNECESSARILY DANGEROUS WORK. SURELY THERE ARE OTHER MINING TECHNOLOGIES USING PARTICLE BEAMS AND TRANSPORTER TECHNOLOGY FROM ORBIT THAT COULD MAKE THIS EASIER.
CERTAINLY. BUT THE DAI-AI HAVE STRICT ENVIRONMENTAL PROTOCOLS THAT WE MUST FOLLOW UNDER THE TERMS OF OUR AGREEMENT. MONTHS OF NEGOTIATIONS ALLOWED US TO REACH A COMPROMISE THAT PERMITTED OUR OPERATIONS TO PROCEED IN THIS VERY PARTICULAR AND, ADMITTEDLY, WORK-INTENSIVE FASHION.
IN OTHER WORDS, THEY DON'T WANT ANYONE FIRING ON THEIR PLANET.
PRECISELY.

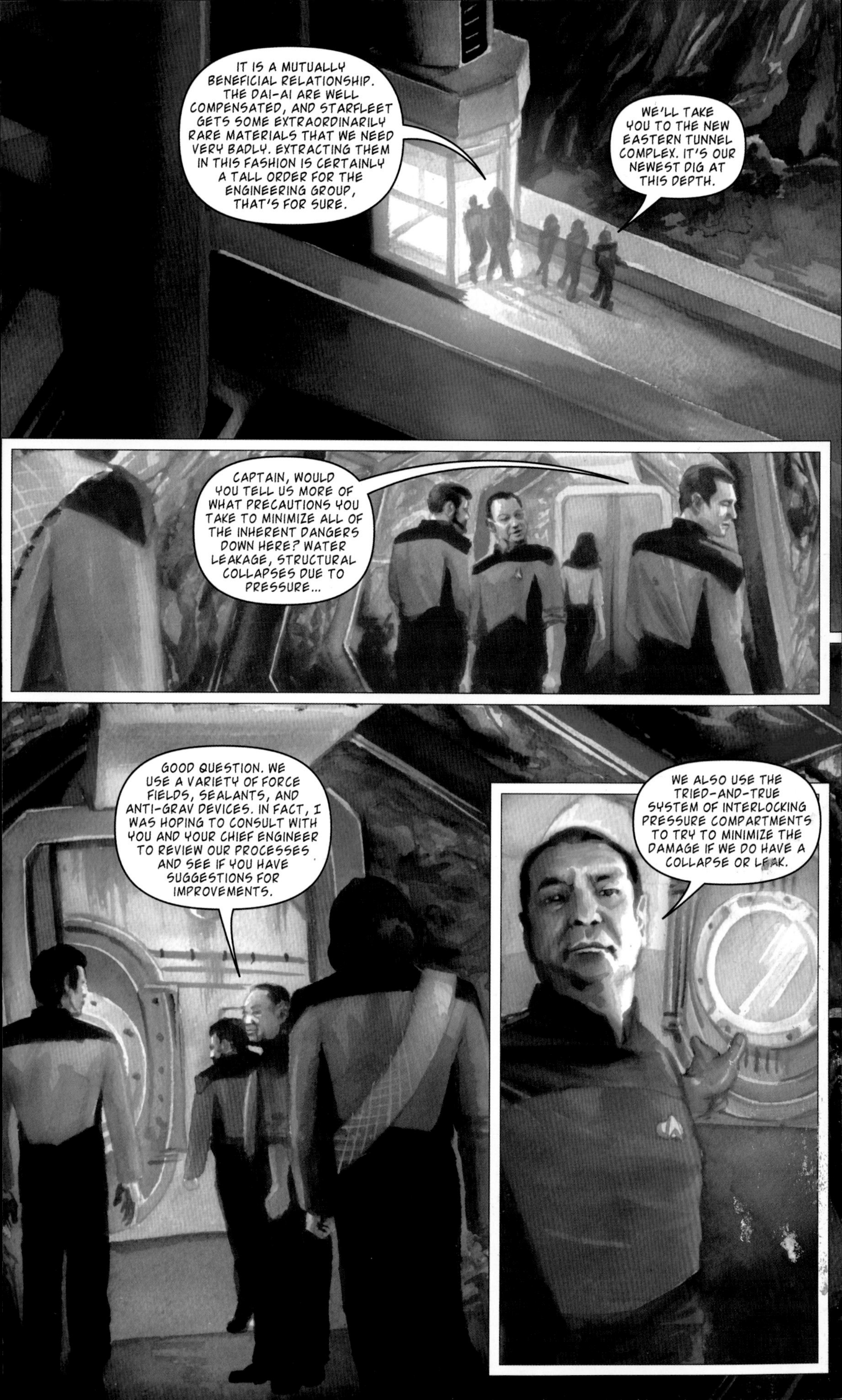
IT IS A MUTUALLY BENEFICIAL RELATIONSHIP. THE DAI-AI ARE WELL COMPENSATED, AND STARFLEET GETS SOME EXTRAORDINARILY RARE MATERIALS THAT WE NEED VERY BADLY. EXTRACTING THEM IN THIS FASHION IS CERTAINLY A TALL ORDER FOR THE ENGINEERING GROUP, THAT'S FOR SURE.
WE'LL TAKE YOU TO THE NEW EASTERN TUNNEL COMPLEX. IT'S OUR NEWEST DIG AT THIS DEPTH.
CAPTAIN, WOULD YOU TELL US MORE OF WHAT PRECAUTIONS YOU TAKE TO MINIMIZE ALL OF THE INHERENT DANGERS DOWN HERE? WATER LEAKAGE, STRUCTURAL COLLAPSES DUE TO PRESSURE...
GOOD QUESTION. WE USE A VARIETY OF FORCE FIELDS, SEALANTS, AND ANTI-GRAV DEVICES. IN FACT, I WAS HOPING TO CONSULT WITH YOU AND YOUR CHIEF ENGINEER TO REVIEW OUR PROCESSES AND SEE IF YOU HAVE SUGGESTIONS FOR IMPROVEMENTS.
WE ALSO USE THE TRIED-AND-TRUE SYSTEM OF INTERLOCKING PRESSURE COMPARTMENTS TO TRY TO MINIMIZE THE DAMAGE IF WE DO HAVE A COLLAPSE OR LEAK.

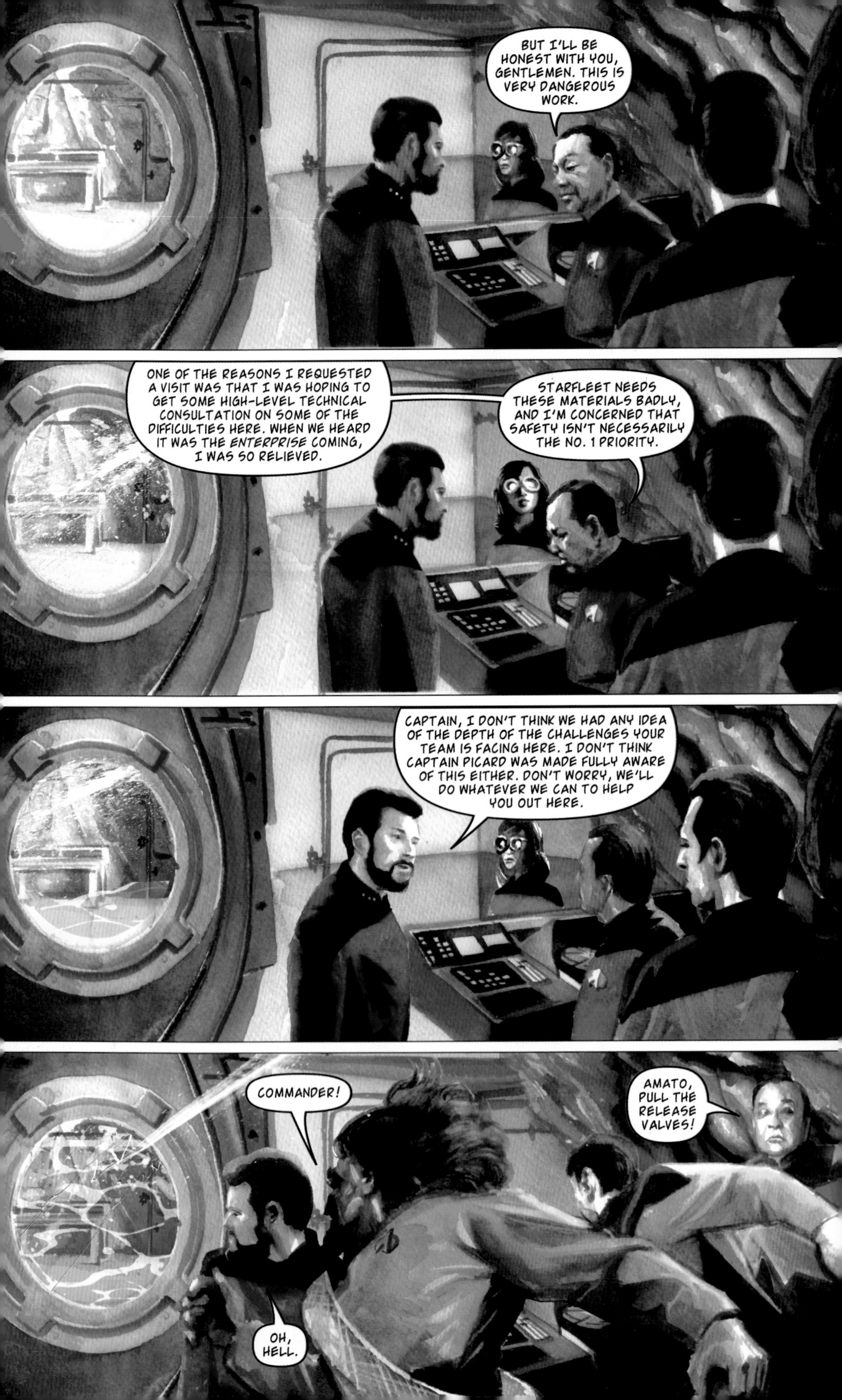
BUT I'LL BE HONEST WITH YOU, GENTLEMEN. THIS IS VERY DANGEROUS WORK.
ONE OF THE REASONS I REQUESTED A VISIT WAS THAT I WAS HOPING TO GET SOME HIGH-LEVEL TECHNICAL CONSULTATION ON SOME OF THE DIFFICULTIES HERE. WHEN WE HEARD IT WAS THE *ENTERPRISE* COMING, I WAS SO RELIEVED.
STARFLEET NEEDS THESE MATERIALS BADLY, AND I'M CONCERNED THAT SAFETY ISN'T NECESSARILY THE NO. 1 PRIORITY.
CAPTAIN, I DON'T THINK WE HAD ANY IDEA OF THE DEPTH OF THE CHALLENGES YOUR TEAM IS FACING HERE. I DON'T THINK CAPTAIN PICARD WAS MADE FULLY AWARE OF THIS EITHER. DON'T WORRY, WE'LL DO WHATEVER WE CAN TO HELP YOU OUT HERE.
COMMANDER!
AMATO, PULL THE RELEASE VALVES!
OH, HELL.

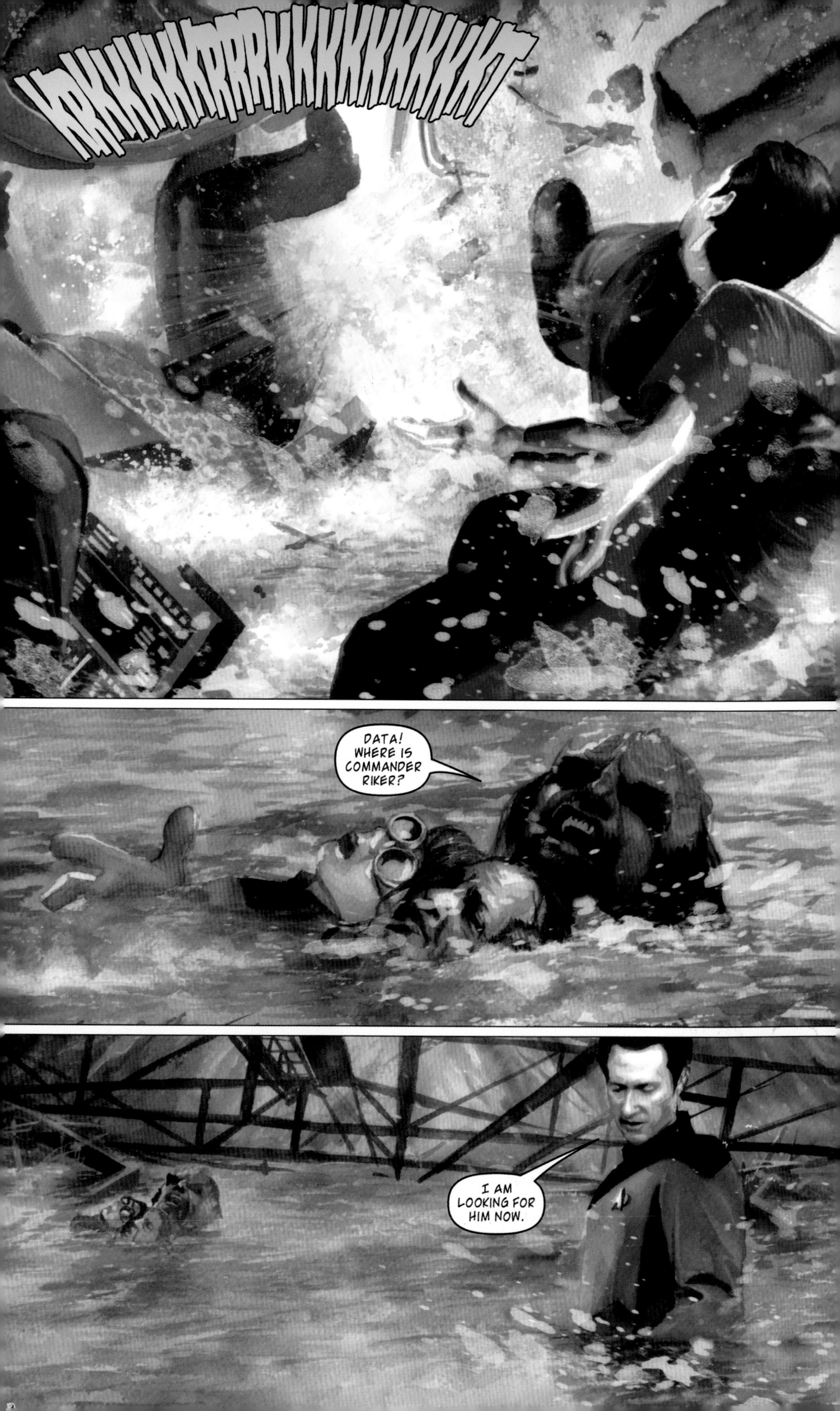
KRKKKKRRRRKKKKKKKKKT
DATA! WHERE IS COMMANDER RIKER?
I AM LOOKING FOR HIM NOW.

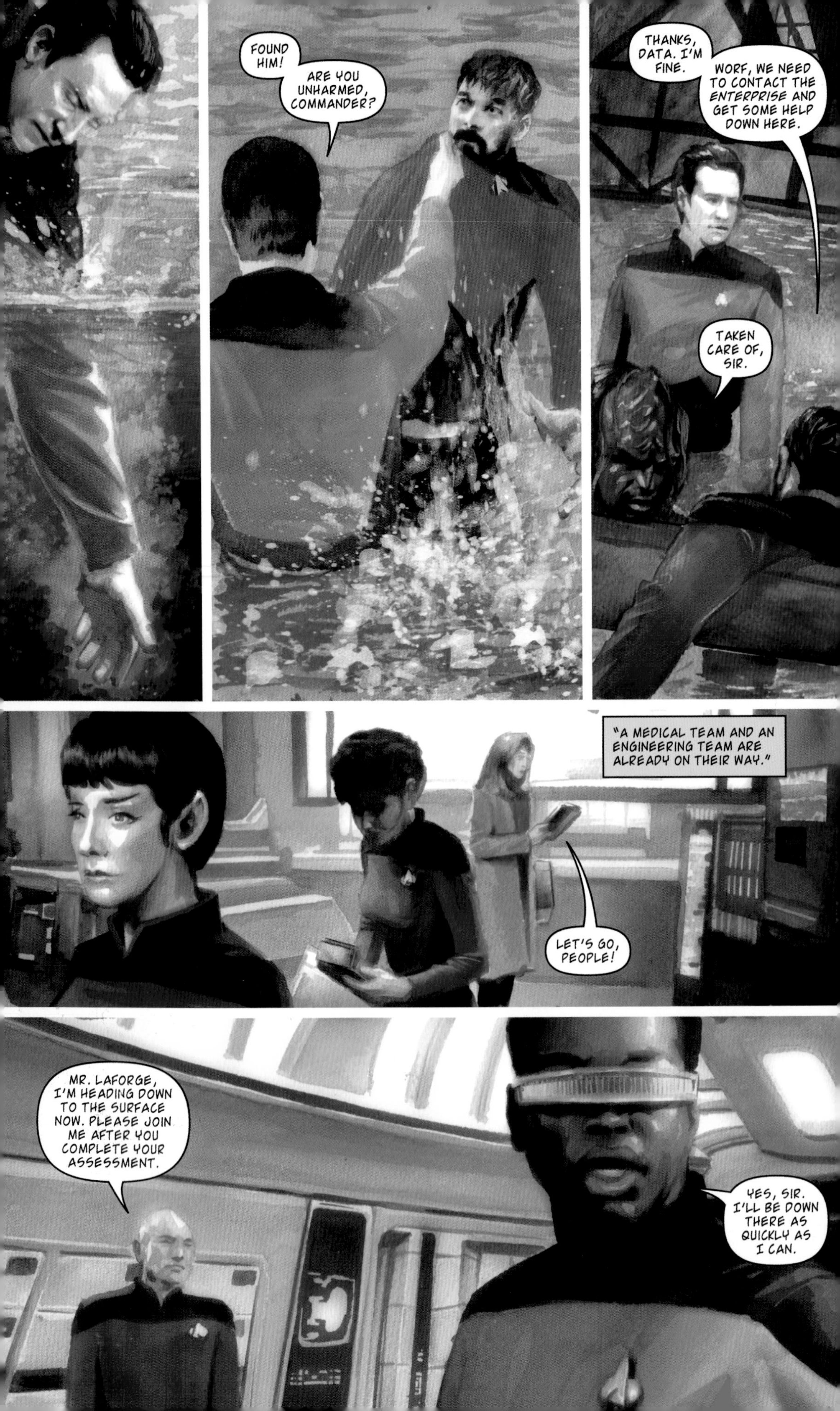
FOUND HIM!
ARE YOU UNHARMED, COMMANDER?
THANKS, DATA. I'M FINE.
WORF, WE NEED TO CONTACT THE *ENTERPRISE* AND GET SOME HELP DOWN HERE.
TAKEN CARE OF, SIR.
"A MEDICAL TEAM AND AN ENGINEERING TEAM ARE ALREADY ON THEIR WAY."
LET'S GO, PEOPLE!
MR. LAFORGE, I'M HEADING DOWN TO THE SURFACE NOW. PLEASE JOIN ME AFTER YOU COMPLETE YOUR ASSESSMENT.
YES, SIR. I'LL BE DOWN THERE AS QUICKLY AS I CAN.

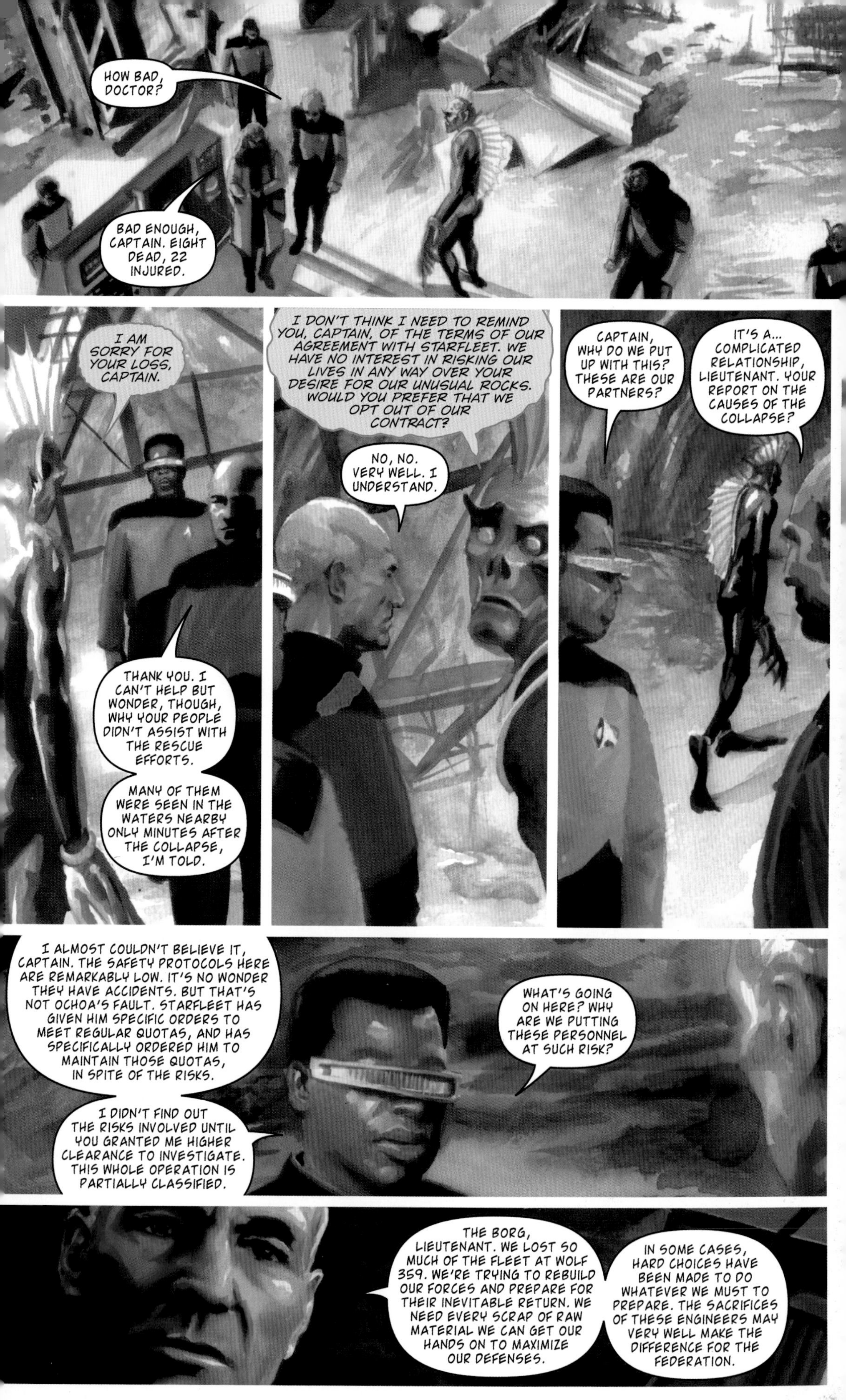
HOW BAD, DOCTOR?
BAD ENOUGH, CAPTAIN. EIGHT DEAD, 22 INJURED.
I AM SORRY FOR YOUR LOSS, CAPTAIN.
THANK YOU. I CAN'T HELP BUT WONDER, THOUGH, WHY YOUR PEOPLE DIDN'T ASSIST WITH THE RESCUE EFFORTS.
MANY OF THEM WERE SEEN IN THE WATERS NEARBY ONLY MINUTES AFTER THE COLLAPSE, I'M TOLD.
I DON'T THINK I NEED TO REMIND YOU, CAPTAIN, OF THE TERMS OF OUR AGREEMENT WITH STARFLEET. WE HAVE NO INTEREST IN RISKING OUR LIVES IN ANY WAY OVER YOUR DESIRE FOR OUR UNUSUAL ROCKS. WOULD YOU PREFER THAT WE OPT OUT OF OUR CONTRACT?
NO, NO. VERY WELL. I UNDERSTAND.
CAPTAIN, WHY DO WE PUT UP WITH THIS? THESE ARE OUR PARTNERS?
IT'S A... COMPLICATED RELATIONSHIP, LIEUTENANT. YOUR REPORT ON THE CAUSES OF THE COLLAPSE?
I ALMOST COULDN'T BELIEVE IT, CAPTAIN. THE SAFETY PROTOCOLS HERE ARE REMARKABLY LOW. IT'S NO WONDER THEY HAVE ACCIDENTS. BUT THAT'S NOT OCHOA'S FAULT. STARFLEET HAS GIVEN HIM SPECIFIC ORDERS TO MEET REGULAR QUOTAS, AND HAS SPECIFICALLY ORDERED HIM TO MAINTAIN THOSE QUOTAS, IN SPITE OF THE RISKS.
I DIDN'T FIND OUT THE RISKS INVOLVED UNTIL YOU GRANTED ME HIGHER CLEARANCE TO INVESTIGATE. THIS WHOLE OPERATION IS PARTIALLY CLASSIFIED.
WHAT'S GOING ON HERE? WHY ARE WE PUTTING THESE PERSONNEL AT SUCH RISK?
THE BORG, LIEUTENANT. WE LOST SO MUCH OF THE FLEET AT WOLF 359. WE'RE TRYING TO REBUILD OUR FORCES AND PREPARE FOR THEIR INEVITABLE RETURN. WE NEED EVERY SCRAP OF RAW MATERIAL WE CAN GET OUR HANDS ON TO MAXIMIZE OUR DEFENSES.
IN SOME CASES, HARD CHOICES HAVE BEEN MADE TO DO WHATEVER WE MUST TO PREPARE. THE SACRIFICES OF THESE ENGINEERS MAY VERY WELL MAKE THE DIFFERENCE FOR THE FEDERATION.

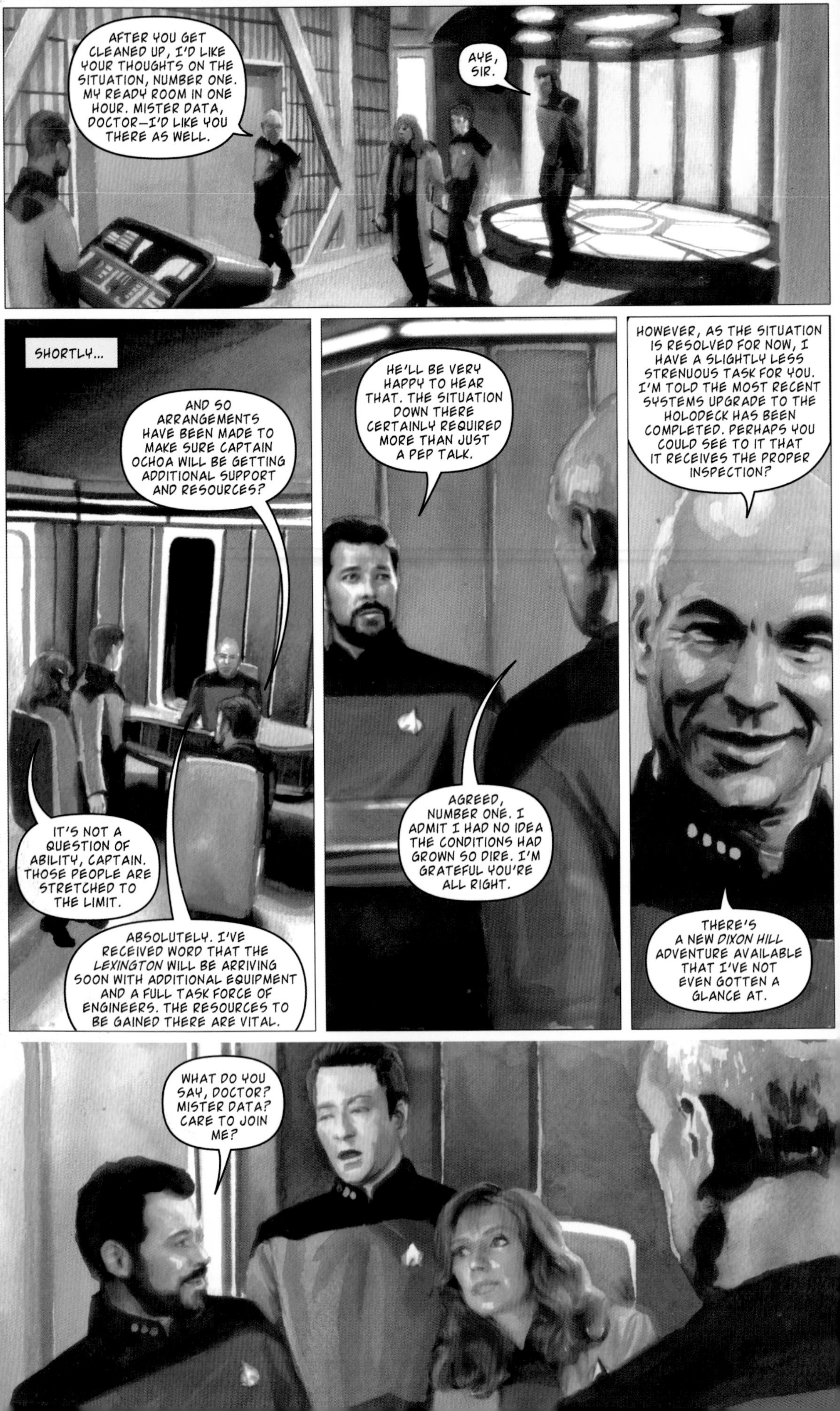
AFTER YOU GET CLEANED UP, I'D LIKE YOUR THOUGHTS ON THE SITUATION, NUMBER ONE. MY READY ROOM IN ONE HOUR. MISTER DATA, DOCTOR—I'D LIKE YOU THERE AS WELL.
AYE, SIR.
SHORTLY...
AND SO ARRANGEMENTS HAVE BEEN MADE TO MAKE SURE CAPTAIN OCHOA WILL BE GETTING ADDITIONAL SUPPORT AND RESOURCES?
IT'S NOT A QUESTION OF ABILITY, CAPTAIN. THOSE PEOPLE ARE STRETCHED TO THE LIMIT.
ABSOLUTELY. I'VE RECEIVED WORD THAT THE *LEXINGTON* WILL BE ARRIVING SOON WITH ADDITIONAL EQUIPMENT AND A FULL TASK FORCE OF ENGINEERS. THE RESOURCES TO BE GAINED THERE ARE VITAL.
HE'LL BE VERY HAPPY TO HEAR THAT. THE SITUATION DOWN THERE CERTAINLY REQUIRED MORE THAN JUST A PEP TALK.
AGREED, NUMBER ONE. I ADMIT I HAD NO IDEA THE CONDITIONS HAD GROWN SO DIRE. I'M GRATEFUL YOU'RE ALL RIGHT.
HOWEVER, AS THE SITUATION IS RESOLVED FOR NOW, I HAVE A SLIGHTLY LESS STRENUOUS TASK FOR YOU. I'M TOLD THE MOST RECENT SYSTEMS UPGRADE TO THE HOLODECK HAS BEEN COMPLETED. PERHAPS YOU COULD SEE TO IT THAT IT RECEIVES THE PROPER INSPECTION?
THERE'S A NEW *DIXON HILL* ADVENTURE AVAILABLE THAT I'VE NOT EVEN GOTTEN A GLANCE AT.
WHAT DO YOU SAY, DOCTOR? MISTER DATA? CARE TO JOIN ME?

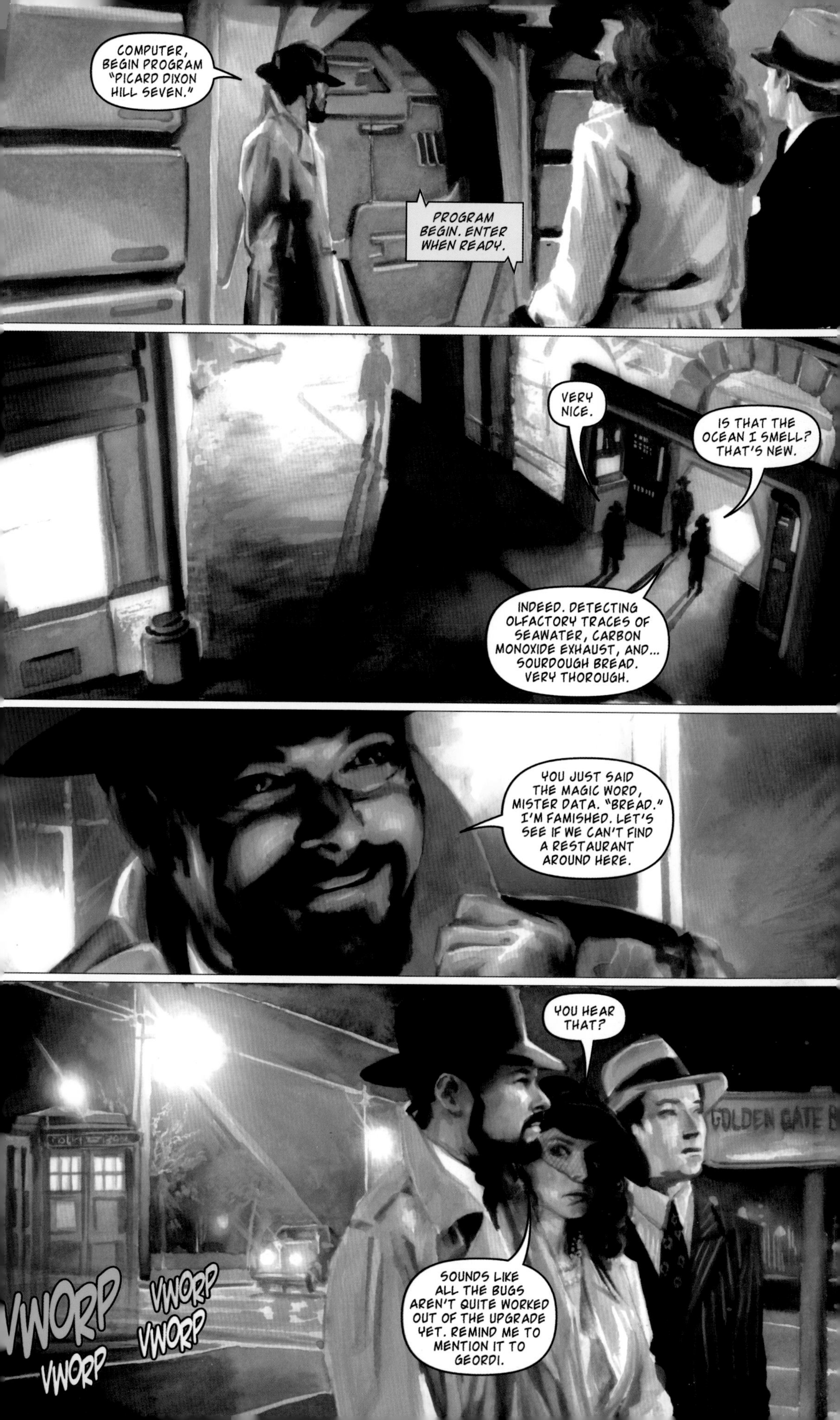
COMPUTER, BEGIN PROGRAM "PICARD DIXON HILL SEVEN."
PROGRAM BEGIN. ENTER WHEN READY.
VERY NICE.
IS THAT THE OCEAN I SMELL? THAT'S NEW.
INDEED. DETECTING OLFACTORY TRACES OF SEAWATER, CARBON MONOXIDE EXHAUST, AND... SOURDOUGH BREAD. VERY THOROUGH.
YOU JUST SAID THE MAGIC WORD, MISTER DATA. "BREAD." I'M FAMISHED. LET'S SEE IF WE CAN'T FIND A RESTAURANT AROUND HERE.
YOU HEAR THAT?
GOLDEN GATE
VWORP VWORP
VWORP VWORP
SOUNDS LIKE ALL THE BUGS AREN'T QUITE WORKED OUT OF THE UPGRADE YET. REMIND ME TO MENTION IT TO GEORDI.

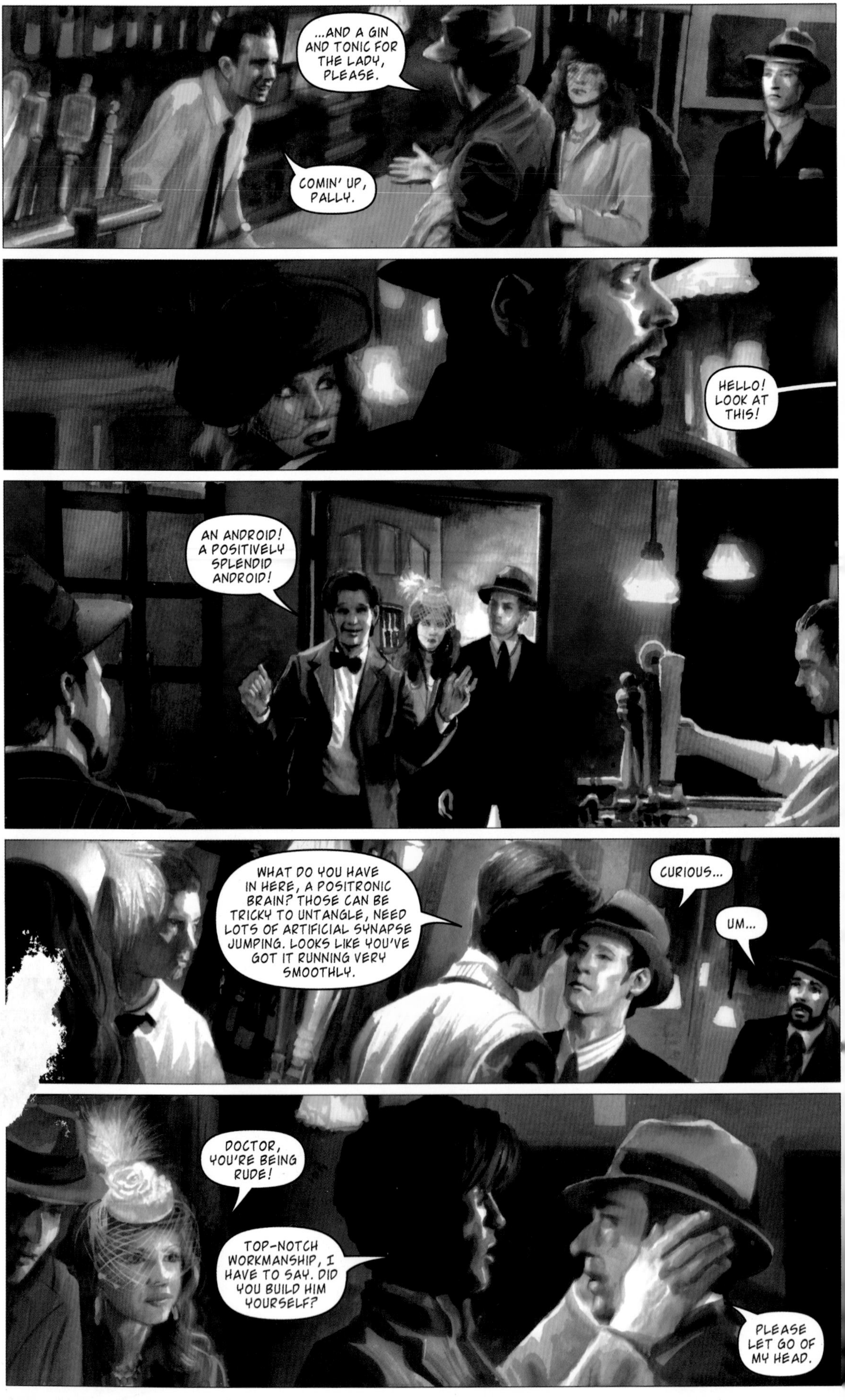
...AND A GIN AND TONIC FOR THE LADY, PLEASE.
COMIN' UP, PALLY.
HELLO! LOOK AT THIS!
AN ANDROID! A POSITIVELY SPLENDID ANDROID!
WHAT DO YOU HAVE IN HERE, A POSITRONIC BRAIN? THOSE CAN BE TRICKY TO UNTANGLE, NEED LOTS OF ARTIFICIAL SYNAPSE JUMPING. LOOKS LIKE YOU'VE GOT IT RUNNING VERY SMOOTHLY.
CURIOUS...
UM...
DOCTOR, YOU'RE BEING RUDE!
TOP-NOTCH WORKMANSHIP, I HAVE TO SAY. DID YOU BUILD HIM YOURSELF?
PLEASE LET GO OF MY HEAD.

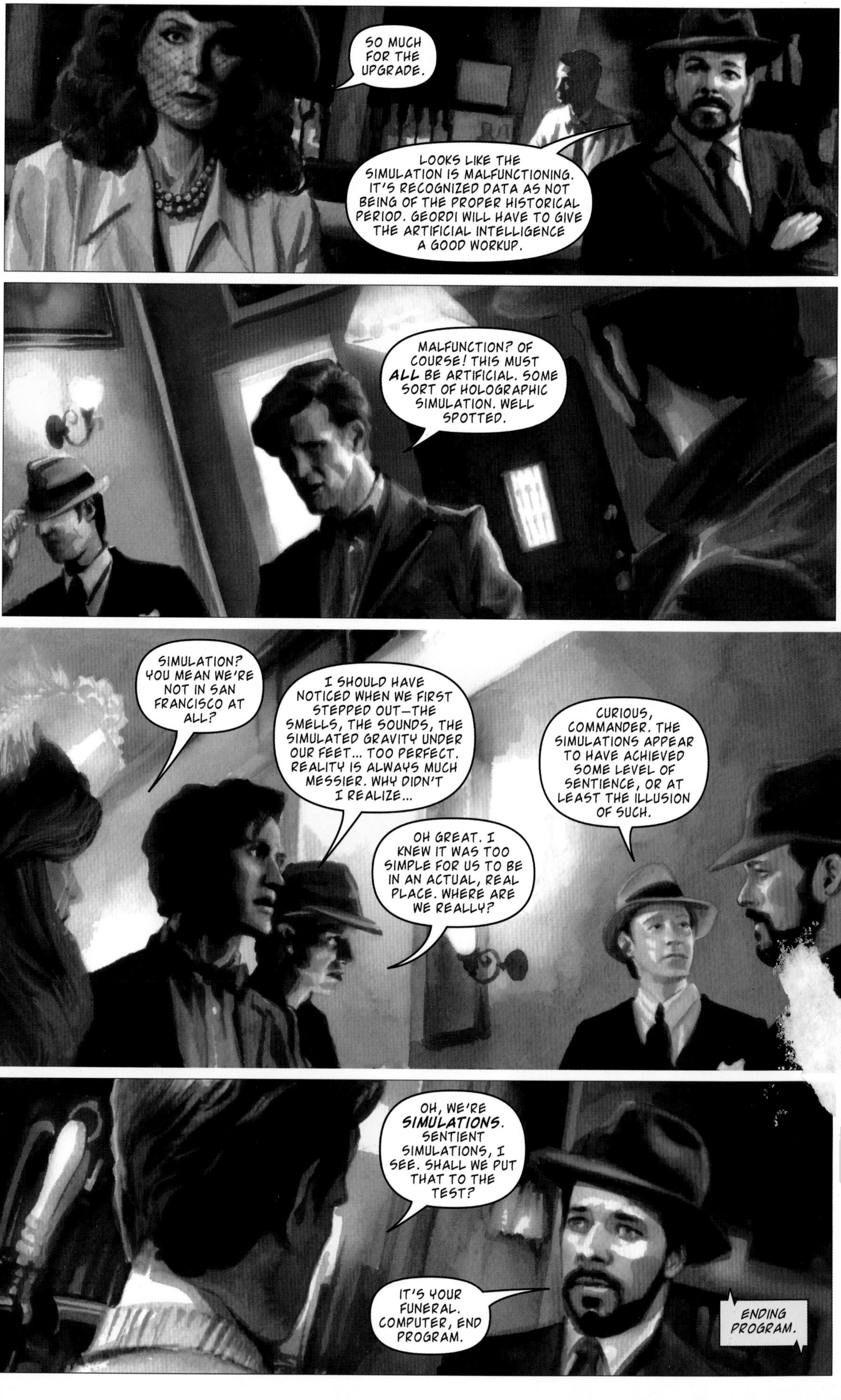
SO MUCH FOR THE UPGRADE.
LOOKS LIKE THE SIMULATION IS MALFUNCTIONING. IT'S RECOGNIZED DATA AS NOT BEING OF THE PROPER HISTORICAL PERIOD. GEORDI WILL HAVE TO GIVE THE ARTIFICIAL INTELLIGENCE A GOOD WORKUP.
MALFUNCTION? OF COURSE! THIS MUST ALL BE ARTIFICIAL. SOME SORT OF HOLOGRAPHIC SIMULATION. WELL SPOTTED.
SIMULATION? YOU MEAN WE'RE NOT IN SAN FRANCISCO AT ALL?
I SHOULD HAVE NOTICED WHEN WE FIRST STEPPED OUT—THE SMELLS, THE SOUNDS, THE SIMULATED GRAVITY UNDER OUR FEET... TOO PERFECT. REALITY IS ALWAYS MUCH MESSIER. WHY DIDN'T I REALIZE...
OH GREAT. I KNEW IT WAS TOO SIMPLE FOR US TO BE IN AN ACTUAL, REAL PLACE. WHERE ARE WE REALLY?
CURIOUS, COMMANDER. THE SIMULATIONS APPEAR TO HAVE ACHIEVED SOME LEVEL OF SENTIENCE, OR AT LEAST THE ILLUSION OF SUCH.
OH, WE'RE SIMULATIONS. SENTIENT SIMULATIONS, I SEE. SHALL WE PUT THAT TO THE TEST?
IT'S YOUR FUNERAL. COMPUTER, END PROGRAM.
ENDING PROGRAM.

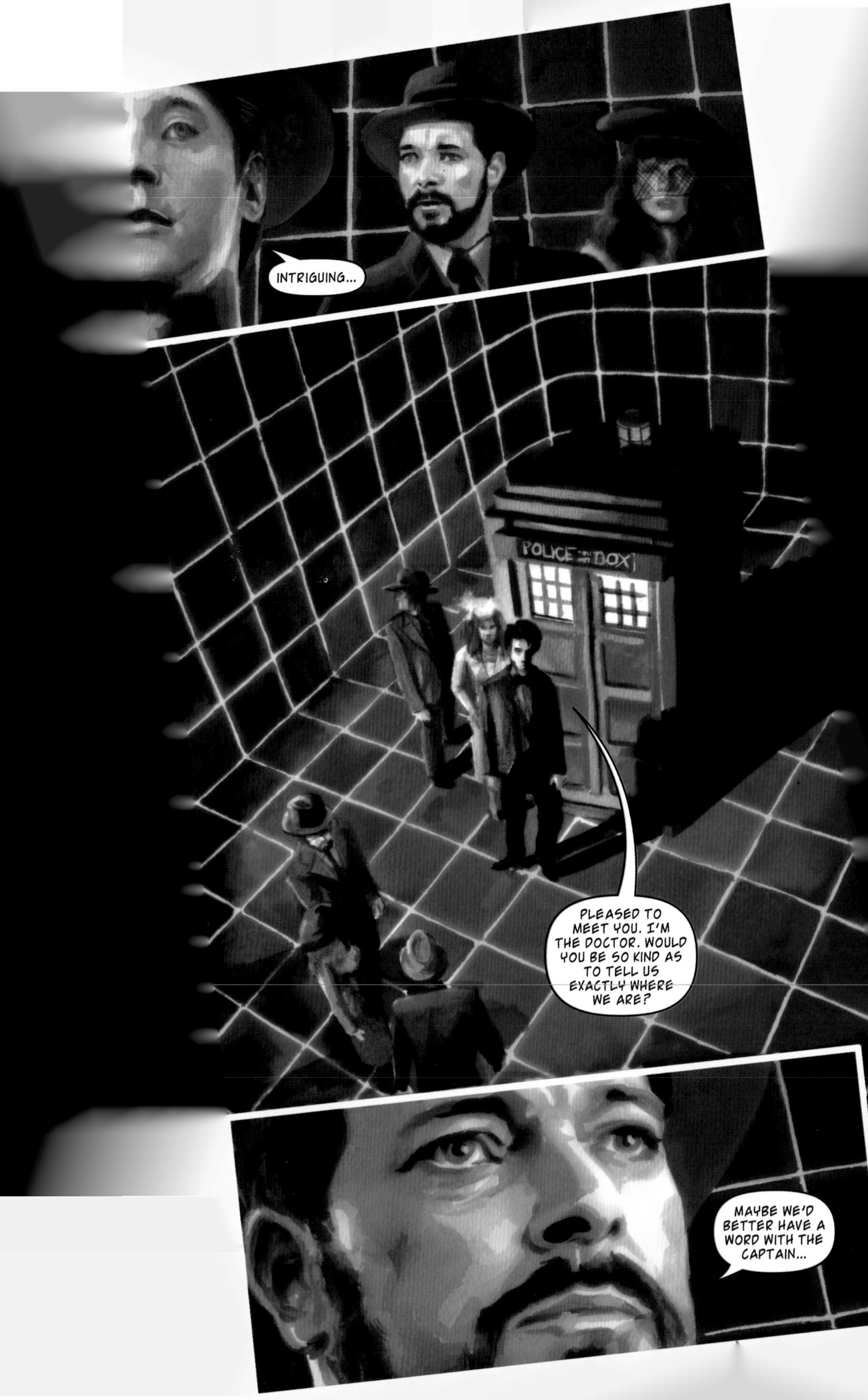
INTRIGUING...
PLEASED TO MEET YOU. I'M THE DOCTOR. WOULD YOU BE SO KIND AS TO TELL US EXACTLY WHERE WE ARE?
MAYBE WE'D BETTER HAVE A WORD WITH THE CAPTAIN...

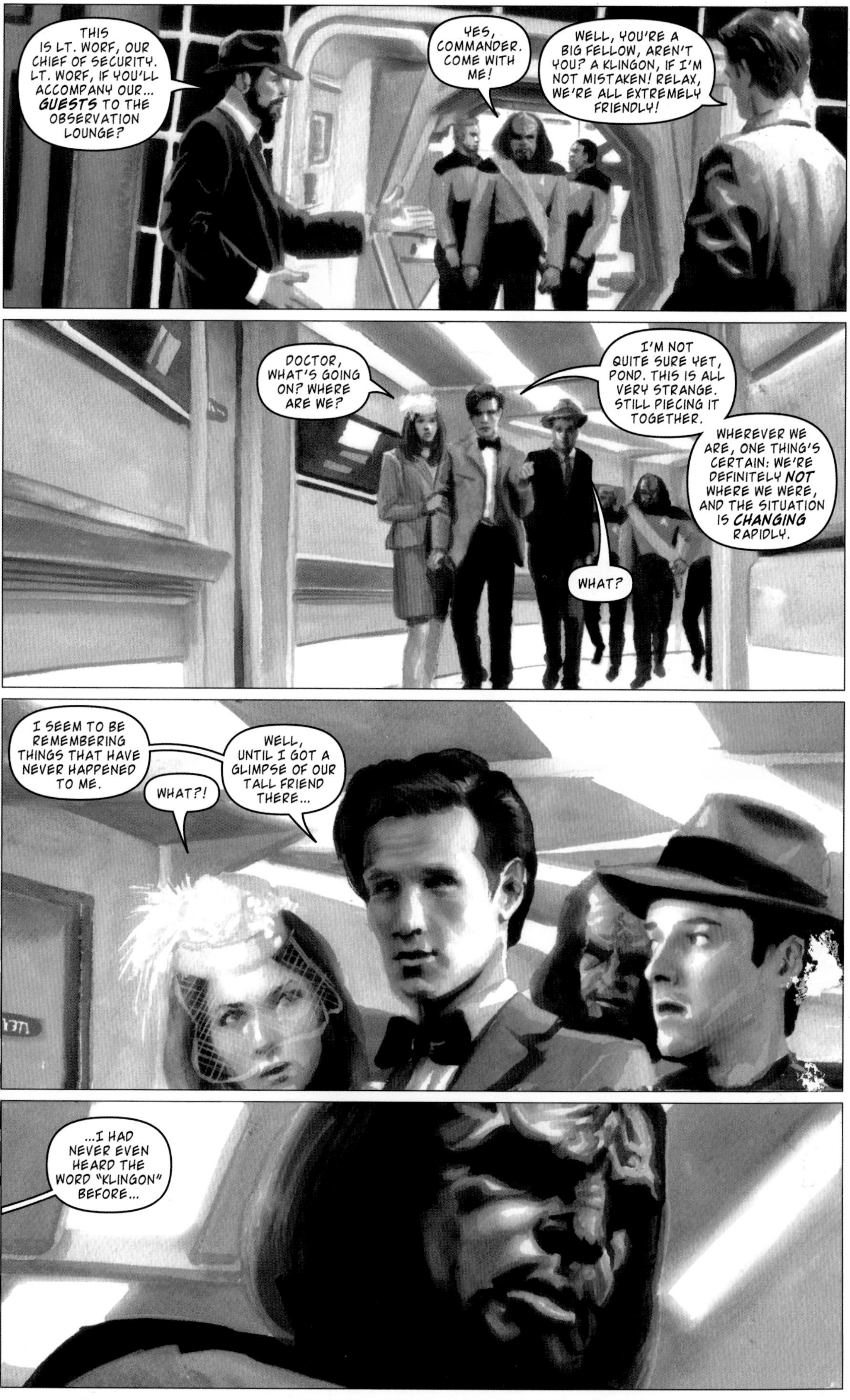
THIS IS LT. WORF, OUR CHIEF OF SECURITY. LT. WORF, IF YOU'LL ACCOMPANY OUR... **GUESTS** TO THE OBSERVATION LOUNGE?
YES, COMMANDER. COME WITH ME!
WELL, YOU'RE A BIG FELLOW, AREN'T YOU? A KLINGON, IF I'M NOT MISTAKEN! RELAX, WE'RE ALL EXTREMELY FRIENDLY!
DOCTOR, WHAT'S GOING ON? WHERE ARE WE?
I'M NOT QUITE SURE YET, POND. THIS IS ALL VERY STRANGE. STILL PIECING IT TOGETHER.
WHEREVER WE ARE, ONE THING'S CERTAIN: WE'RE DEFINITELY **NOT** WHERE WE WERE, AND THE SITUATION IS **CHANGING** RAPIDLY.
WHAT?
I SEEM TO BE REMEMBERING THINGS THAT HAVE NEVER HAPPENED TO ME.
WHAT?!
WELL, UNTIL I GOT A GLIMPSE OF OUR TALL FRIEND THERE...
...I HAD NEVER EVEN HEARD THE WORD "KLINGON" BEFORE...

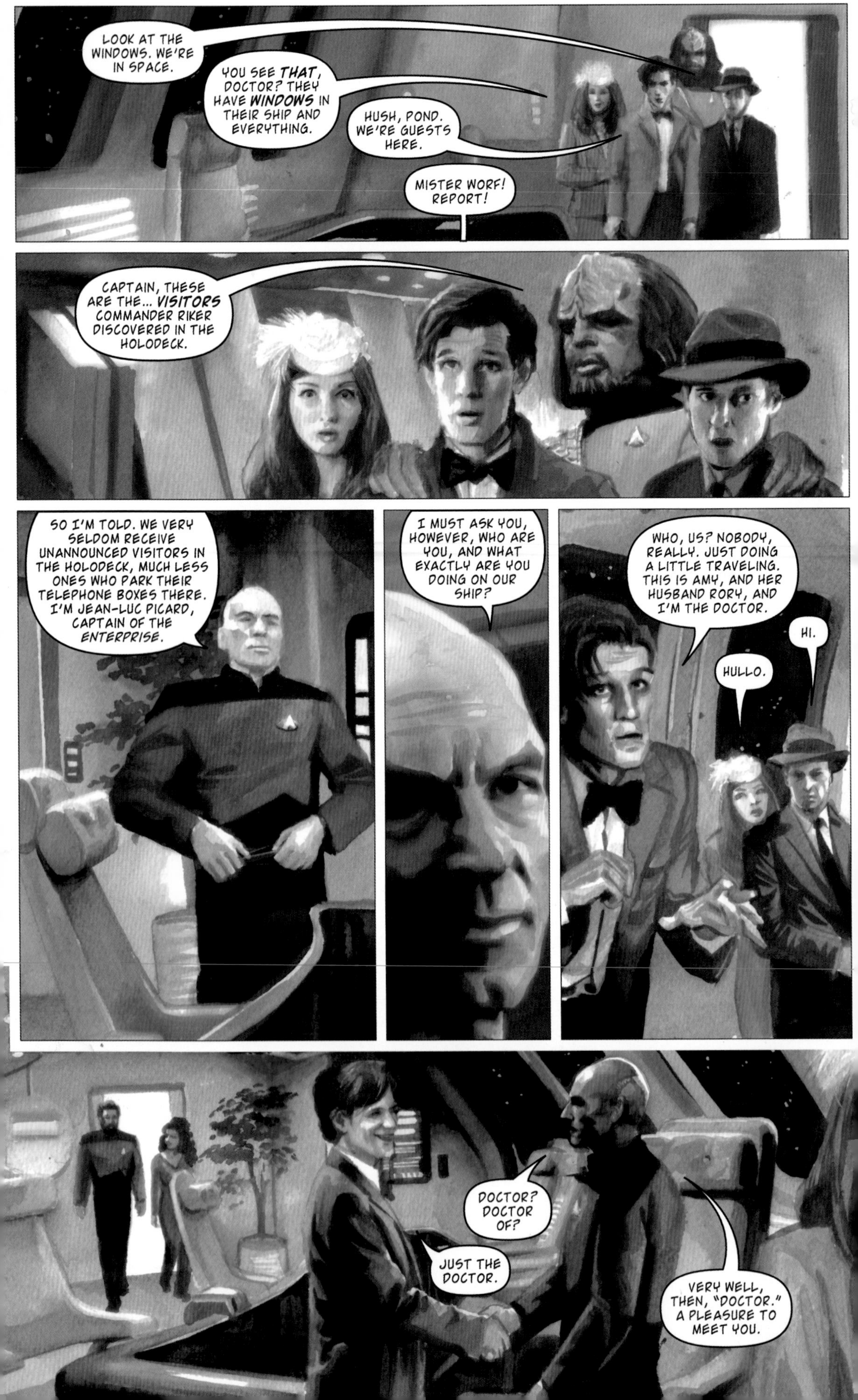
LOOK AT THE WINDOWS. WE'RE IN SPACE.
YOU SEE **THAT**, DOCTOR? THEY HAVE **WINDOWS** IN THEIR SHIP AND EVERYTHING.
HUSH, POND. WE'RE GUESTS HERE.
MISTER WORF! REPORT!
CAPTAIN, THESE ARE THE... ***VISITORS*** COMMANDER RIKER DISCOVERED IN THE HOLODECK.
SO I'M TOLD. WE VERY SELDOM RECEIVE UNANNOUNCED VISITORS IN THE HOLODECK, MUCH LESS ONES WHO PARK THEIR TELEPHONE BOXES THERE. I'M JEAN-LUC PICARD, CAPTAIN OF THE *ENTERPRISE*.
I MUST ASK YOU, HOWEVER, WHO ARE YOU, AND WHAT EXACTLY ARE YOU DOING ON OUR SHIP?
WHO, US? NOBODY, REALLY. JUST DOING A LITTLE TRAVELING. THIS IS AMY, AND HER HUSBAND RORY, AND I'M THE DOCTOR.
HI.
HULLO.
DOCTOR? DOCTOR OF?
JUST THE DOCTOR.
VERY WELL, THEN, "DOCTOR." A PLEASURE TO MEET YOU.

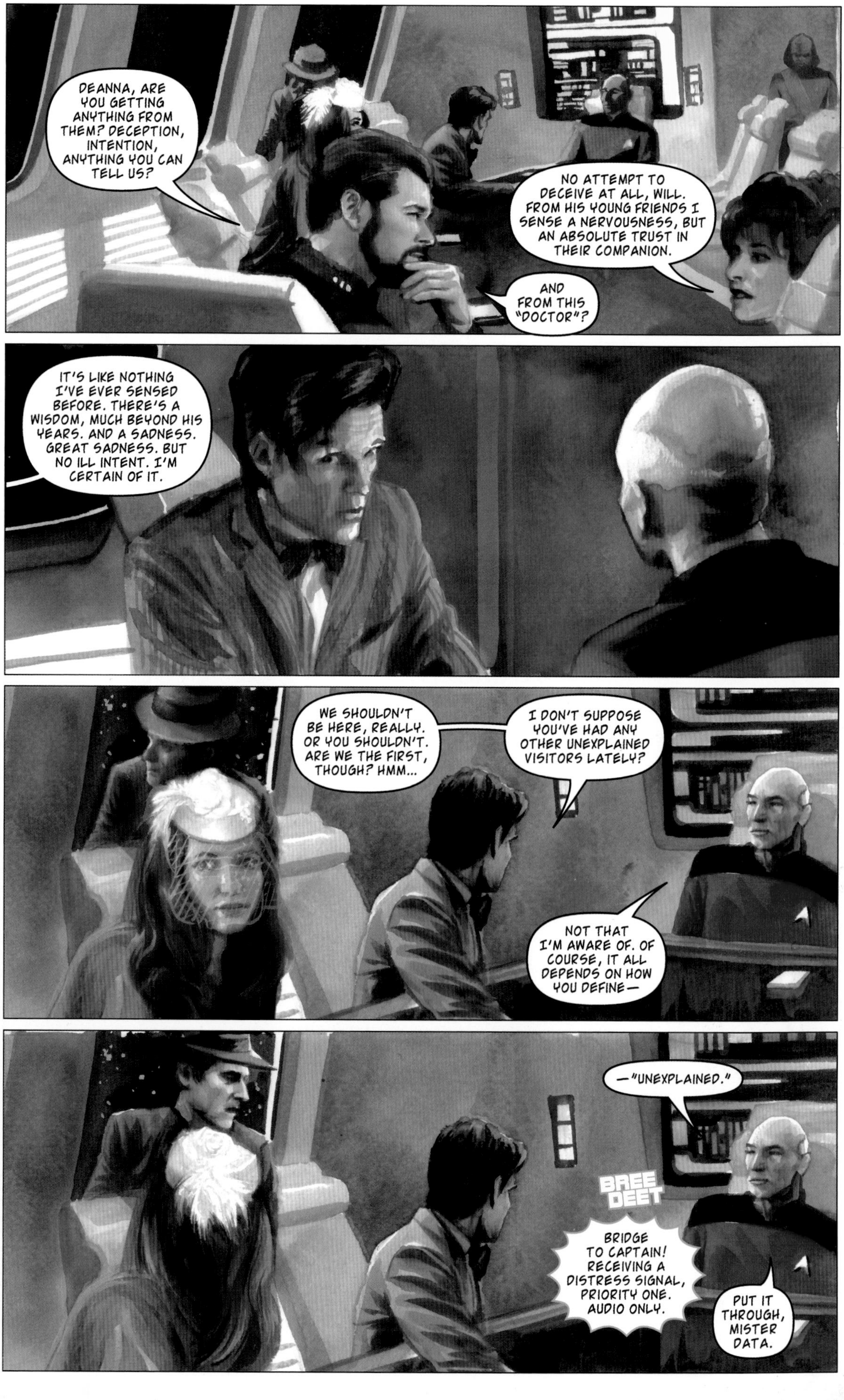
DEANNA, ARE YOU GETTING ANYTHING FROM THEM? DECEPTION, INTENTION, ANYTHING YOU CAN TELL US?
NO ATTEMPT TO DECEIVE AT ALL, WILL. FROM HIS YOUNG FRIENDS I SENSE A NERVOUSNESS, BUT AN ABSOLUTE TRUST IN THEIR COMPANION.
AND FROM THIS "DOCTOR"?
IT'S LIKE NOTHING I'VE EVER SENSED BEFORE. THERE'S A WISDOM, MUCH BEYOND HIS YEARS. AND A SADNESS. GREAT SADNESS. BUT NO ILL INTENT. I'M CERTAIN OF IT.
WE SHOULDN'T BE HERE, REALLY. OR YOU SHOULDN'T. ARE WE THE FIRST, THOUGH? HMM...
I DON'T SUPPOSE YOU'VE HAD ANY OTHER UNEXPLAINED VISITORS LATELY?
NOT THAT I'M AWARE OF. OF COURSE, IT ALL DEPENDS ON HOW YOU DEFINE—
—"UNEXPLAINED."
BREE DEET
BRIDGE TO CAPTAIN! RECEIVING A DISTRESS SIGNAL, PRIORITY ONE. AUDIO ONLY.
PUT IT THROUGH, MISTER DATA.

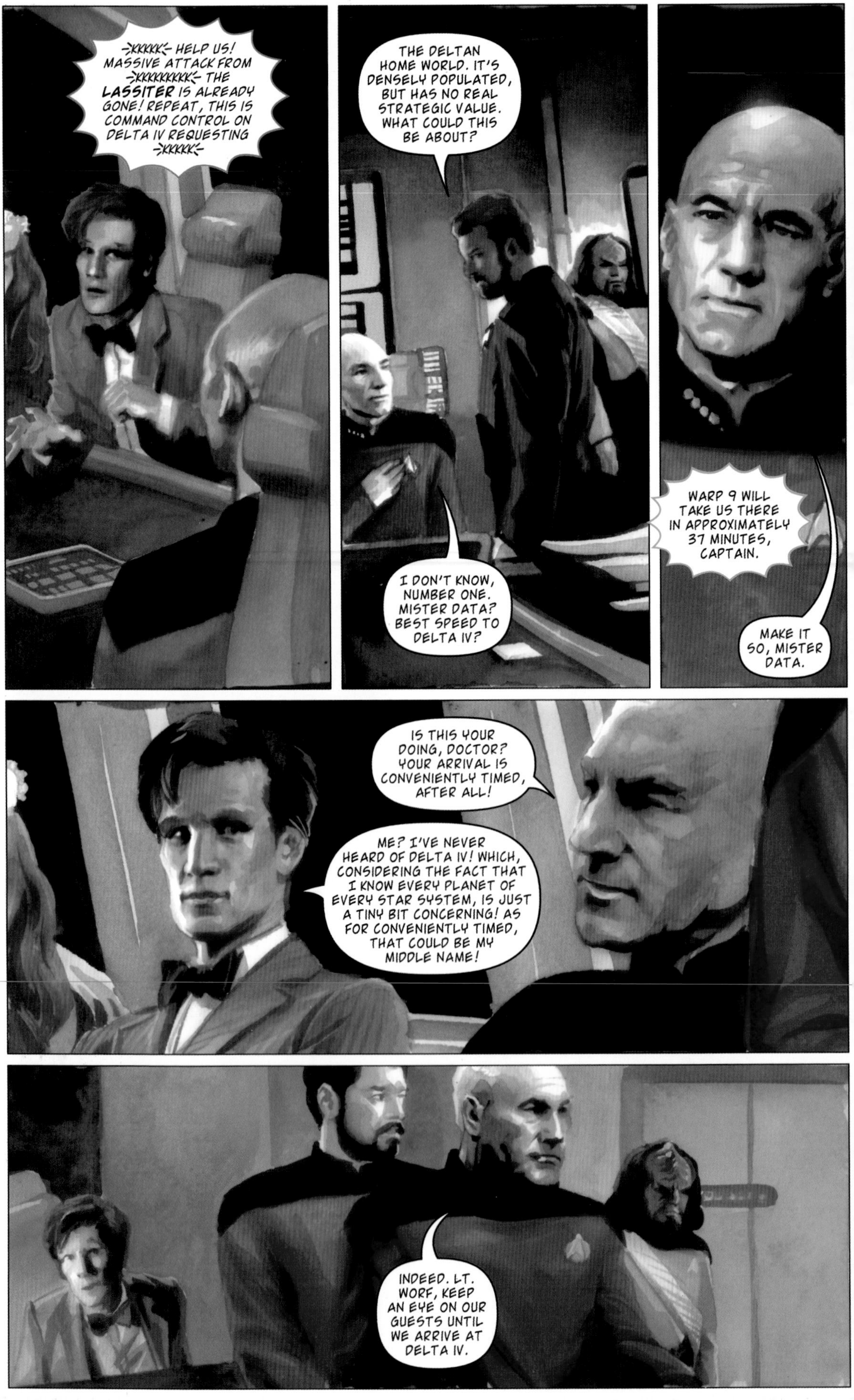
-KKKKK- HELP US! MASSIVE ATTACK FROM -KKKKKKKKK- THE LASSITER IS ALREADY GONE! REPEAT, THIS IS COMMAND CONTROL ON DELTA IV REQUESTING -KKKKK-
THE DELTAN HOME WORLD. IT'S DENSELY POPULATED, BUT HAS NO REAL STRATEGIC VALUE. WHAT COULD THIS BE ABOUT?
I DON'T KNOW, NUMBER ONE. MISTER DATA? BEST SPEED TO DELTA IV?
WARP 9 WILL TAKE US THERE IN APPROXIMATELY 37 MINUTES, CAPTAIN.
MAKE IT SO, MISTER DATA.
IS THIS YOUR DOING, DOCTOR? YOUR ARRIVAL IS CONVENIENTLY TIMED, AFTER ALL!
ME? I'VE NEVER HEARD OF DELTA IV! WHICH, CONSIDERING THE FACT THAT I KNOW EVERY PLANET OF EVERY STAR SYSTEM, IS JUST A TINY BIT CONCERNING! AS FOR CONVENIENTLY TIMED, THAT COULD BE MY MIDDLE NAME!
INDEED. LT. WORF, KEEP AN EYE ON OUR GUESTS UNTIL WE ARRIVE AT DELTA IV.

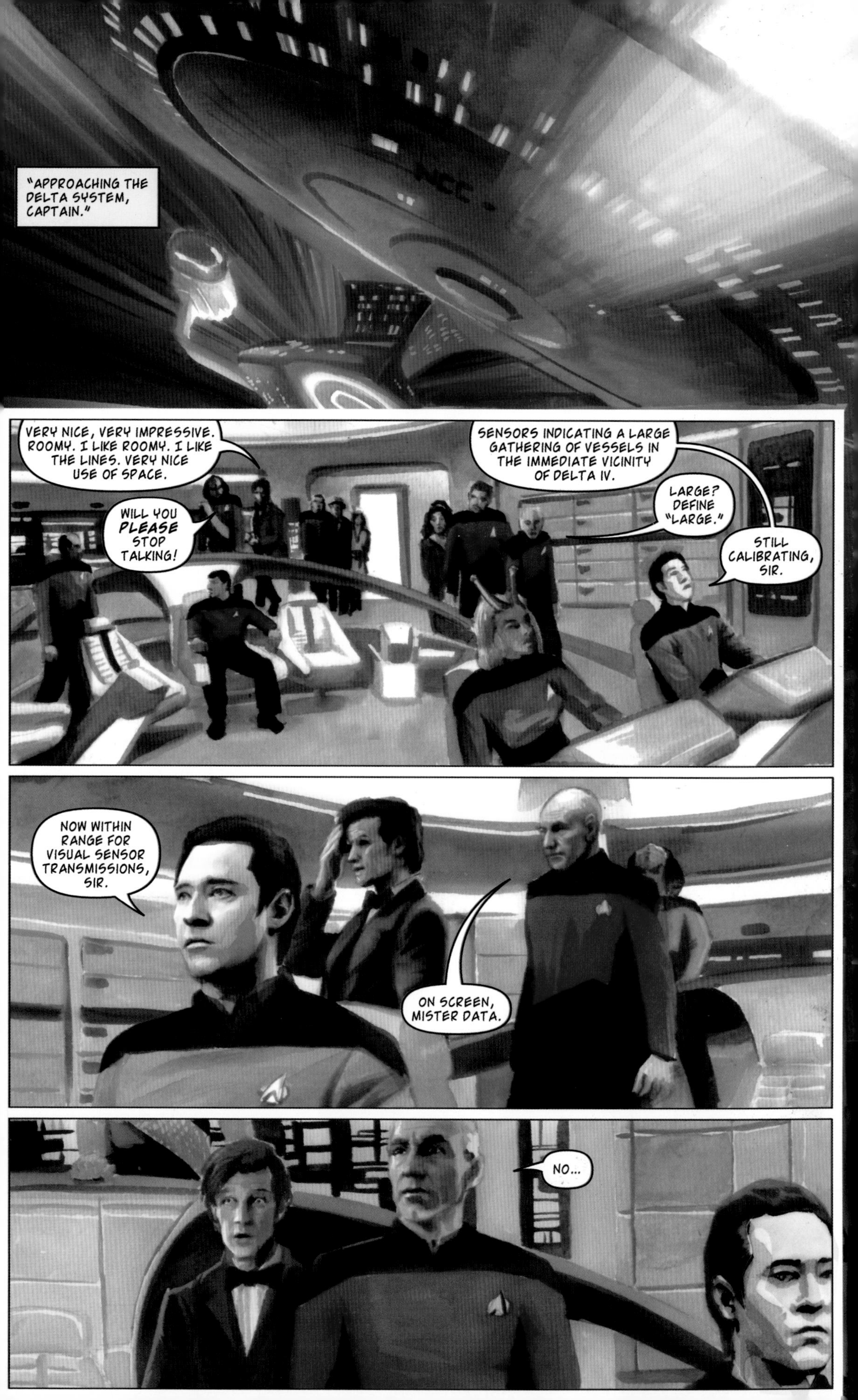
"APPROACHING THE DELTA SYSTEM, CAPTAIN."
VERY NICE, VERY IMPRESSIVE. ROOMY. I LIKE ROOMY. I LIKE THE LINES. VERY NICE USE OF SPACE.
WILL YOU PLEASE STOP TALKING!
SENSORS INDICATING A LARGE GATHERING OF VESSELS IN THE IMMEDIATE VICINITY OF DELTA IV.
LARGE? DEFINE "LARGE."
STILL CALIBRATING, SIR.
NOW WITHIN RANGE FOR VISUAL SENSOR TRANSMISSIONS, SIR.
ON SCREEN, MISTER DATA.
NO...

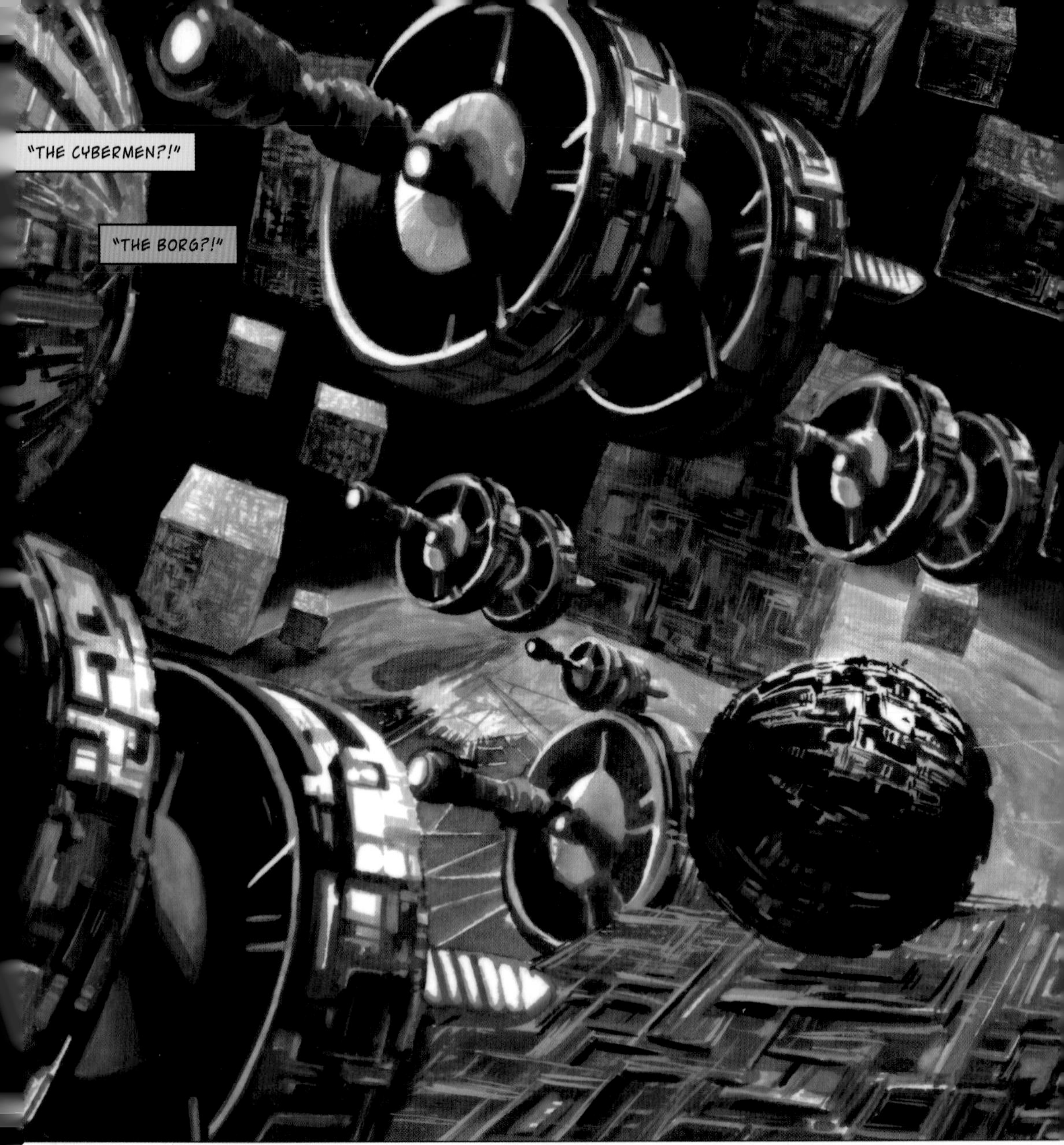
"THE CYBERMEN?!"
"THE BORG?!"

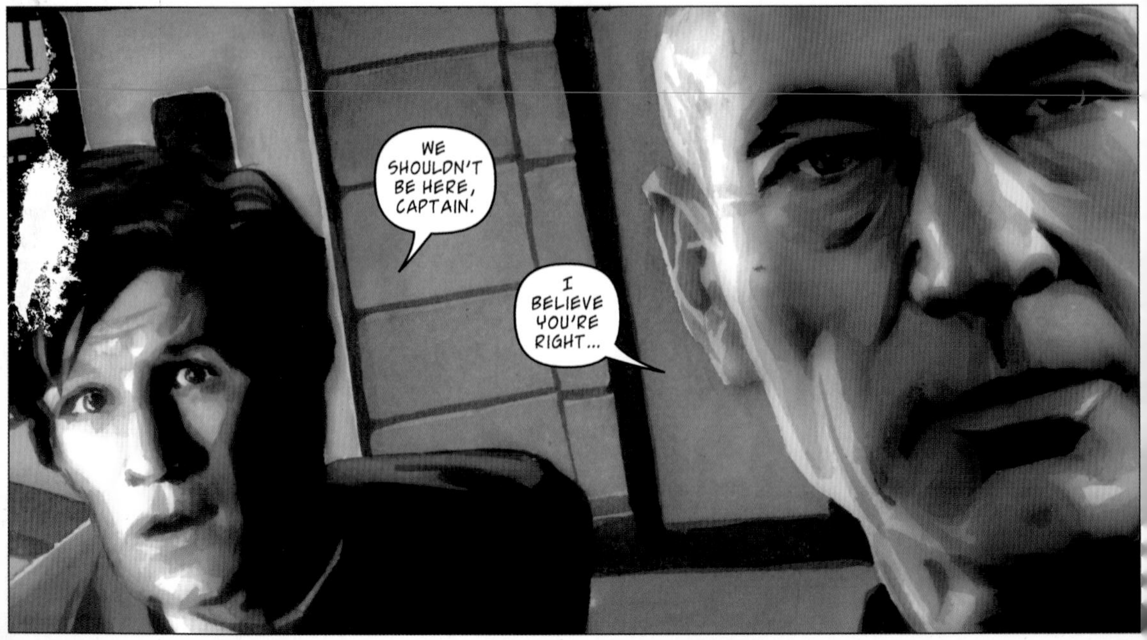
WE SHOULDN'T BE HERE, CAPTAIN.
I BELIEVE YOU'RE RIGHT...

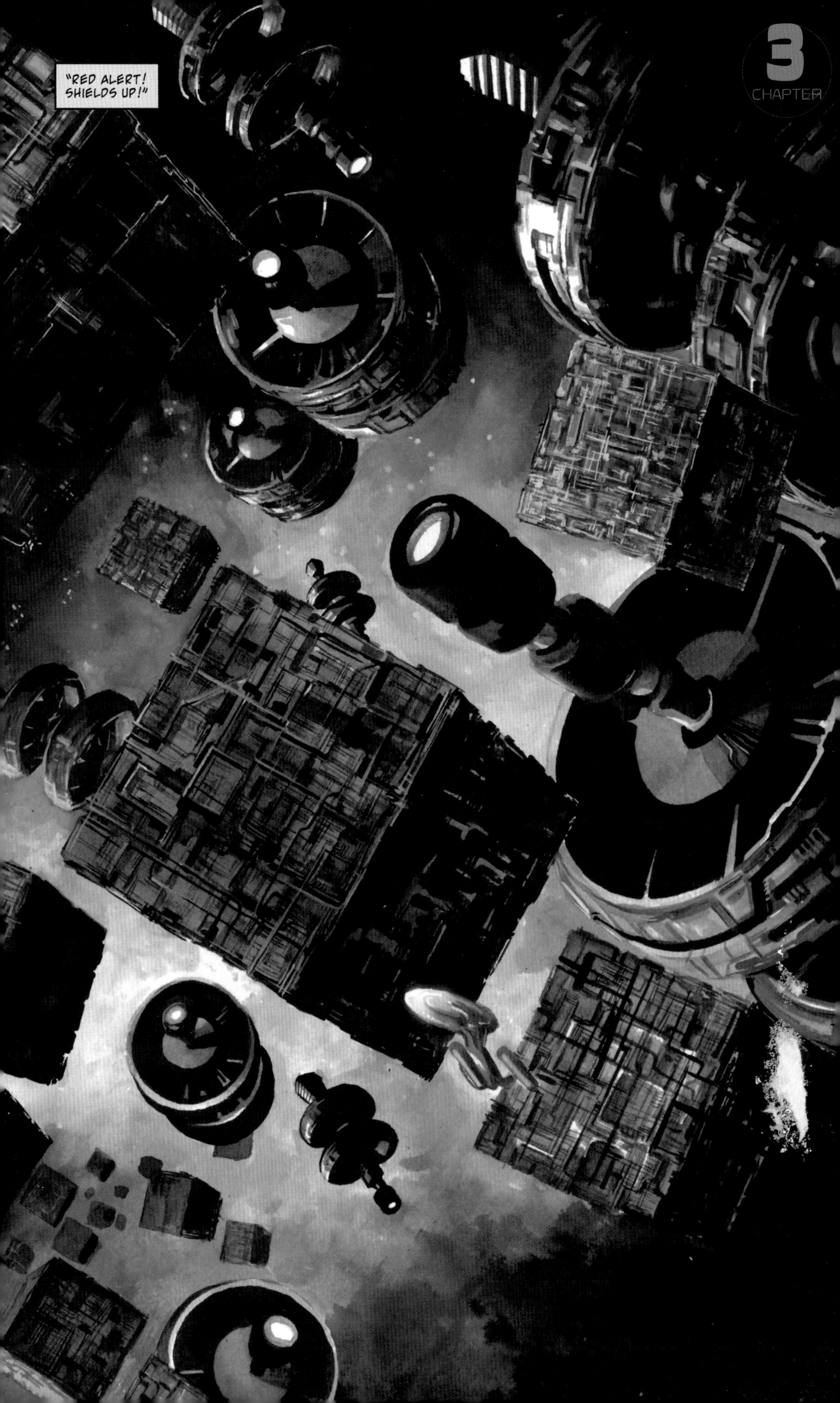
"RED ALERT! SHIELDS UP!"
3
CHAPTER

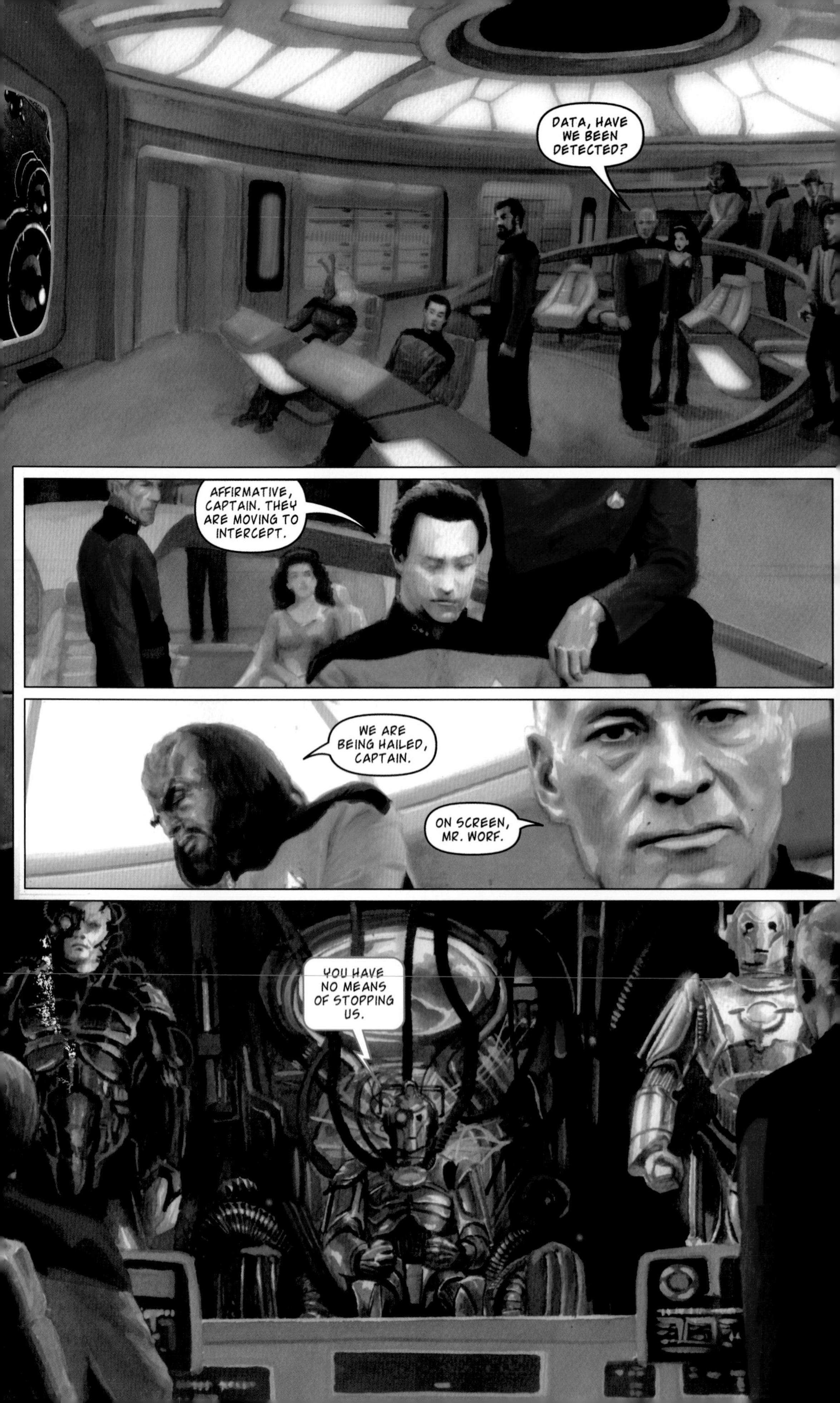
DATA, HAVE WE BEEN DETECTED?
AFFIRMATIVE, CAPTAIN. THEY ARE MOVING TO INTERCEPT.
WE ARE BEING HAILED, CAPTAIN.
ON SCREEN, MR. WORF.
YOU HAVE NO MEANS OF STOPPING US.

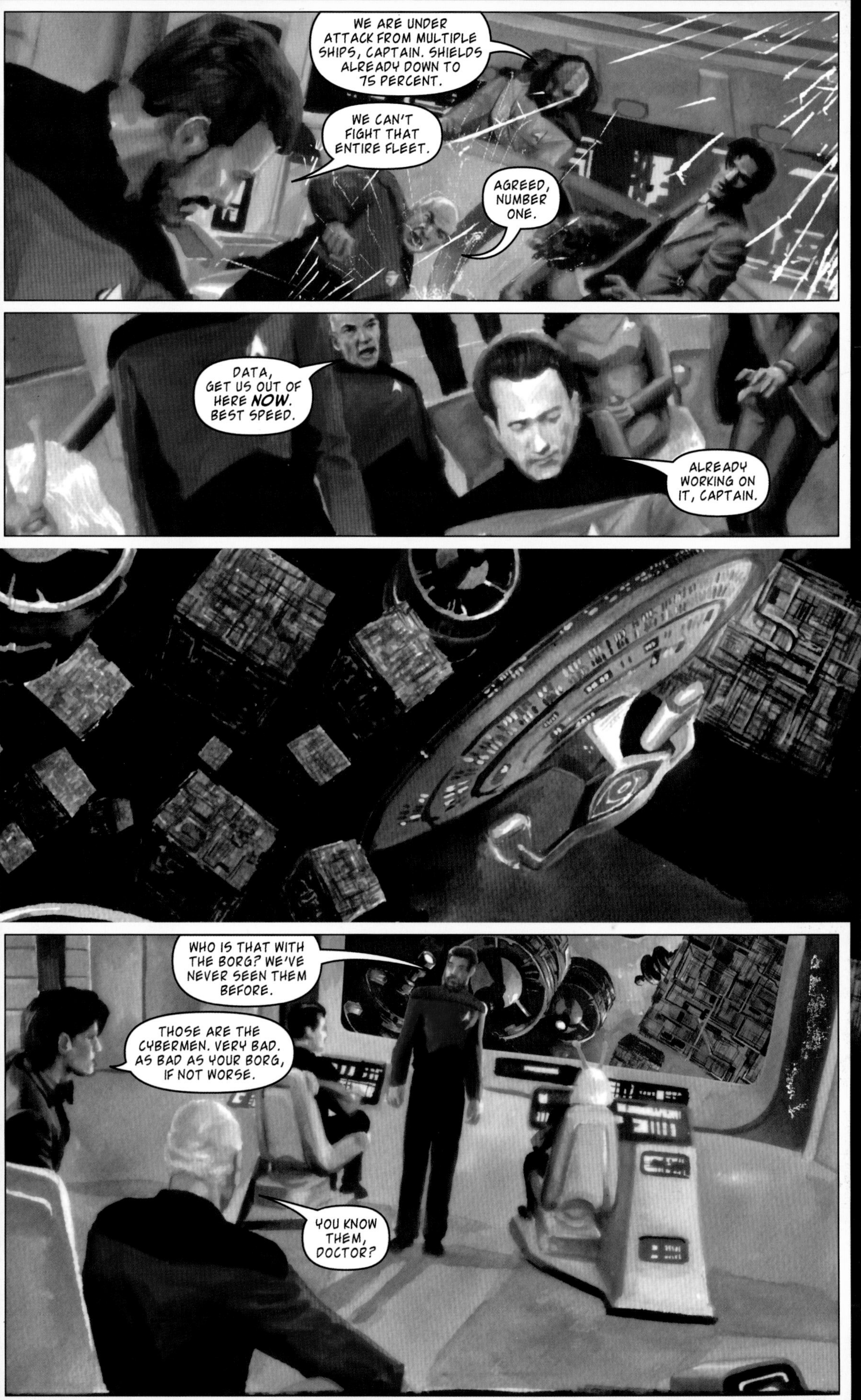

WE ARE UNDER ATTACK FROM MULTIPLE SHIPS, CAPTAIN. SHIELDS ALREADY DOWN TO 75 PERCENT.
WE CAN'T FIGHT THAT ENTIRE FLEET.
AGREED, NUMBER ONE.
DATA, GET US OUT OF HERE **NOW**. BEST SPEED.
ALREADY WORKING ON IT, CAPTAIN.
WHO IS THAT WITH THE BORG? WE'VE NEVER SEEN THEM BEFORE.
THOSE ARE THE CYBERMEN. VERY BAD. AS BAD AS YOUR BORG, IF NOT WORSE.
YOU KNOW THEM, DOCTOR?

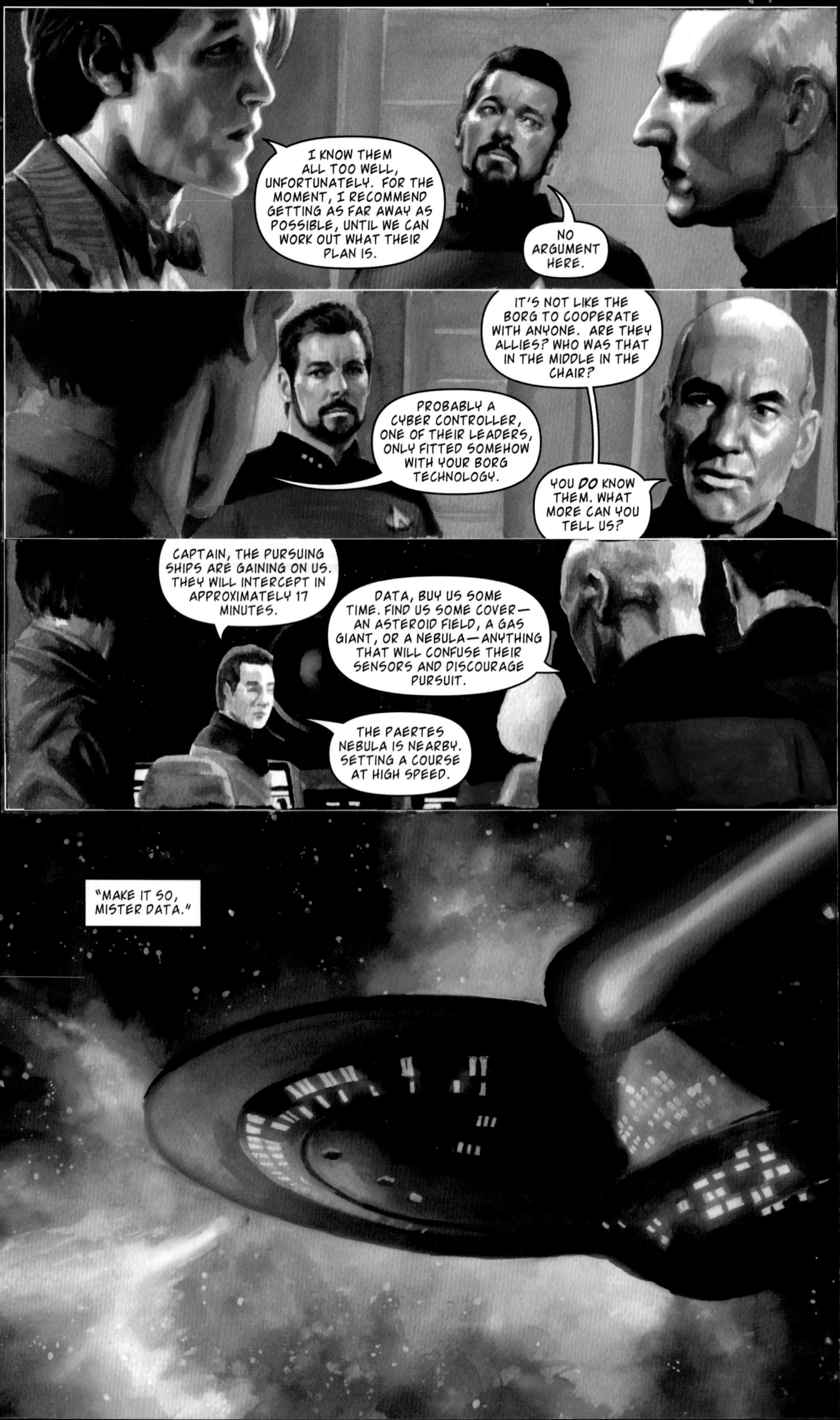
I KNOW THEM ALL TOO WELL, UNFORTUNATELY. FOR THE MOMENT, I RECOMMEND GETTING AS FAR AWAY AS POSSIBLE, UNTIL WE CAN WORK OUT WHAT THEIR PLAN IS.
NO ARGUMENT HERE.
IT'S NOT LIKE THE BORG TO COOPERATE WITH ANYONE. ARE THEY ALLIES? WHO WAS THAT IN THE MIDDLE IN THE CHAIR?
PROBABLY A CYBER CONTROLLER, ONE OF THEIR LEADERS, ONLY FITTED SOMEHOW WITH YOUR BORG TECHNOLOGY.
YOU DO KNOW THEM. WHAT MORE CAN YOU TELL US?
CAPTAIN, THE PURSUING SHIPS ARE GAINING ON US. THEY WILL INTERCEPT IN APPROXIMATELY 17 MINUTES.
DATA, BUY US SOME TIME. FIND US SOME COVER— AN ASTEROID FIELD, A GAS GIANT, OR A NEBULA— ANYTHING THAT WILL CONFUSE THEIR SENSORS AND DISCOURAGE PURSUIT.
THE PAERTES NEBULA IS NEARBY. SETTING A COURSE AT HIGH SPEED.
"MAKE IT SO, MISTER DATA."

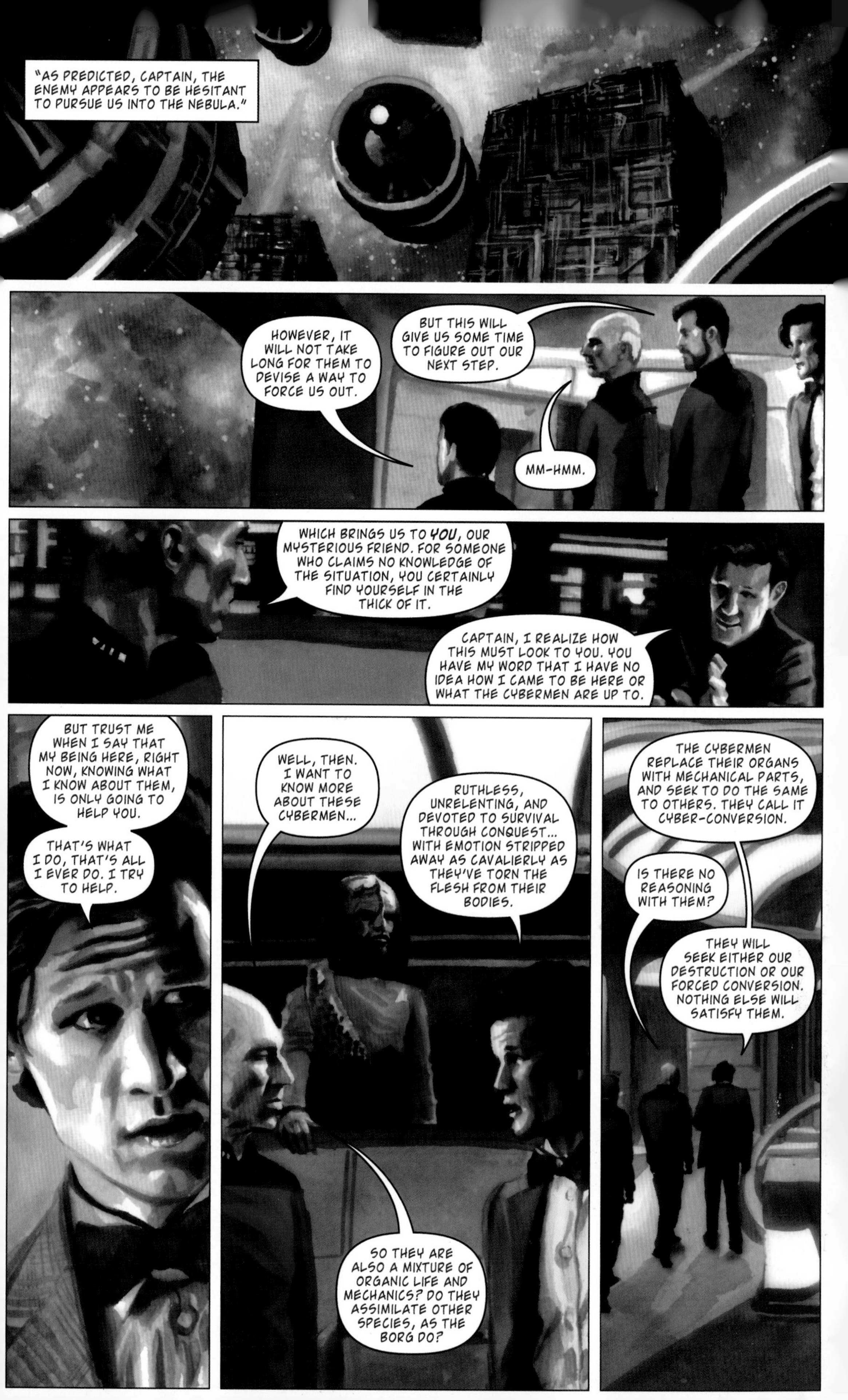
"AS PREDICTED, CAPTAIN, THE ENEMY APPEARS TO BE HESITANT TO PURSUE US INTO THE NEBULA."
HOWEVER, IT WILL NOT TAKE LONG FOR THEM TO DEVISE A WAY TO FORCE US OUT.
BUT THIS WILL GIVE US SOME TIME TO FIGURE OUT OUR NEXT STEP.
MM-HMM.
WHICH BRINGS US TO YOU, OUR MYSTERIOUS FRIEND. FOR SOMEONE WHO CLAIMS NO KNOWLEDGE OF THE SITUATION, YOU CERTAINLY FIND YOURSELF IN THE THICK OF IT.
CAPTAIN, I REALIZE HOW THIS MUST LOOK TO YOU. YOU HAVE MY WORD THAT I HAVE NO IDEA HOW I CAME TO BE HERE OR WHAT THE CYBERMEN ARE UP TO.
BUT TRUST ME WHEN I SAY THAT MY BEING HERE, RIGHT NOW, KNOWING WHAT I KNOW ABOUT THEM, IS ONLY GOING TO HELP YOU.
THAT'S WHAT I DO, THAT'S ALL I EVER DO. I TRY TO HELP.
WELL, THEN. I WANT TO KNOW MORE ABOUT THESE CYBERMEN...
RUTHLESS, UNRELENTING, AND DEVOTED TO SURVIVAL THROUGH CONQUEST... WITH EMOTION STRIPPED AWAY AS CAVALIERLY AS THEY'VE TORN THE FLESH FROM THEIR BODIES.
SO THEY ARE ALSO A MIXTURE OF ORGANIC LIFE AND MECHANICS? DO THEY ASSIMILATE OTHER SPECIES, AS THE BORG DO?
THE CYBERMEN REPLACE THEIR ORGANS WITH MECHANICAL PARTS, AND SEEK TO DO THE SAME TO OTHERS. THEY CALL IT CYBER-CONVERSION.
IS THERE NO REASONING WITH THEM?
THEY WILL SEEK EITHER OUR DESTRUCTION OR OUR FORCED CONVERSION. NOTHING ELSE WILL SATISFY THEM.

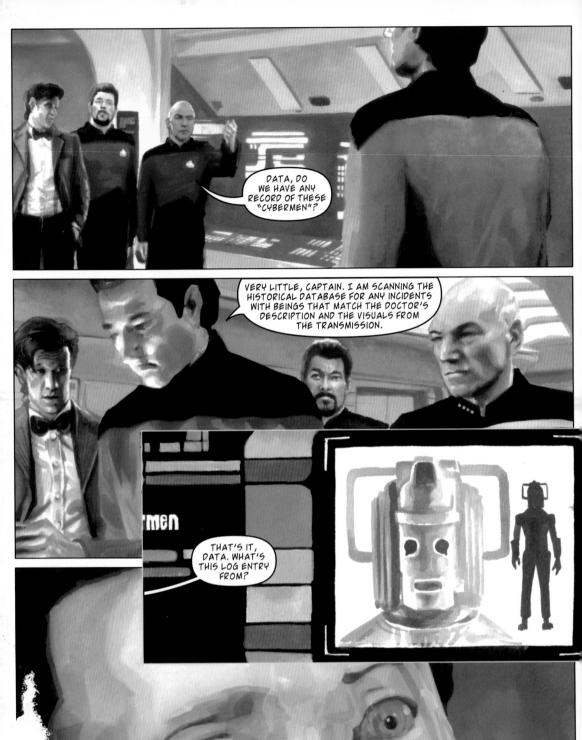

DATA, DO WE HAVE ANY RECORD OF THESE "CYBERMEN"?

VERY LITTLE, CAPTAIN. I AM SCANNING THE HISTORICAL DATABASE FOR ANY INCIDENTS WITH BEINGS THAT MATCH THE DOCTOR'S DESCRIPTION AND THE VISUALS FROM THE TRANSMISSION.

THAT'S IT, DATA. WHAT'S THIS LOG ENTRY FROM?

THIS LOG ENTRY IS... FROM THE ENTERPRISE.

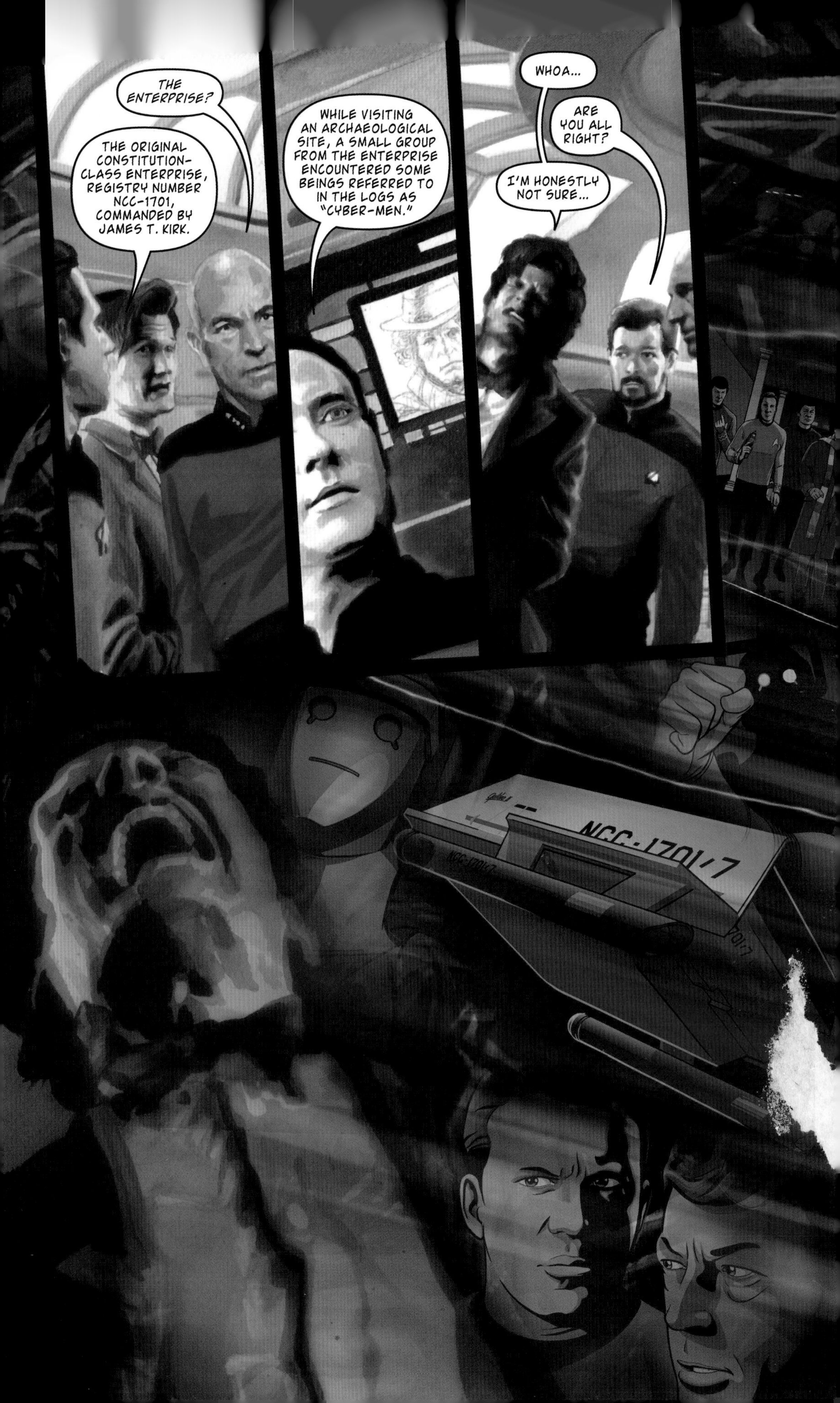

THE ENTERPRISE?
THE ORIGINAL CONSTITUTION-CLASS ENTERPRISE, REGISTRY NUMBER NCC-1701, COMMANDED BY JAMES T. KIRK.
WHILE VISITING AN ARCHAEOLOGICAL SITE, A SMALL GROUP FROM THE ENTERPRISE ENCOUNTERED SOME BEINGS REFERRED TO IN THE LOGS AS "CYBER-MEN."
WHOA...
ARE YOU ALL RIGHT?
I'M HONESTLY NOT SURE...
NCC-1701/7

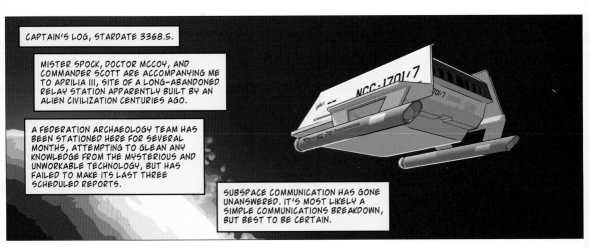

CAPTAIN'S LOG, STARDATE 3368.5.

MISTER SPOCK, DOCTOR MCCOY, AND COMMANDER SCOTT ARE ACCOMPANYING ME TO APRILIA III, SITE OF A LONG-ABANDONED RELAY STATION APPARENTLY BUILT BY AN ALIEN CIVILIZATION CENTURIES AGO.

A FEDERATION ARCHAEOLOGY TEAM HAS BEEN STATIONED HERE FOR SEVERAL MONTHS, ATTEMPTING TO GLEAN ANY KNOWLEDGE FROM THE MYSTERIOUS AND UNWORKABLE TECHNOLOGY, BUT HAS FAILED TO MAKE ITS LAST THREE SCHEDULED REPORTS.

SUBSPACE COMMUNICATION HAS GONE UNANSWERED. IT'S MOST LIKELY A SIMPLE COMMUNICATIONS BREAKDOWN, BUT BEST TO BE CERTAIN.

THE PLANET'S UNIQUE RADIATION ALSO PREVENTS THE USE OF THE TRANSPORTER, NECESSITATING OUR VISIT VIA SHUTTLECRAFT.

LOOKING CLEAR FOR LANDING, CAPTAIN.

TAKE US DOWN, SCOTTY.

AYE, SIR.

SEEMS QUIET ENOUGH.

YES. YES, IT DOES...

HELLO THERE!

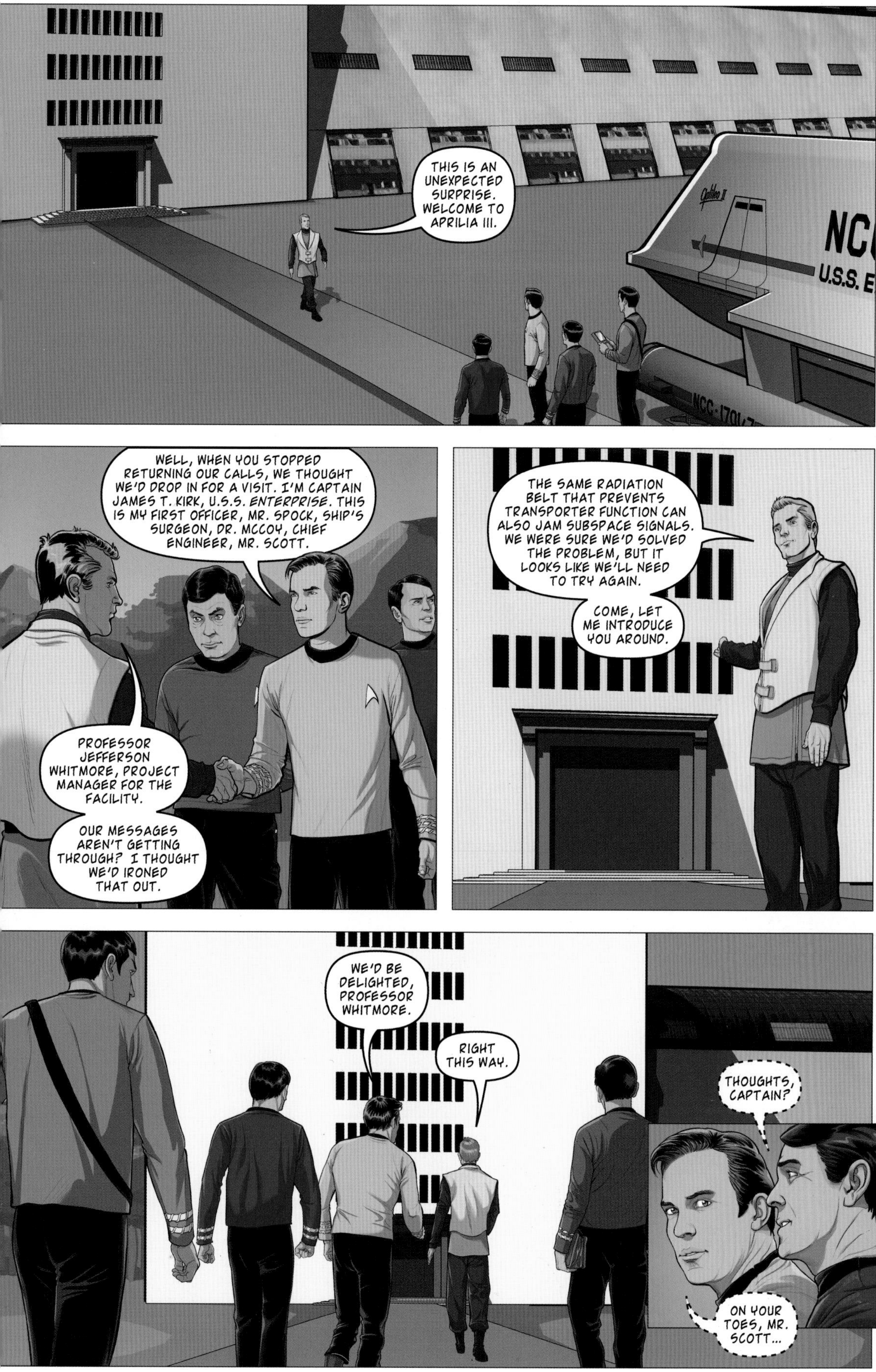
THIS IS AN UNEXPECTED SURPRISE. WELCOME TO APRILIA III.
NCC
U.S.S. E
NCC-1701/7
WELL, WHEN YOU STOPPED RETURNING OUR CALLS, WE THOUGHT WE'D DROP IN FOR A VISIT. I'M CAPTAIN JAMES T. KIRK, U.S.S. *ENTERPRISE*. THIS IS MY FIRST OFFICER, MR. SPOCK, SHIP'S SURGEON, DR. MCCOY, CHIEF ENGINEER, MR. SCOTT.
PROFESSOR JEFFERSON WHITMORE, PROJECT MANAGER FOR THE FACILITY.
OUR MESSAGES AREN'T GETTING THROUGH? I THOUGHT WE'D IRONED THAT OUT.
THE SAME RADIATION BELT THAT PREVENTS TRANSPORTER FUNCTION CAN ALSO JAM SUBSPACE SIGNALS. WE WERE SURE WE'D SOLVED THE PROBLEM, BUT IT LOOKS LIKE WE'LL NEED TO TRY AGAIN.
COME, LET ME INTRODUCE YOU AROUND.
WE'D BE DELIGHTED, PROFESSOR WHITMORE.
RIGHT THIS WAY.
THOUGHTS, CAPTAIN?
ON YOUR TOES, MR. SCOTT...

THIS IS THE MAIN RELAY STATION THAT WAS DISCOVERED. WE STILL HAVEN'T BEEN ABLE TO FIGURE OUT HOW TO ACTIVATE IT, ALTHOUGH WE HAVE DETERMINED THAT THERE IS STILL POWER CIRCULATING THROUGH IT. WHERE THAT'S COMING FROM IS SOMETHING ELSE WE'RE NOT SURE ABOUT...

WE HAVE GUESTS, PROFESSOR?

MY APOLOGIES, DOCTOR. CAPTAIN JAMES KIRK OF THE U.S.S. ENTERPRISE. CAPTAIN, THIS IS DOCTOR PAULA ZARLENGA, ONE OF OUR RESEARCHERS.

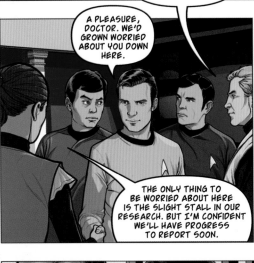

A PLEASURE, DOCTOR. WE'D GROWN WORRIED ABOUT YOU DOWN HERE.

THE ONLY THING TO BE WORRIED ABOUT HERE IS THE SLIGHT STALL IN OUR RESEARCH. BUT I'M CONFIDENT WE'LL HAVE PROGRESS TO REPORT SOON.

ABSOLUTELY. NOW, IF YOU'LL EXCUSE US, CAPTAIN, WE REALLY MUST RETURN TO OUR WORK, UNLESS YOU HAVE OTHER CONCERNS.

NO CONCERNS, PROFESSOR WHITMORE. SORRY TO HAVE BOTHERED YOU.

NOT AT ALL, CAPTAIN. THANK YOU FOR CHECKING IN.

SCOTTY, YOU CONVINCED?

NOT ONE BIT, CAP'N.

ME NEITHER.

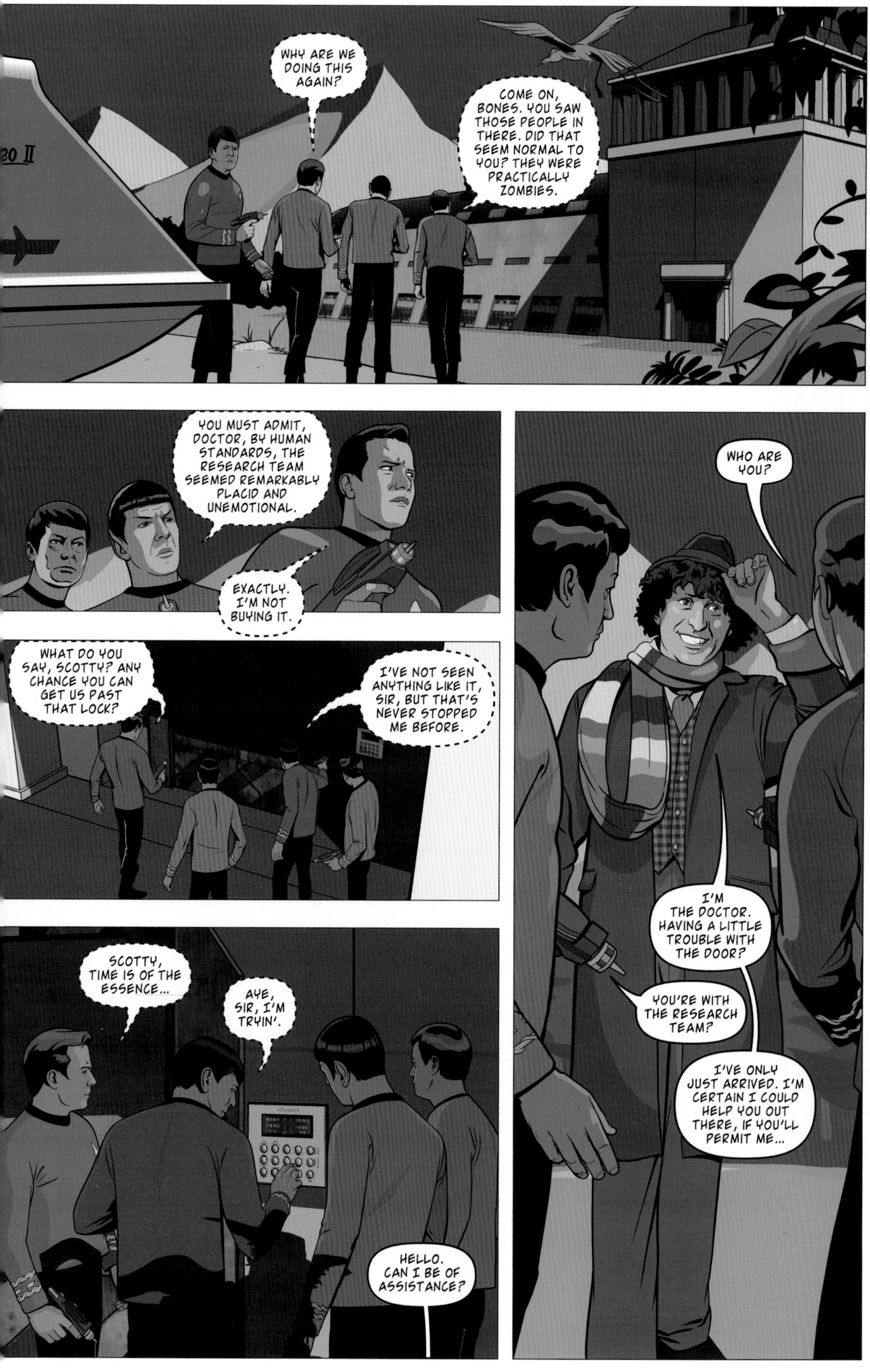
WHY ARE WE DOING THIS AGAIN?
COME ON, BONES. YOU SAW THOSE PEOPLE IN THERE. DID THAT SEEM NORMAL TO YOU? THEY WERE PRACTICALLY ZOMBIES.
YOU MUST ADMIT, DOCTOR, BY HUMAN STANDARDS, THE RESEARCH TEAM SEEMED REMARKABLY PLACID AND UNEMOTIONAL.
EXACTLY. I'M NOT BUYING IT.
WHAT DO YOU SAY, SCOTTY? ANY CHANCE YOU CAN GET US PAST THAT LOCK?
I'VE NOT SEEN ANYTHING LIKE IT, SIR, BUT THAT'S NEVER STOPPED ME BEFORE.
SCOTTY, TIME IS OF THE ESSENCE...
AYE, SIR, I'M TRYIN'.
HELLO. CAN I BE OF ASSISTANCE?
WHO ARE YOU?
I'M THE DOCTOR. HAVING A LITTLE TROUBLE WITH THE DOOR?
YOU'RE WITH THE RESEARCH TEAM?
I'VE ONLY JUST ARRIVED. I'M CERTAIN I COULD HELP YOU OUT THERE, IF YOU'LL PERMIT ME...

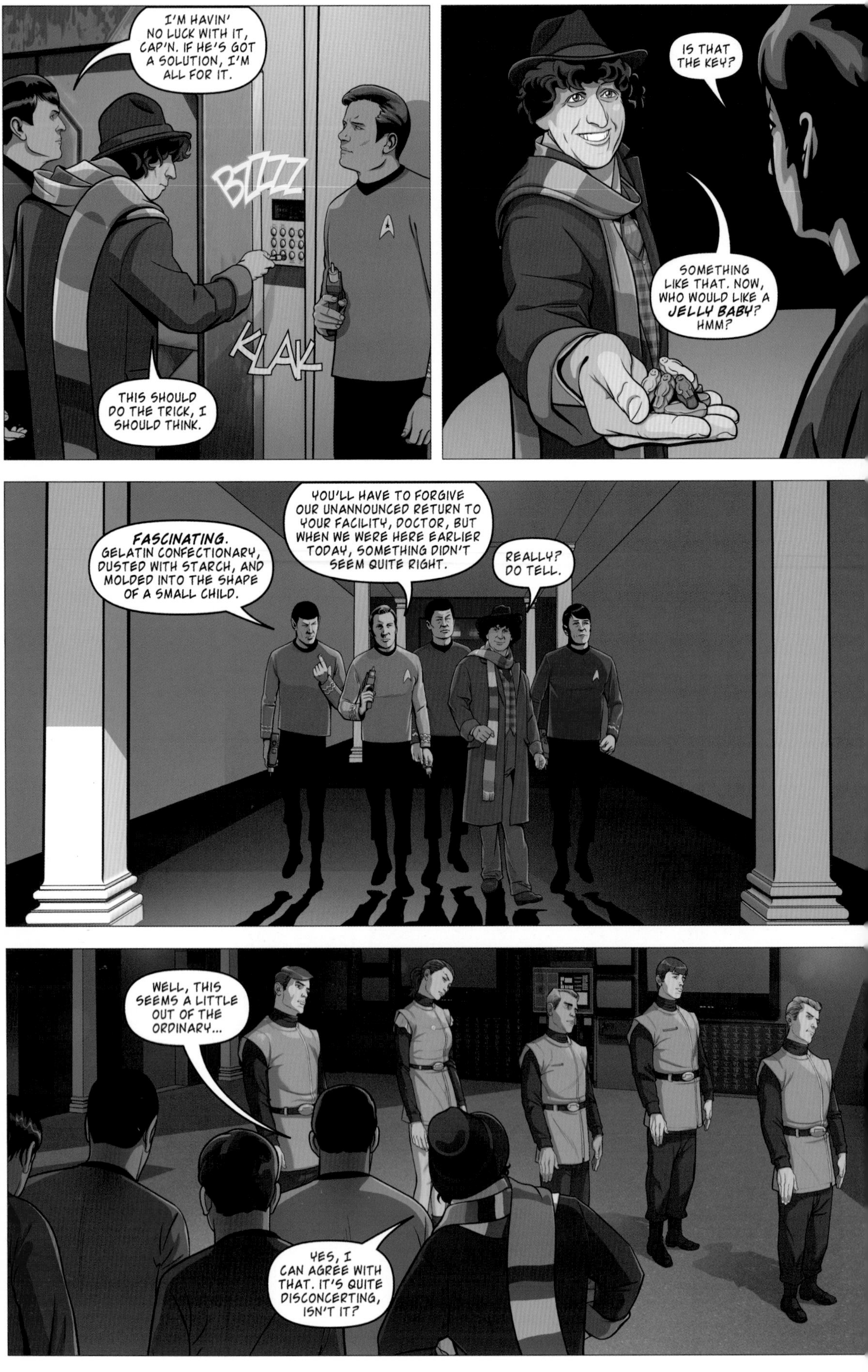
I'M HAVIN' NO LUCK WITH IT, CAP'N. IF HE'S GOT A SOLUTION, I'M ALL FOR IT.
BZZZ
KLAK
THIS SHOULD DO THE TRICK, I SHOULD THINK.
IS THAT THE KEY?
SOMETHING LIKE THAT. NOW, WHO WOULD LIKE A *JELLY BABY*? HMM?
FASCINATING. GELATIN CONFECTIONARY, DUSTED WITH STARCH, AND MOLDED INTO THE SHAPE OF A SMALL CHILD.
YOU'LL HAVE TO FORGIVE OUR UNANNOUNCED RETURN TO YOUR FACILITY, DOCTOR, BUT WHEN WE WERE HERE EARLIER TODAY, SOMETHING DIDN'T SEEM QUITE RIGHT.
REALLY? DO TELL.
WELL, THIS SEEMS A LITTLE OUT OF THE ORDINARY...
YES, I CAN AGREE WITH THAT. IT'S QUITE DISCONCERTING, ISN'T IT?

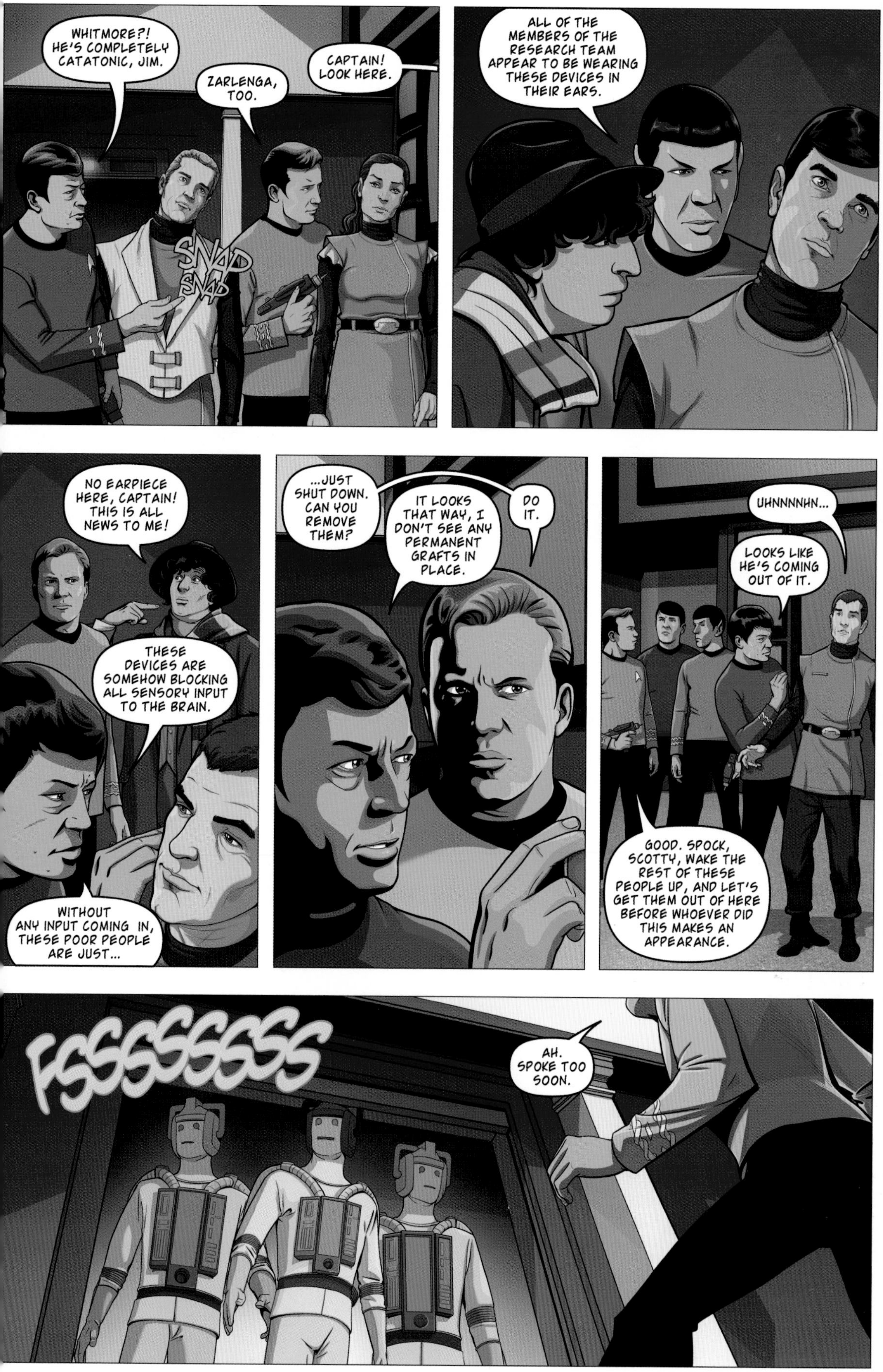
WHITMORE?! HE'S COMPLETELY CATATONIC, JIM.
ZARLENGA, TOO.
CAPTAIN! LOOK HERE.
SNAP SNAP
ALL OF THE MEMBERS OF THE RESEARCH TEAM APPEAR TO BE WEARING THESE DEVICES IN THEIR EARS.
NO EARPIECE HERE, CAPTAIN! THIS IS ALL NEWS TO ME!
THESE DEVICES ARE SOMEHOW BLOCKING ALL SENSORY INPUT TO THE BRAIN.
WITHOUT ANY INPUT COMING IN, THESE POOR PEOPLE ARE JUST...
...JUST SHUT DOWN. CAN YOU REMOVE THEM?
IT LOOKS THAT WAY, I DON'T SEE ANY PERMANENT GRAFTS IN PLACE.
DO IT.
UHNNNNHN...
LOOKS LIKE HE'S COMING OUT OF IT.
GOOD. SPOCK, SCOTTY, WAKE THE REST OF THESE PEOPLE UP, AND LET'S GET THEM OUT OF HERE BEFORE WHOEVER DID THIS MAKES AN APPEARANCE.
FSSSSSSSS
AH. SPOKE TOO SOON.

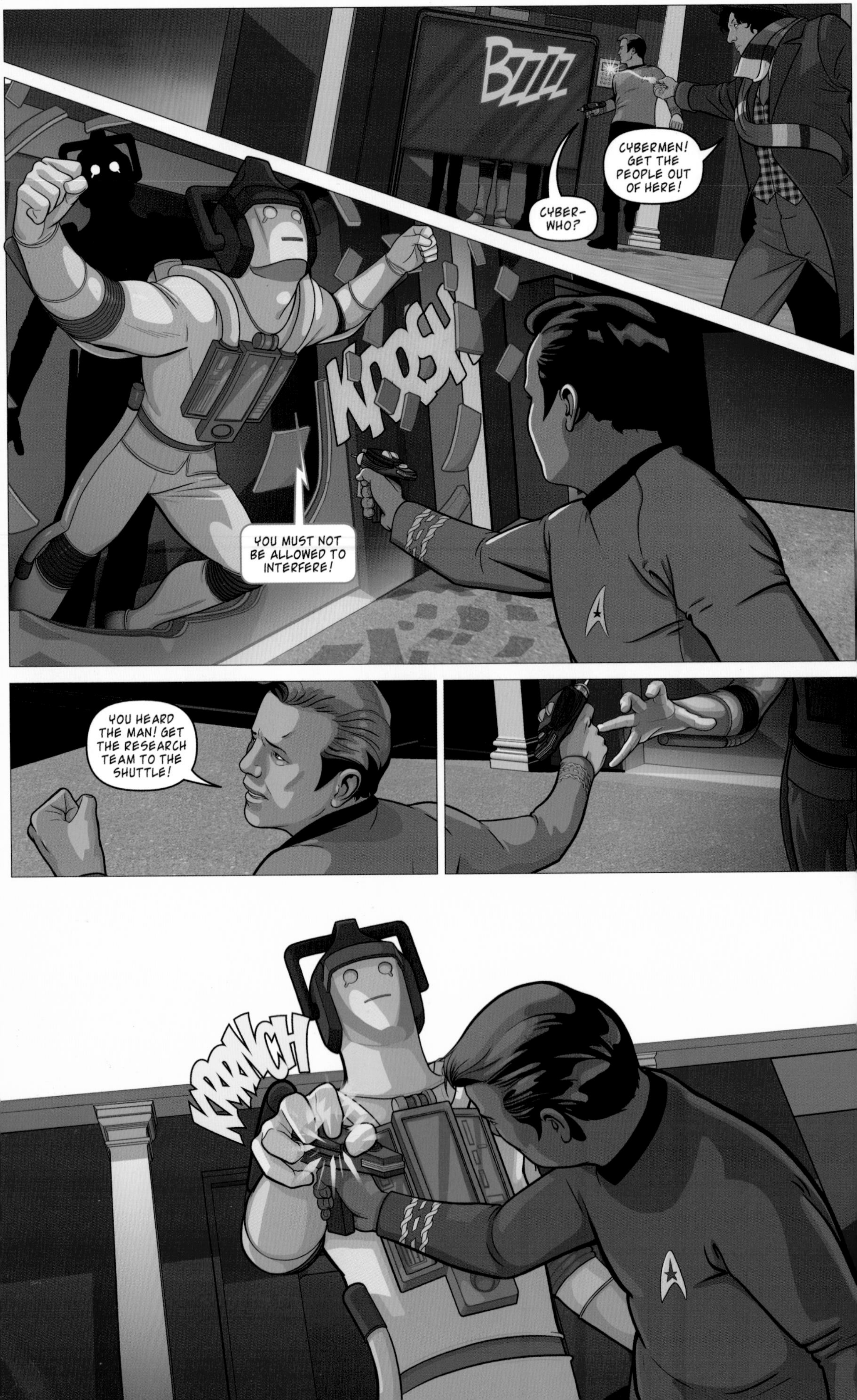
BZZZ
CYBERMEN! GET THE PEOPLE OUT OF HERE!
CYBER-WHO?
KRASH
YOU MUST NOT BE ALLOWED TO INTERFERE!
YOU HEARD THE MAN! GET THE RESEARCH TEAM TO THE SHUTTLE!
KRRNCH

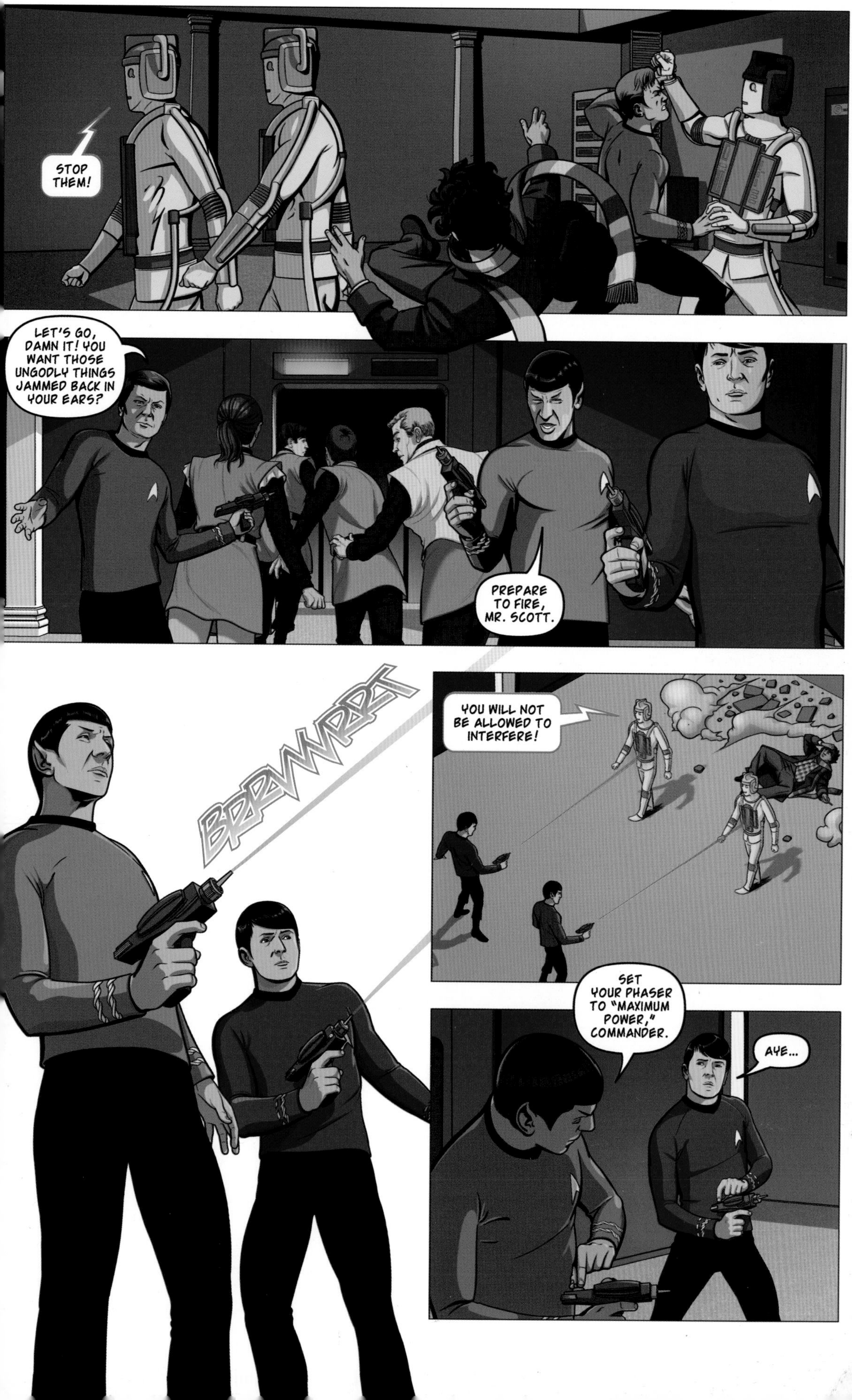
STOP THEM!
LET'S GO, DAMN IT! YOU WANT THOSE UNGODLY THINGS JAMMED BACK IN YOUR EARS?
PREPARE TO FIRE, MR. SCOTT.
BRRWWRRT
YOU WILL NOT BE ALLOWED TO INTERFERE!
SET YOUR PHASER TO "MAXIMUM POWER," COMMANDER.
AYE...

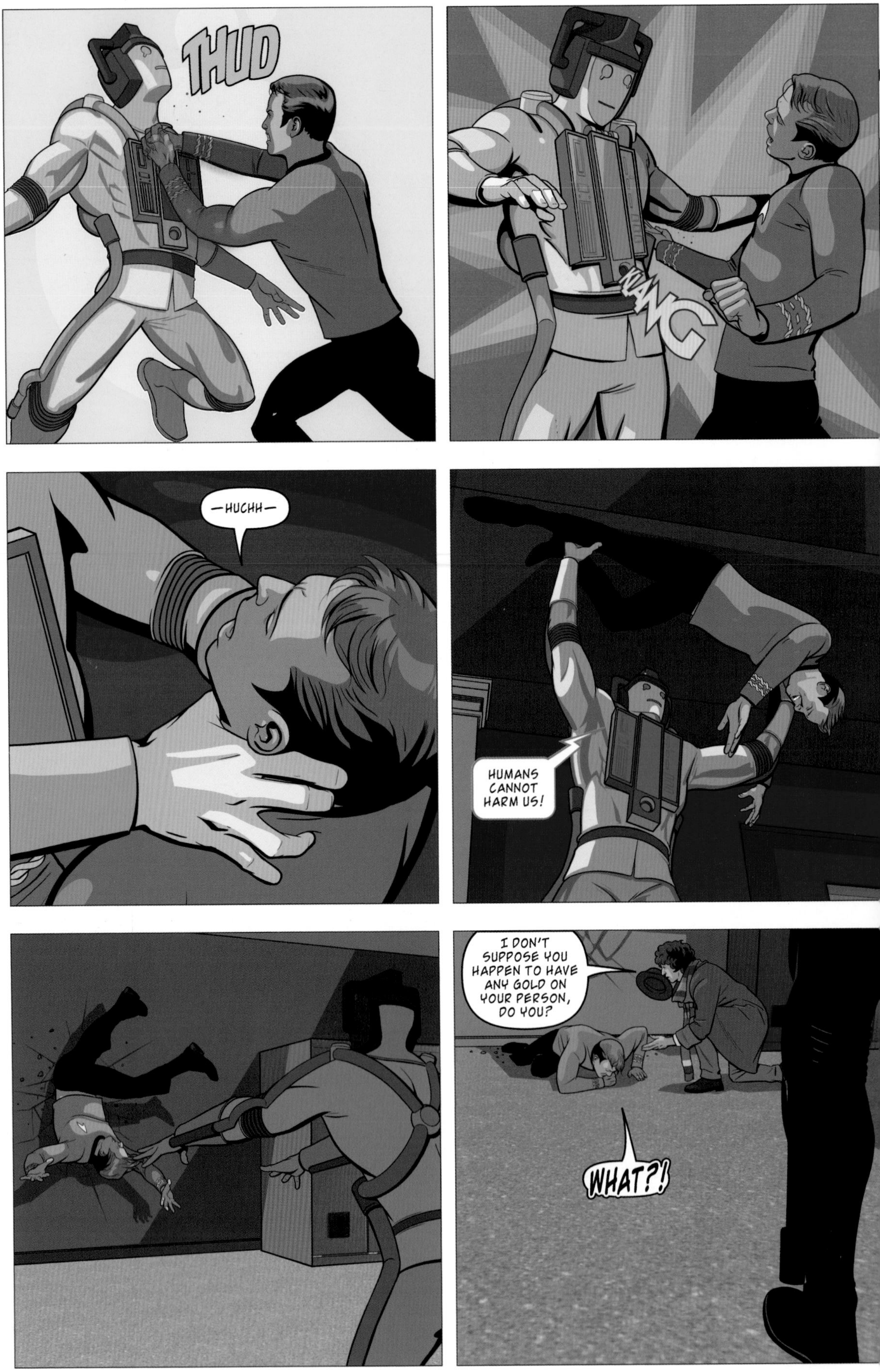
THUD
KLANG
—HUCHH—
HUMANS CANNOT HARM US!
I DON'T SUPPOSE YOU HAPPEN TO HAVE ANY GOLD ON YOUR PERSON, DO YOU?
WHAT?!

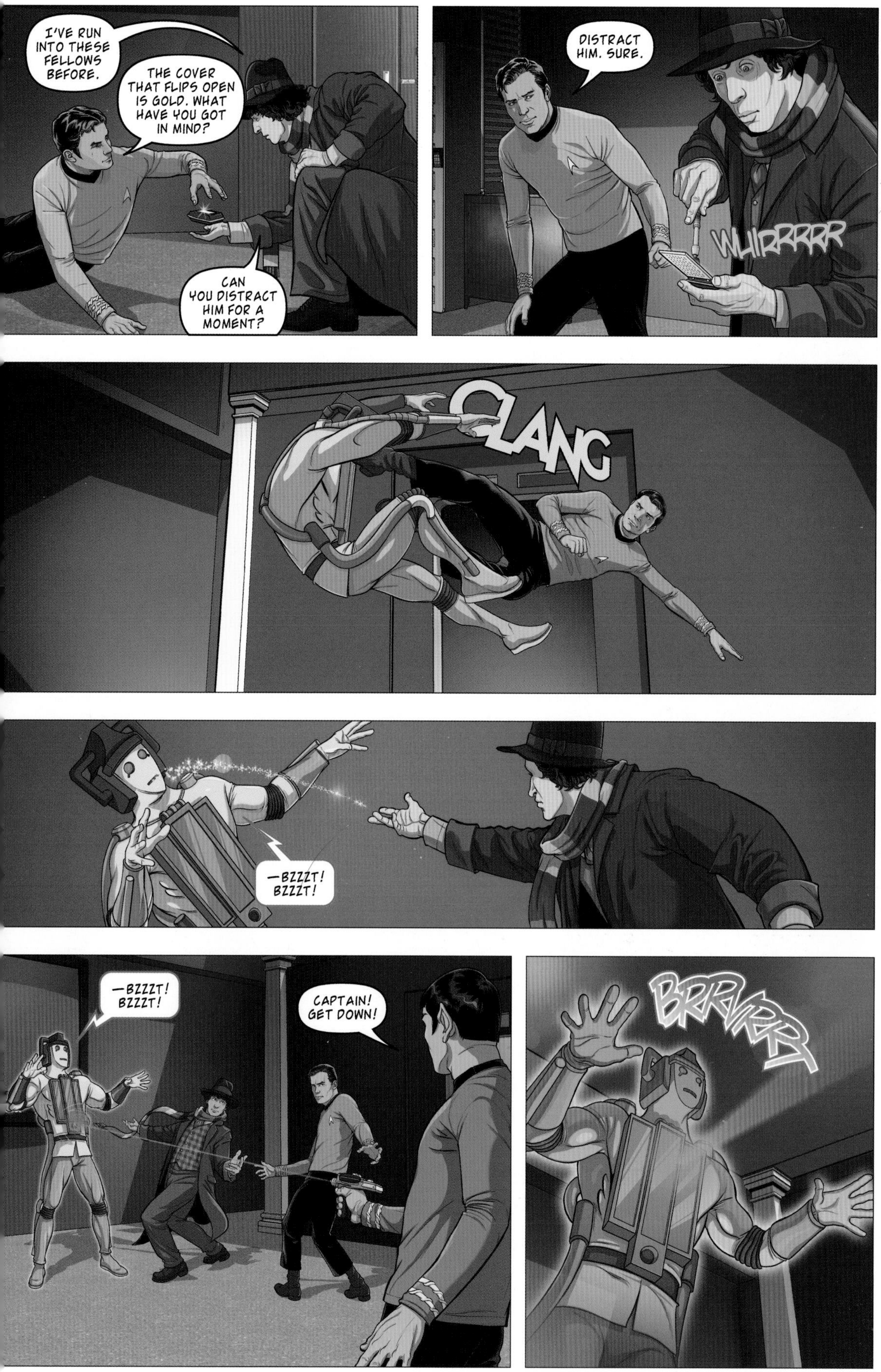
I'VE RUN INTO THESE FELLOWS BEFORE.
THE COVER THAT FLIPS OPEN IS GOLD. WHAT HAVE YOU GOT IN MIND?
CAN YOU DISTRACT HIM FOR A MOMENT?
DISTRACT HIM. SURE.
WHIRRRRR
CLANG
—BZZZT! BZZZT!
—BZZZT! BZZZT!
CAPTAIN! GET DOWN!
BRRVRRT

YOU SEE, THE GOLD FLAKE INTERFERES WITH THEIR RESPIRATORY SYSTEM.

RESPIRATORY SYSTEM? YOU MEAN THOSE THINGS ACTUALLY *BREATHE*?

THE OTHER TWO ARE DOWN, CAPTAIN. ALL THE RESEARCHERS ARE SAFE.

SEARCH THE FACILITY. I DON'T WANT ANY MORE SURPRISES.

LATER...

NO SIGN OF ANY MORE OF THESE "CYBER-MEN," CAPTAIN.

AND THERE LOOKS TO BE NO DAMAGE TO THE FACILITY?

NONE THAT WE CAN ASCERTAIN.

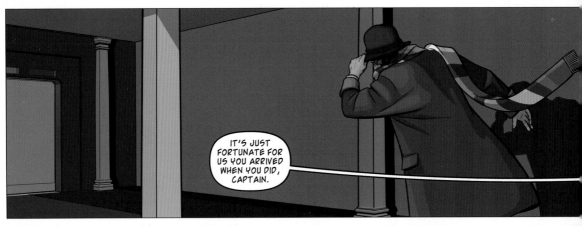

IT'S JUST FORTUNATE FOR US YOU ARRIVED WHEN YOU DID, CAPTAIN.

"I DON'T BELIEVE IN BEING LUCKY TWICE, PROFESSOR WHITMORE. WE'LL BE ARRANGING FOR A PERMANENT GARRISON OF SECURITY PERSONNEL HERE, JUST IN CASE YOU HAVE ANY MORE UNEXPECTED VISITORS."

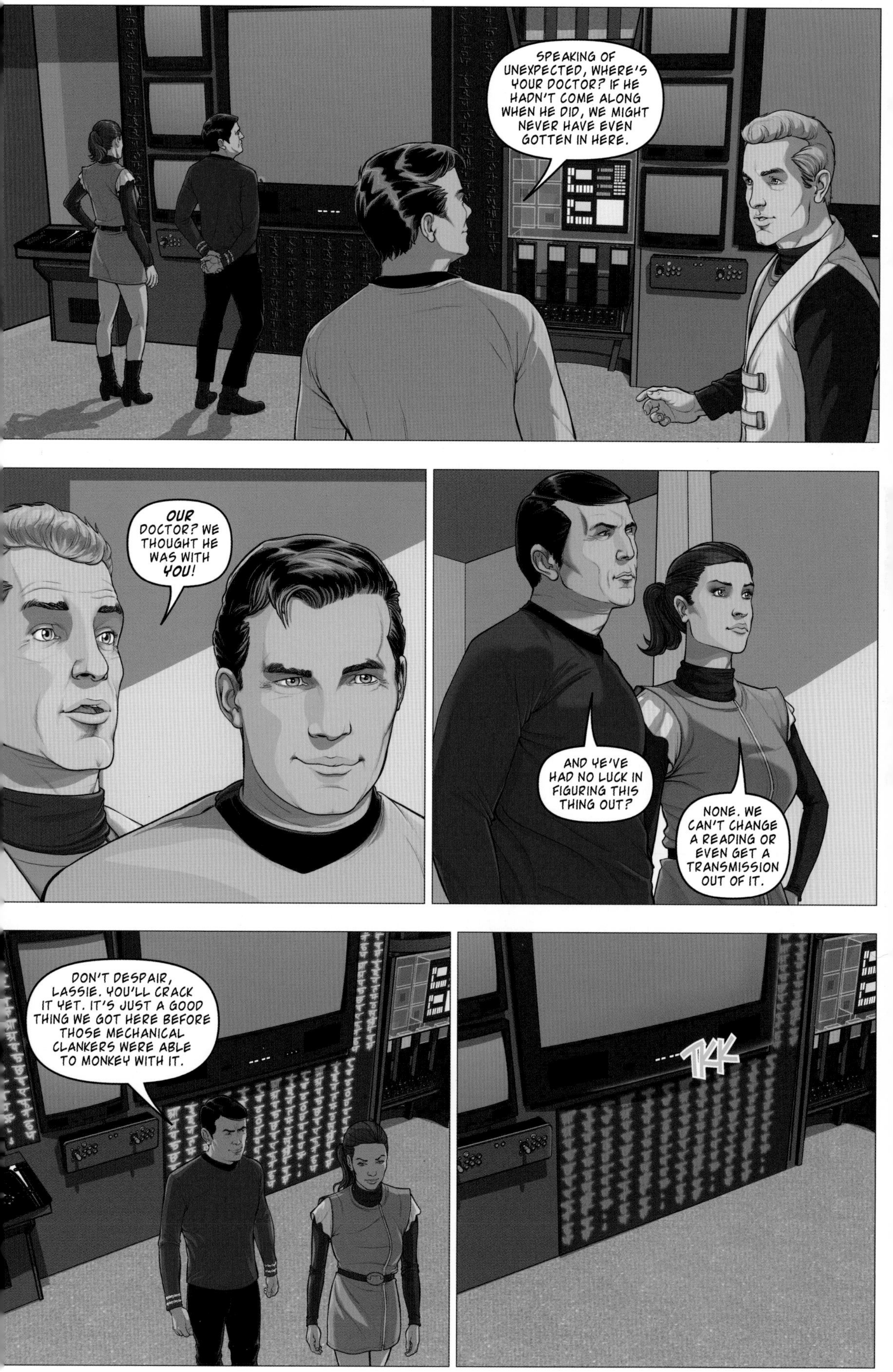
SPEAKING OF UNEXPECTED, WHERE'S YOUR DOCTOR? IF HE HADN'T COME ALONG WHEN HE DID, WE MIGHT NEVER HAVE EVEN GOTTEN IN HERE.
OUR DOCTOR? WE THOUGHT HE WAS WITH YOU!
AND YE'VE HAD NO LUCK IN FIGURING THIS THING OUT?
NONE. WE CAN'T CHANGE A READING OR EVEN GET A TRANSMISSION OUT OF IT.
DON'T DESPAIR, LASSIE. YOU'LL CRACK IT YET. IT'S JUST A GOOD THING WE GOT HERE BEFORE THOSE MECHANICAL CLANKERS WERE ABLE TO MONKEY WITH IT.
TKK

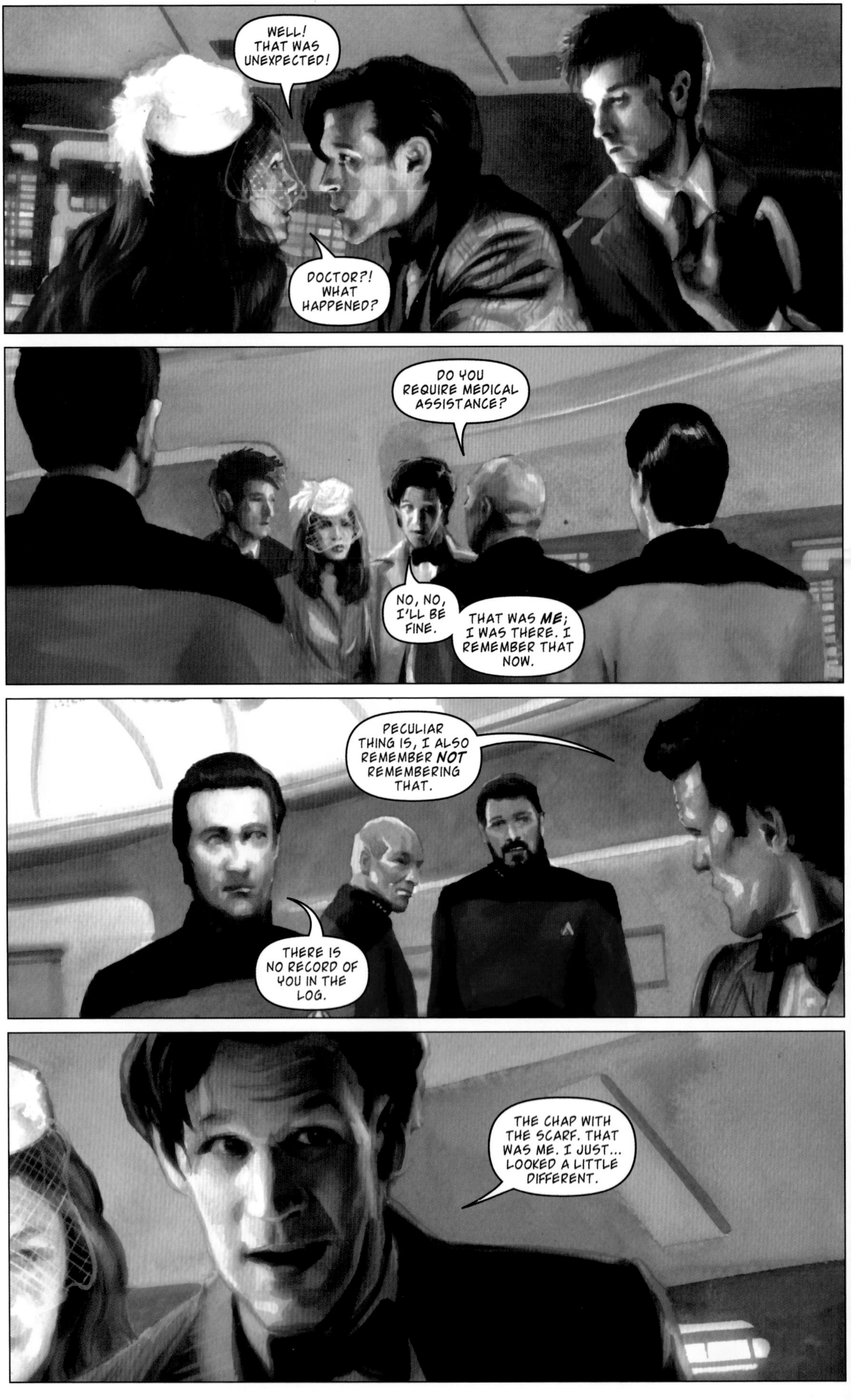

WELL! THAT WAS UNEXPECTED!
DOCTOR?! WHAT HAPPENED?
DO YOU REQUIRE MEDICAL ASSISTANCE?
NO, NO, I'LL BE FINE.
THAT WAS ME; I WAS THERE. I REMEMBER THAT NOW.
PECULIAR THING IS, I ALSO REMEMBER NOT REMEMBERING THAT.
THERE IS NO RECORD OF YOU IN THE LOG.
THE CHAP WITH THE SCARF. THAT WAS ME. I JUST... LOOKED A LITTLE DIFFERENT.

HOW COULD YOU HAVE BEEN THERE?

IT'S A LITTLE HARD TO EXPLAIN, REALLY.

HE DOES TRAVEL A LOT, YOU KNOW...

THAT WOULD MAKE YOU MORE THAN A HUNDRED YEARS OLD?

DON'T BE RIDICULOUS, COMMANDER. I'M NOWHERE NEAR 100.

CAPTAIN, IF I'M REMEMBERING THINGS THAT SHOULD NOT BE, WE'RE ALL IN EVEN GREATER DANGER THAN I REALIZED.

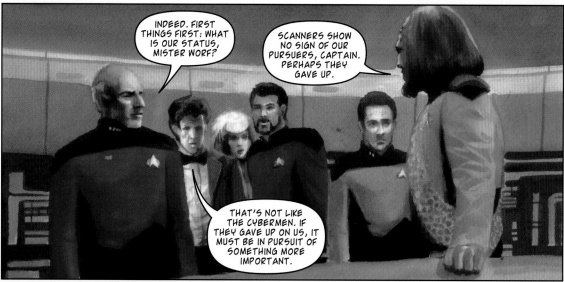

INDEED. FIRST THINGS FIRST: WHAT IS OUR STATUS, MISTER WORF?

SCANNERS SHOW NO SIGN OF OUR PURSUERS, CAPTAIN. PERHAPS THEY GAVE UP.

THAT'S NOT LIKE THE CYBERMEN. IF THEY GAVE UP ON US, IT MUST BE IN PURSUIT OF SOMETHING MORE IMPORTANT.

BIGGER FISH TO FRY. YOU MAY BE RIGHT, DOCTOR, BUT LET US TAKE ADVANTAGE OF THIS RESPITE TO ATTEMPT TO FIND SOME ANSWERS. AND I BELIEVE I MAY KNOW WHERE TO START.

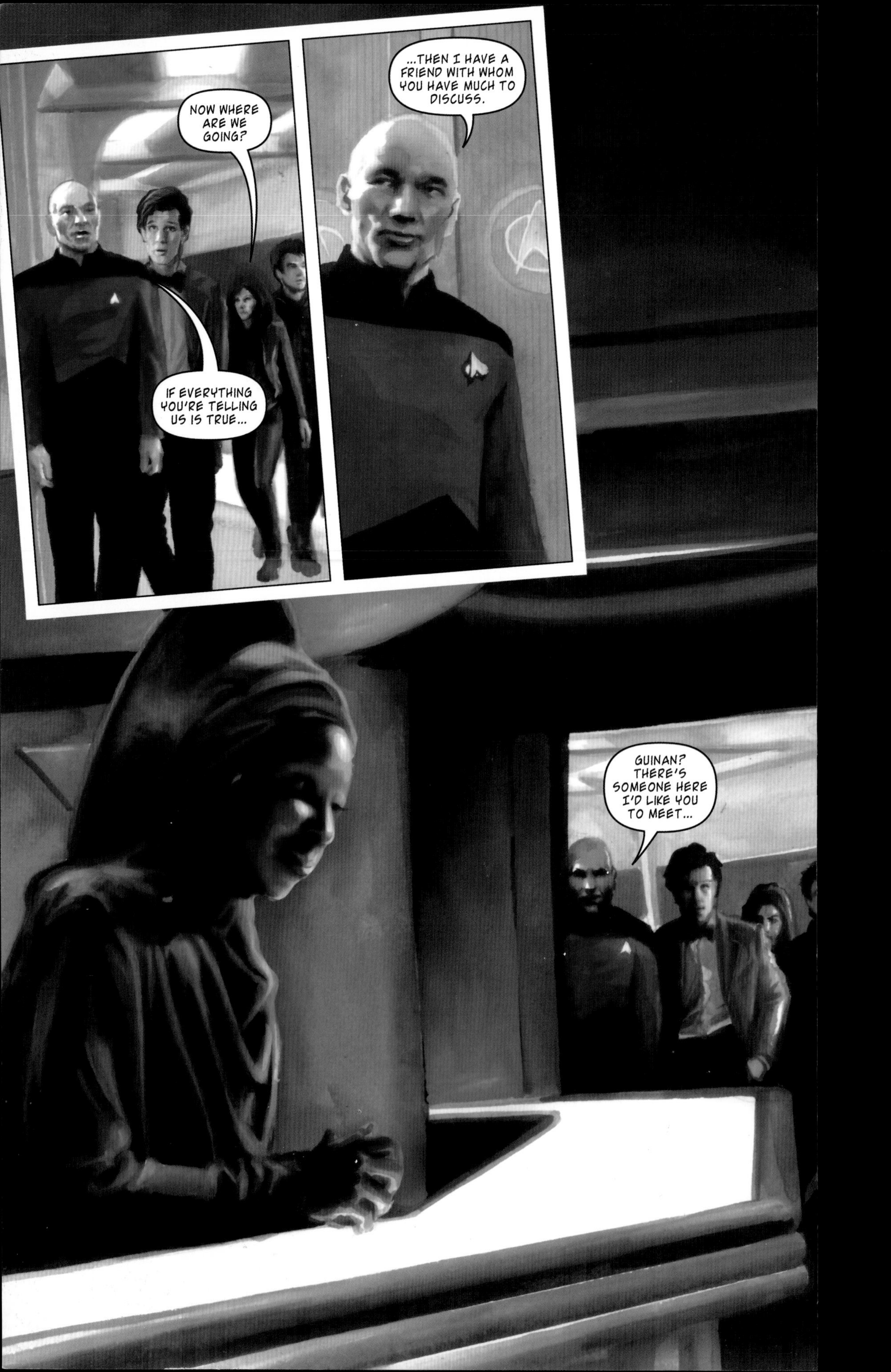
NOW WHERE ARE WE GOING?
IF EVERYTHING YOU'RE TELLING US IS TRUE...
...THEN I HAVE A FRIEND WITH WHOM YOU HAVE MUCH TO DISCUSS.
GUINAN? THERE'S SOMEONE HERE I'D LIKE YOU TO MEET...

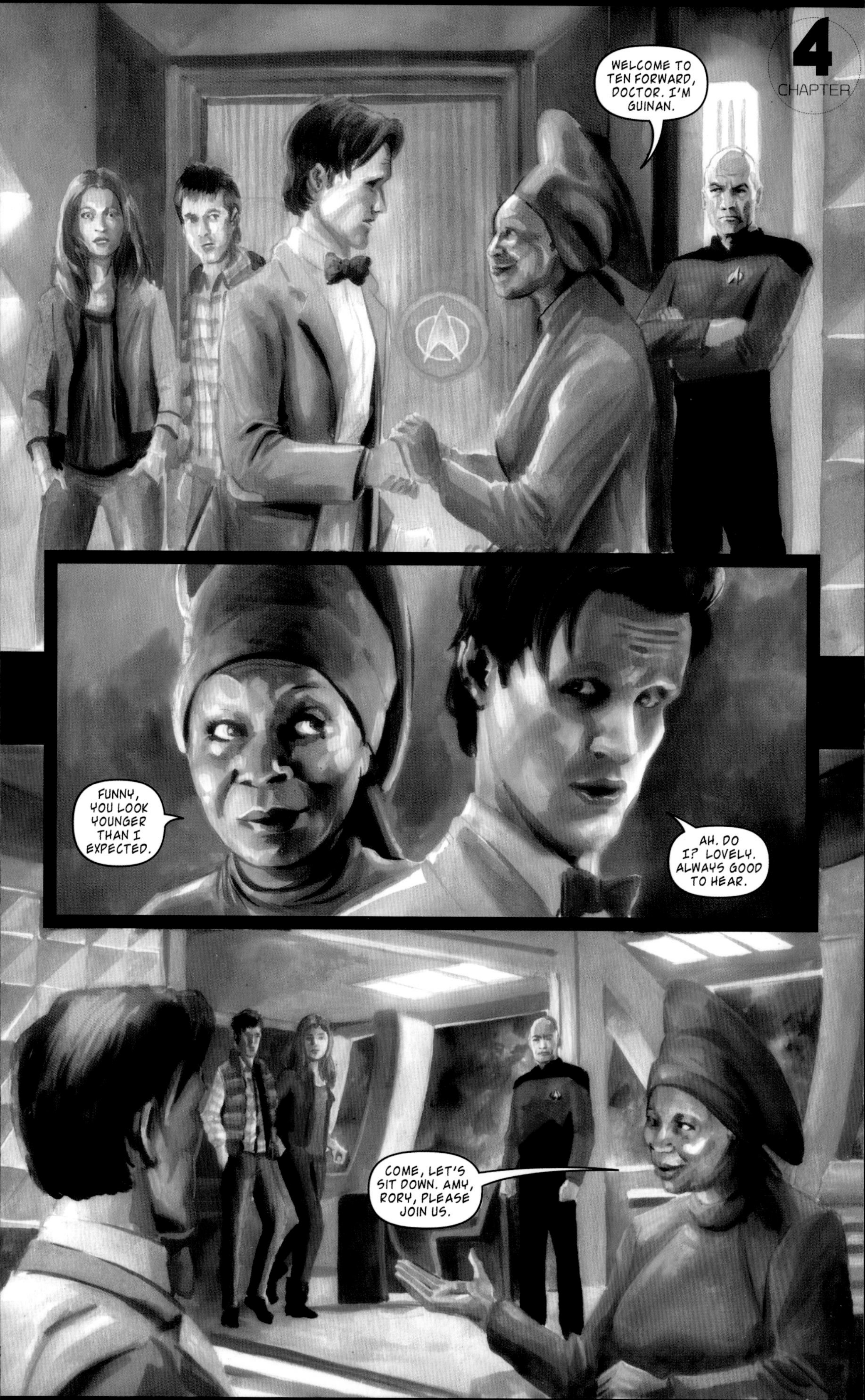
4
CHAPTER
WELCOME TO TEN FORWARD, DOCTOR. I'M GUINAN.
FUNNY, YOU LOOK YOUNGER THAN I EXPECTED.
AH. DO I? LOVELY. ALWAYS GOOD TO HEAR.
COME, LET'S SIT DOWN. AMY, RORY, PLEASE JOIN US.

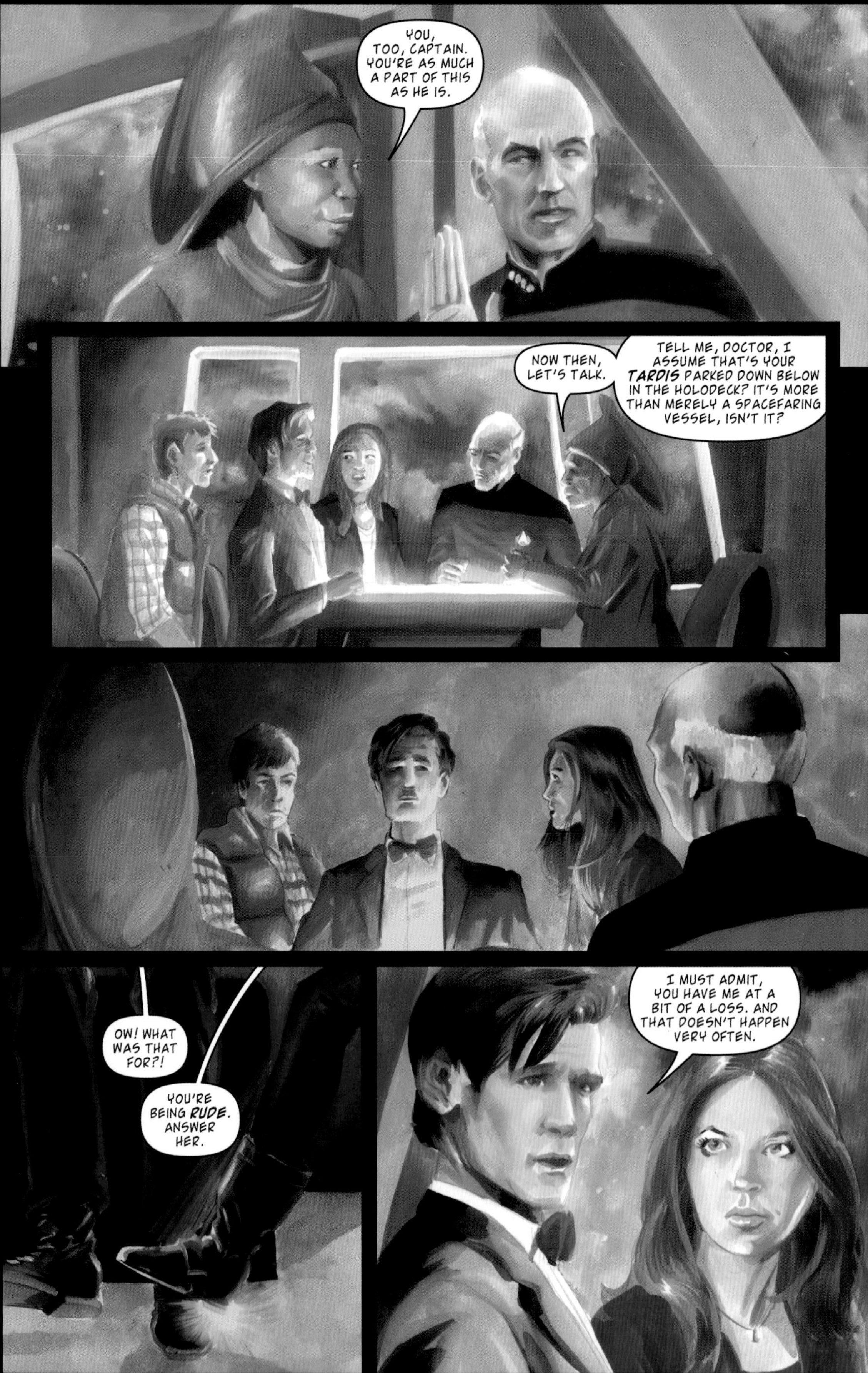
YOU, TOO, CAPTAIN. YOU'RE AS MUCH A PART OF THIS AS HE IS.
NOW THEN, LET'S TALK.
TELL ME, DOCTOR, I ASSUME THAT'S YOUR *TARDIS* PARKED DOWN BELOW IN THE HOLODECK? IT'S MORE THAN MERELY A SPACEFARING VESSEL, ISN'T IT?
OW! WHAT WAS THAT FOR?!
YOU'RE BEING *RUDE*. ANSWER HER.
I MUST ADMIT, YOU HAVE ME AT A BIT OF A LOSS. AND THAT DOESN'T HAPPEN VERY OFTEN.

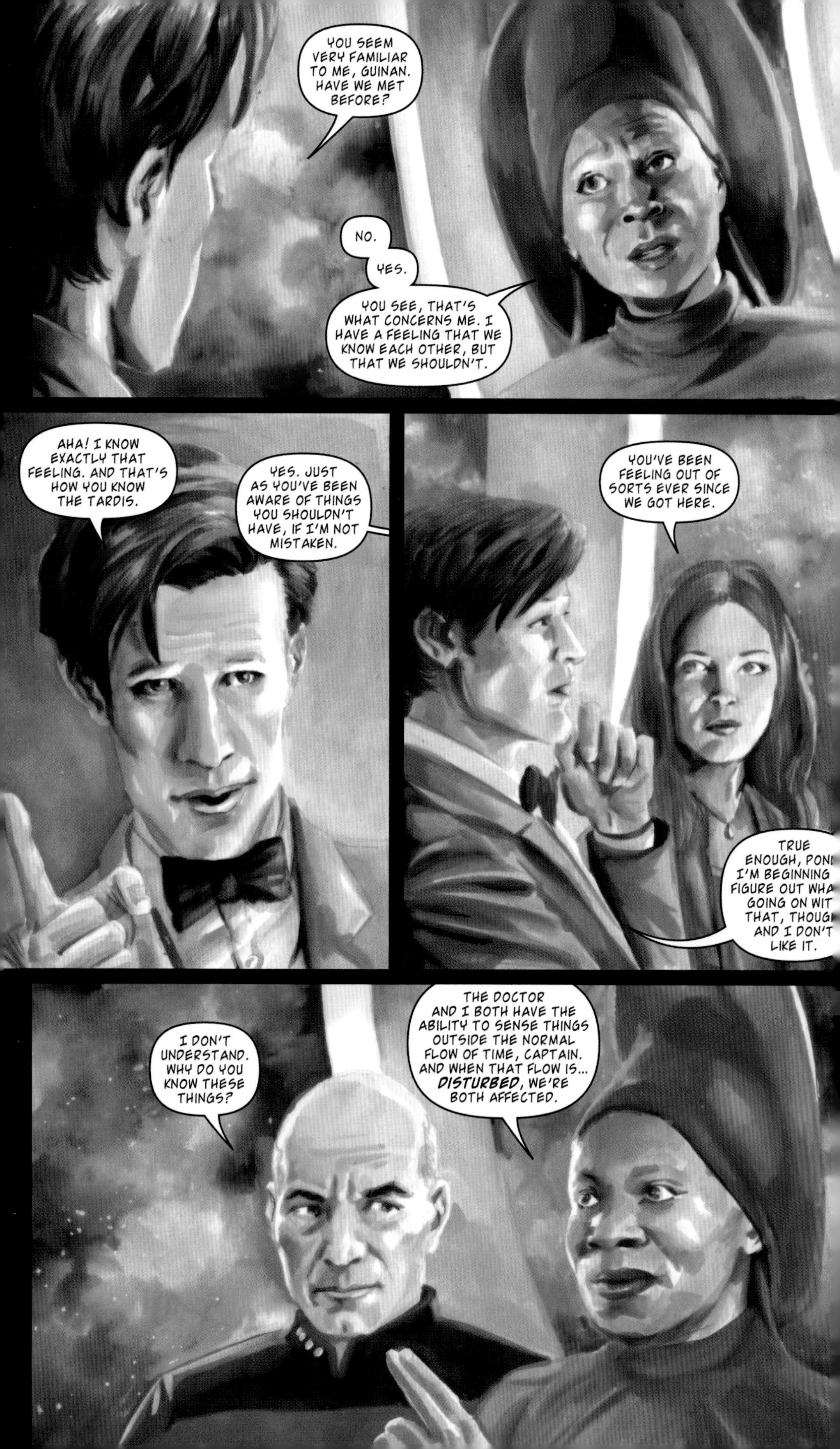
YOU SEEM VERY FAMILIAR TO ME, GUINAN. HAVE WE MET BEFORE?
NO.
YES.
YOU SEE, THAT'S WHAT CONCERNS ME. I HAVE A FEELING THAT WE KNOW EACH OTHER, BUT THAT WE SHOULDN'T.
AHA! I KNOW EXACTLY THAT FEELING. AND THAT'S HOW YOU KNOW THE TARDIS.
YES. JUST AS YOU'VE BEEN AWARE OF THINGS YOU SHOULDN'T HAVE, IF I'M NOT MISTAKEN.
YOU'VE BEEN FEELING OUT OF SORTS EVER SINCE WE GOT HERE.
TRUE ENOUGH, PON
I'M BEGINNING
FIGURE OUT WHA
GOING ON WIT
THAT, THOUG
AND I DON'T
LIKE IT.
I DON'T UNDERSTAND. WHY DO YOU KNOW THESE THINGS?
THE DOCTOR AND I BOTH HAVE THE ABILITY TO SENSE THINGS OUTSIDE THE NORMAL FLOW OF TIME, CAPTAIN. AND WHEN THAT FLOW IS... ***DISTURBED***, WE'RE BOTH AFFECTED.

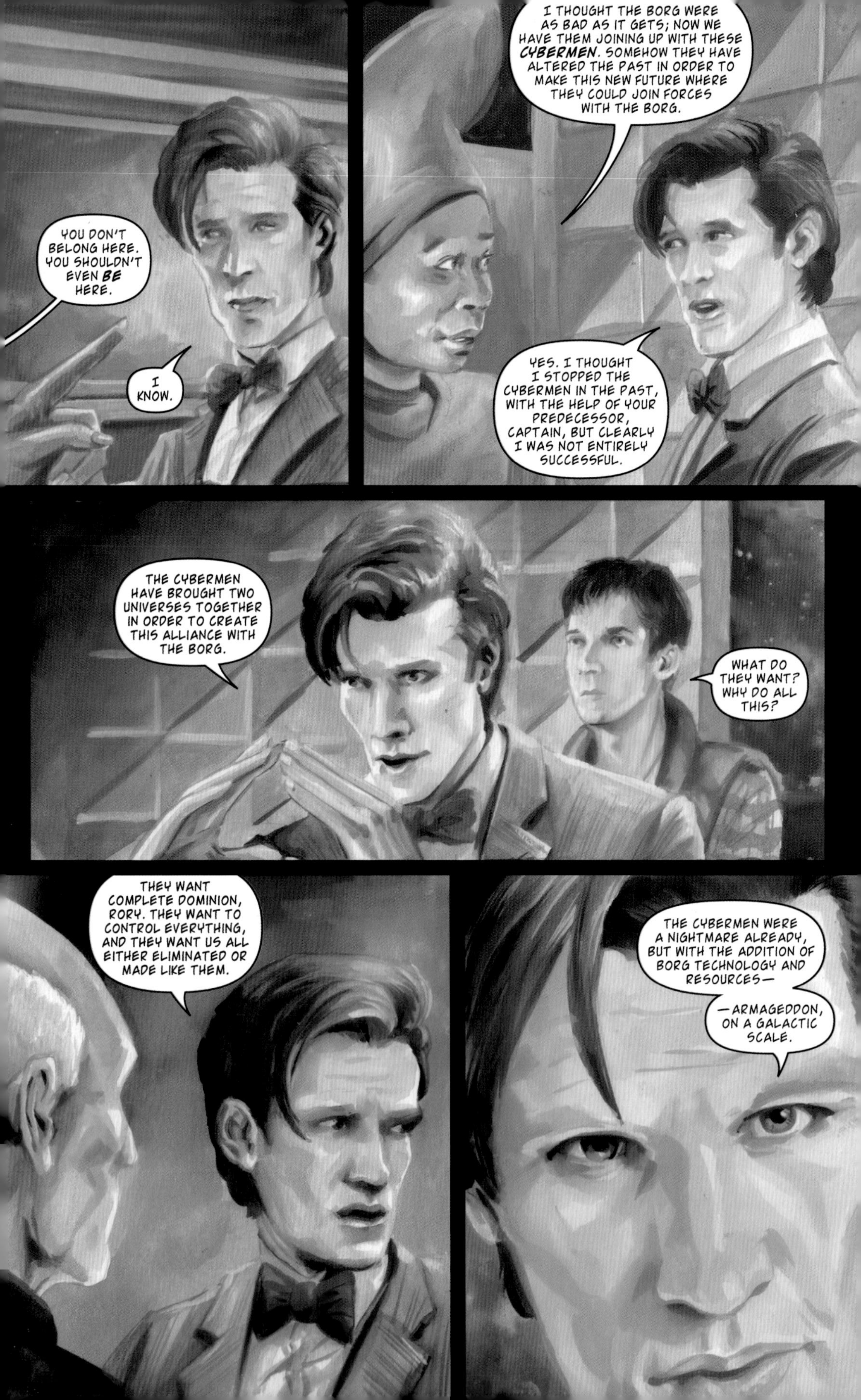
YOU DON'T BELONG HERE. YOU SHOULDN'T EVEN **BE** HERE.
I KNOW.
I THOUGHT THE BORG WERE AS BAD AS IT GETS; NOW WE HAVE THEM JOINING UP WITH THESE *CYBERMEN*. SOMEHOW THEY HAVE ALTERED THE PAST IN ORDER TO MAKE THIS NEW FUTURE WHERE THEY COULD JOIN FORCES WITH THE BORG.
YES. I THOUGHT I STOPPED THE CYBERMEN IN THE PAST, WITH THE HELP OF YOUR PREDECESSOR, CAPTAIN, BUT CLEARLY I WAS NOT ENTIRELY SUCCESSFUL.
THE CYBERMEN HAVE BROUGHT TWO UNIVERSES TOGETHER IN ORDER TO CREATE THIS ALLIANCE WITH THE BORG.
WHAT DO THEY WANT? WHY DO ALL THIS?
THEY WANT COMPLETE DOMINION, RORY. THEY WANT TO CONTROL EVERYTHING, AND THEY WANT US ALL EITHER ELIMINATED OR MADE LIKE THEM.
THE CYBERMEN WERE A NIGHTMARE ALREADY, BUT WITH THE ADDITION OF BORG TECHNOLOGY AND RESOURCES—
—ARMAGEDDON, ON A GALACTIC SCALE.

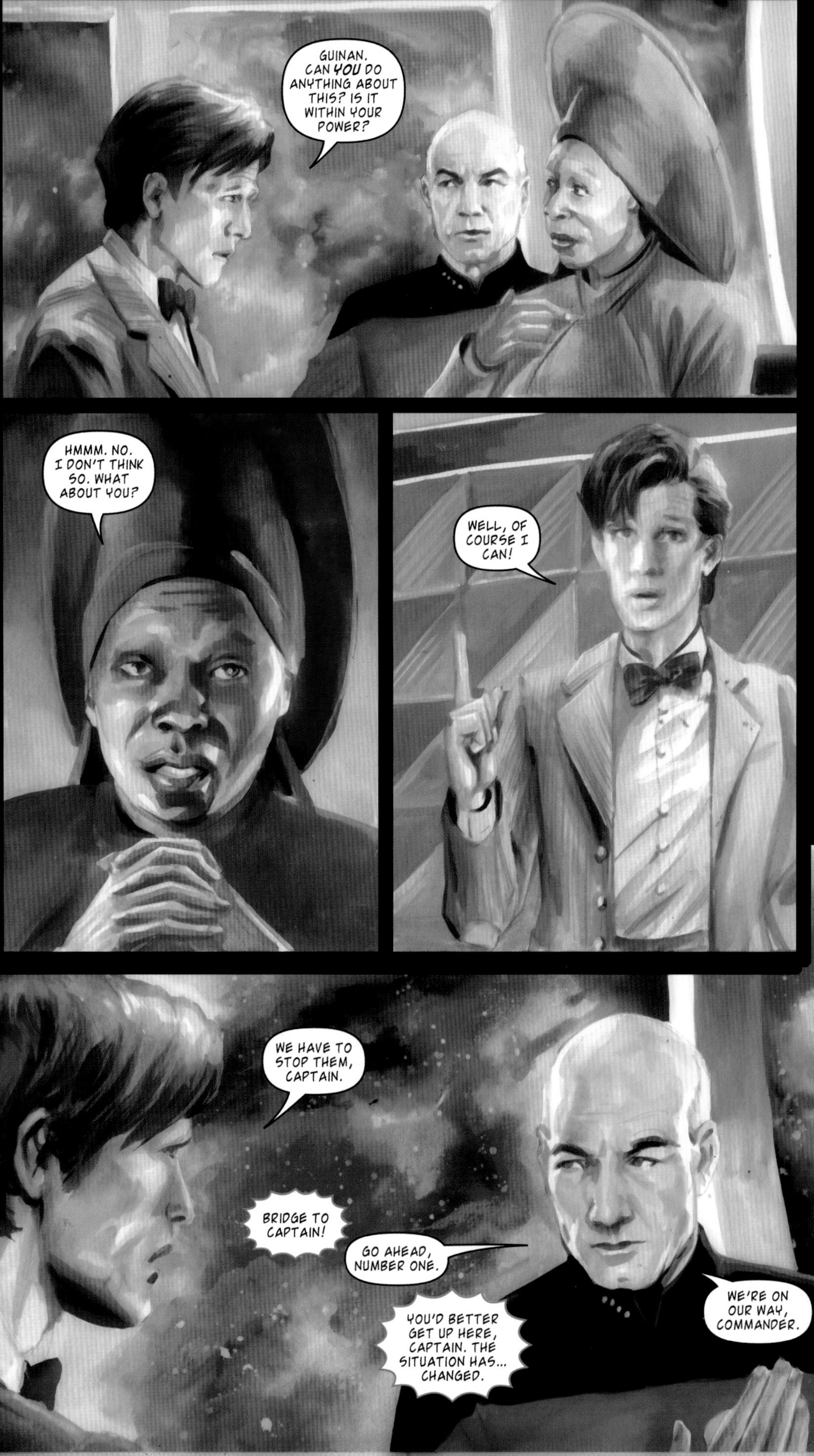
GUINAN. CAN YOU DO ANYTHING ABOUT THIS? IS IT WITHIN YOUR POWER?
HMMM. NO. I DON'T THINK SO. WHAT ABOUT YOU?
WELL, OF COURSE I CAN!
WE HAVE TO STOP THEM, CAPTAIN.
BRIDGE TO CAPTAIN!
GO AHEAD, NUMBER ONE.
YOU'D BETTER GET UP HERE, CAPTAIN. THE SITUATION HAS... CHANGED.
WE'RE ON OUR WAY, COMMANDER.

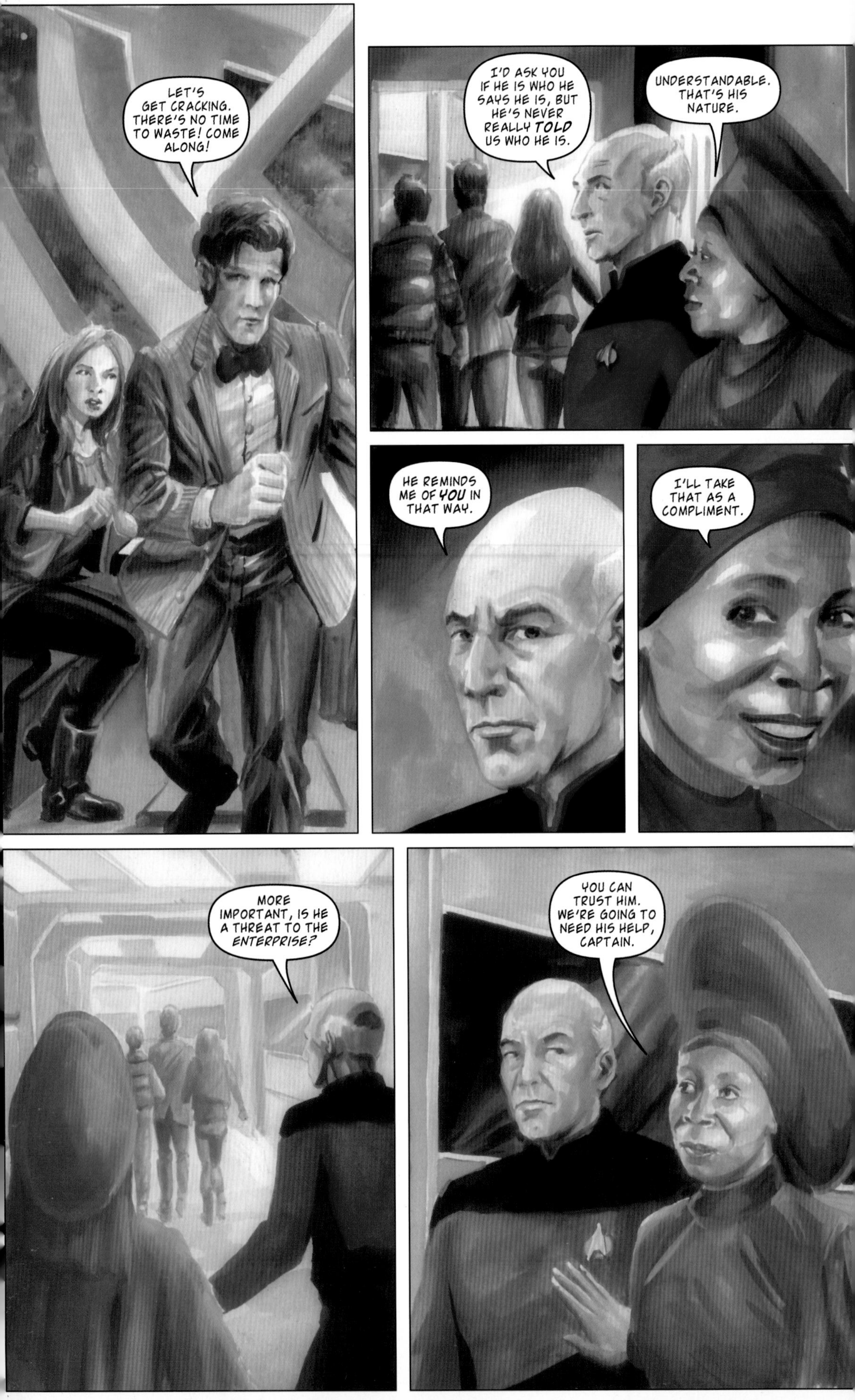
LET'S GET CRACKING. THERE'S NO TIME TO WASTE! COME ALONG!
I'D ASK YOU IF HE IS WHO HE SAYS HE IS, BUT HE'S NEVER REALLY TOLD US WHO HE IS.
UNDERSTANDABLE. THAT'S HIS NATURE.
HE REMINDS ME OF YOU IN THAT WAY.
I'LL TAKE THAT AS A COMPLIMENT.
MORE IMPORTANT, IS HE A THREAT TO THE ENTERPRISE?
YOU CAN TRUST HIM. WE'RE GOING TO NEED HIS HELP, CAPTAIN.

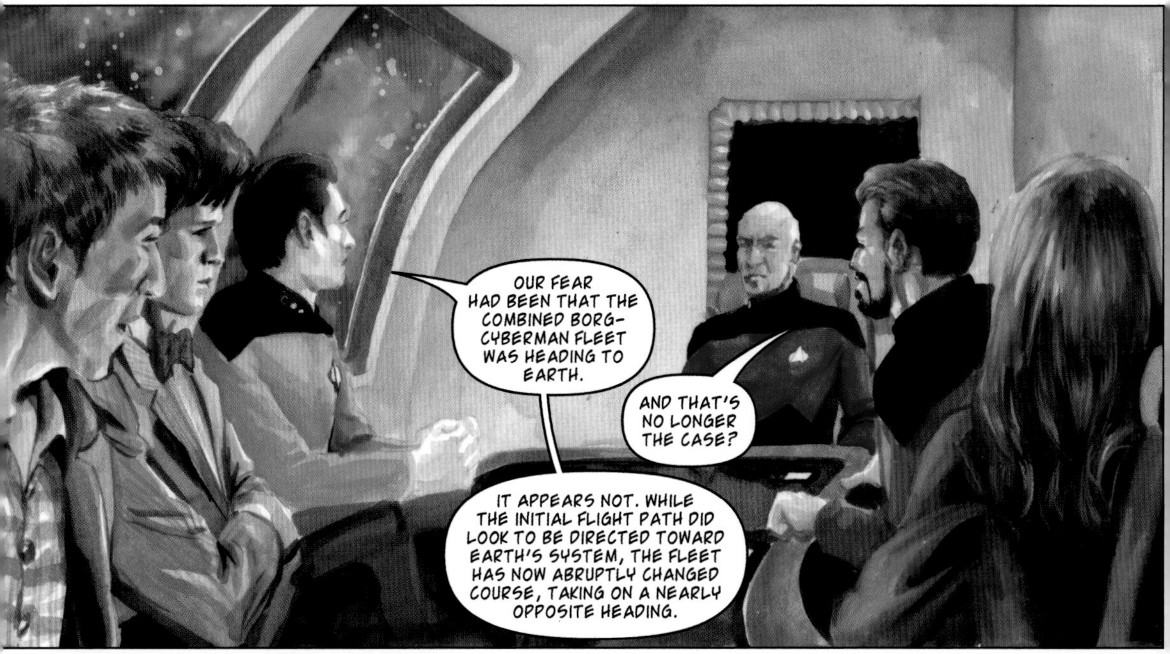
OUR FEAR HAD BEEN THAT THE COMBINED BORG-CYBERMAN FLEET WAS HEADING TO EARTH.
AND THAT'S NO LONGER THE CASE?
IT APPEARS NOT. WHILE THE INITIAL FLIGHT PATH DID LOOK TO BE DIRECTED TOWARD EARTH'S SYSTEM, THE FLEET HAS NOW ABRUPTLY CHANGED COURSE, TAKING ON A NEARLY OPPOSITE HEADING.

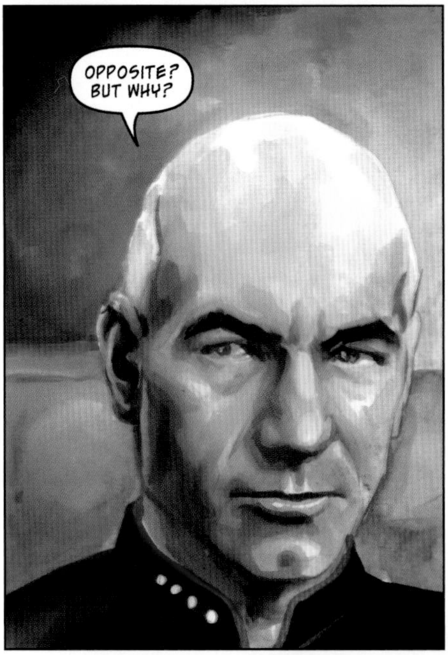
OPPOSITE? BUT WHY?

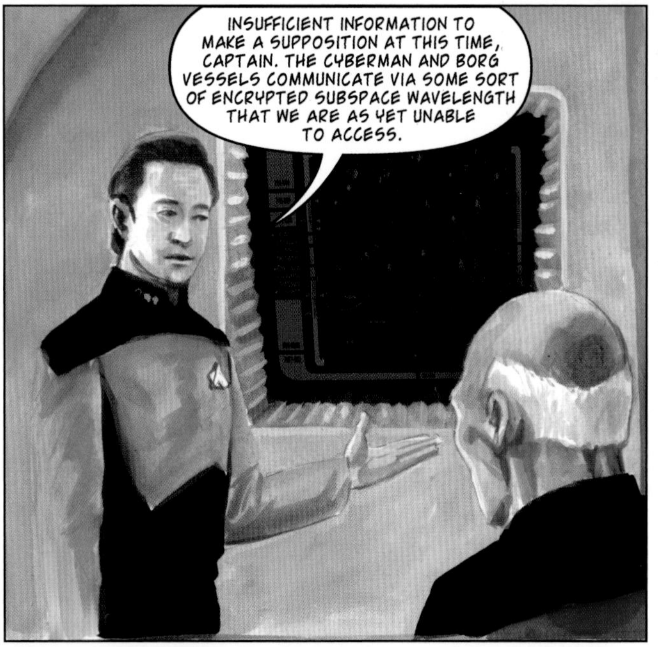
INSUFFICIENT INFORMATION TO MAKE A SUPPOSITION AT THIS TIME, CAPTAIN. THE CYBERMAN AND BORG VESSELS COMMUNICATE VIA SOME SORT OF ENCRYPTED SUBSPACE WAVELENGTH THAT WE ARE AS YET UNABLE TO ACCESS.

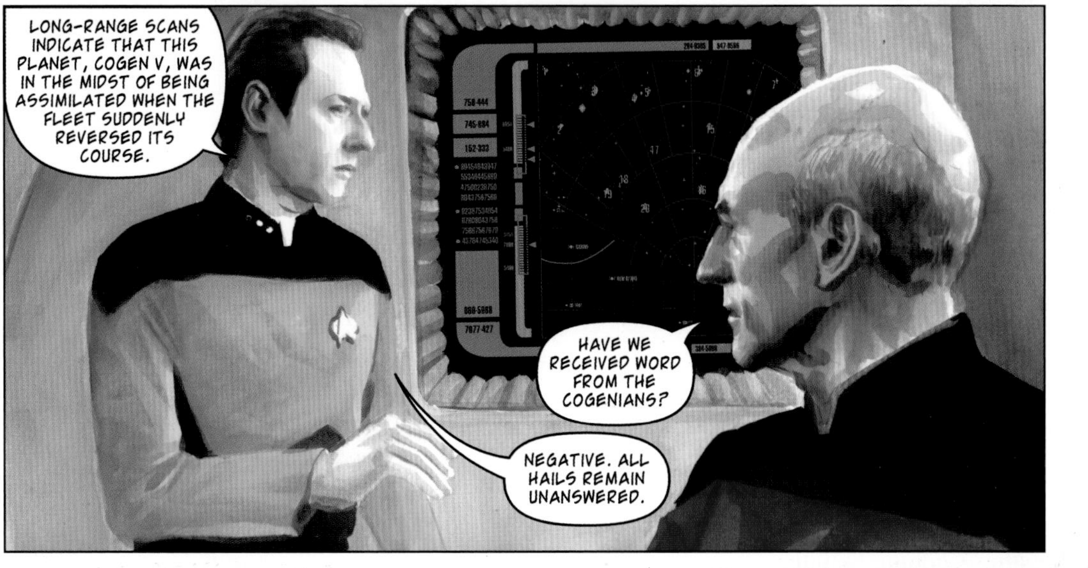
LONG-RANGE SCANS INDICATE THAT THIS PLANET, COGEN V, WAS IN THE MIDST OF BEING ASSIMILATED WHEN THE FLEET SUDDENLY REVERSED ITS COURSE.
HAVE WE RECEIVED WORD FROM THE COGENIANS?
NEGATIVE. ALL HAILS REMAIN UNANSWERED.

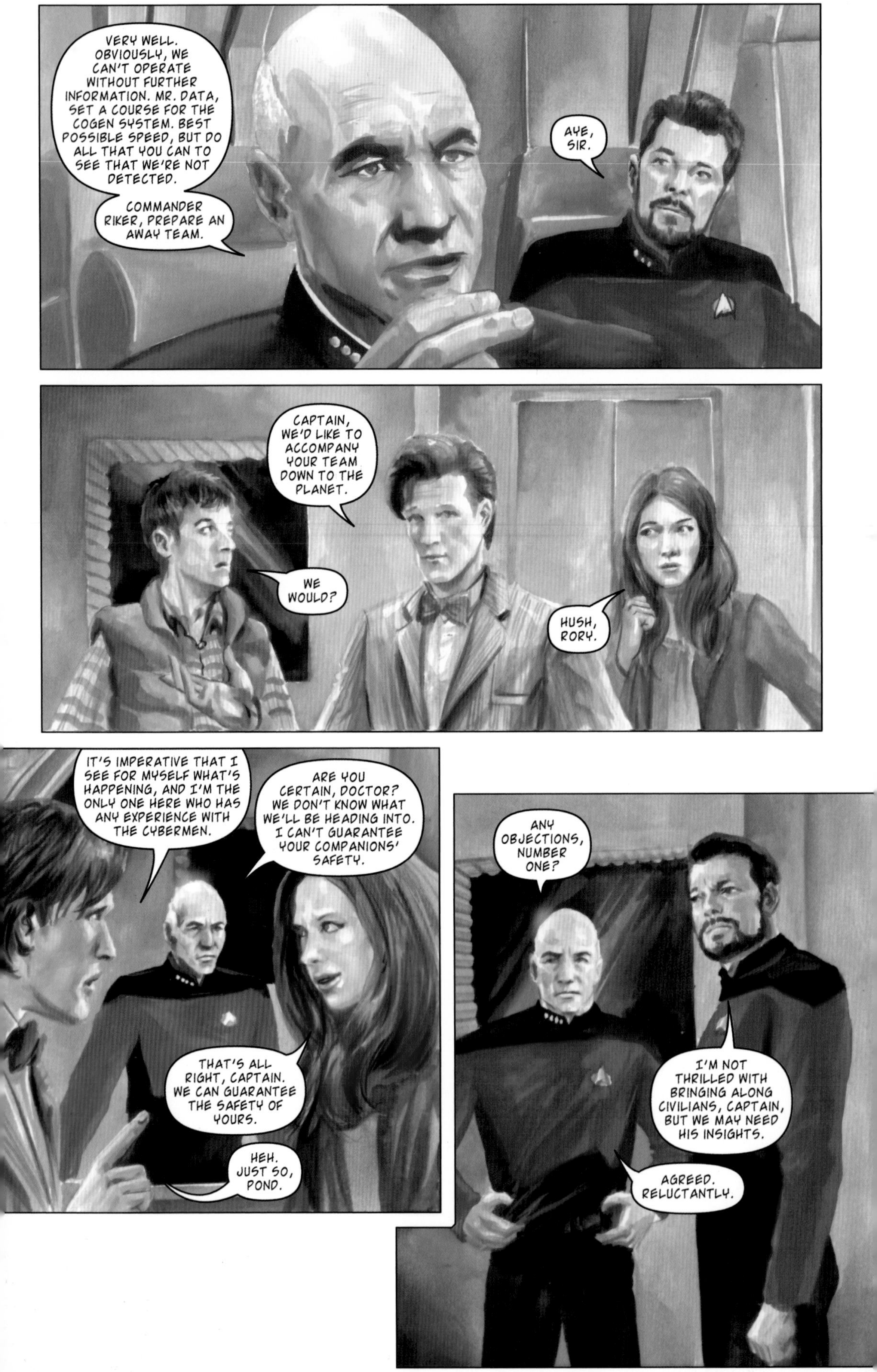

VERY WELL. OBVIOUSLY, WE CAN'T OPERATE WITHOUT FURTHER INFORMATION. MR. DATA, SET A COURSE FOR THE COGEN SYSTEM. BEST POSSIBLE SPEED, BUT DO ALL THAT YOU CAN TO SEE THAT WE'RE NOT DETECTED.
COMMANDER RIKER, PREPARE AN AWAY TEAM.
AYE, SIR.
CAPTAIN, WE'D LIKE TO ACCOMPANY YOUR TEAM DOWN TO THE PLANET.
WE WOULD?
HUSH, RORY.
IT'S IMPERATIVE THAT I SEE FOR MYSELF WHAT'S HAPPENING, AND I'M THE ONLY ONE HERE WHO HAS ANY EXPERIENCE WITH THE CYBERMEN.
ARE YOU CERTAIN, DOCTOR? WE DON'T KNOW WHAT WE'LL BE HEADING INTO. I CAN'T GUARANTEE YOUR COMPANIONS' SAFETY.
THAT'S ALL RIGHT, CAPTAIN. WE CAN GUARANTEE THE SAFETY OF YOURS.
HEH. JUST SO, POND.
ANY OBJECTIONS, NUMBER ONE?
I'M NOT THRILLED WITH BRINGING ALONG CIVILIANS, CAPTAIN, BUT WE MAY NEED HIS INSIGHTS.
AGREED. RELUCTANTLY.

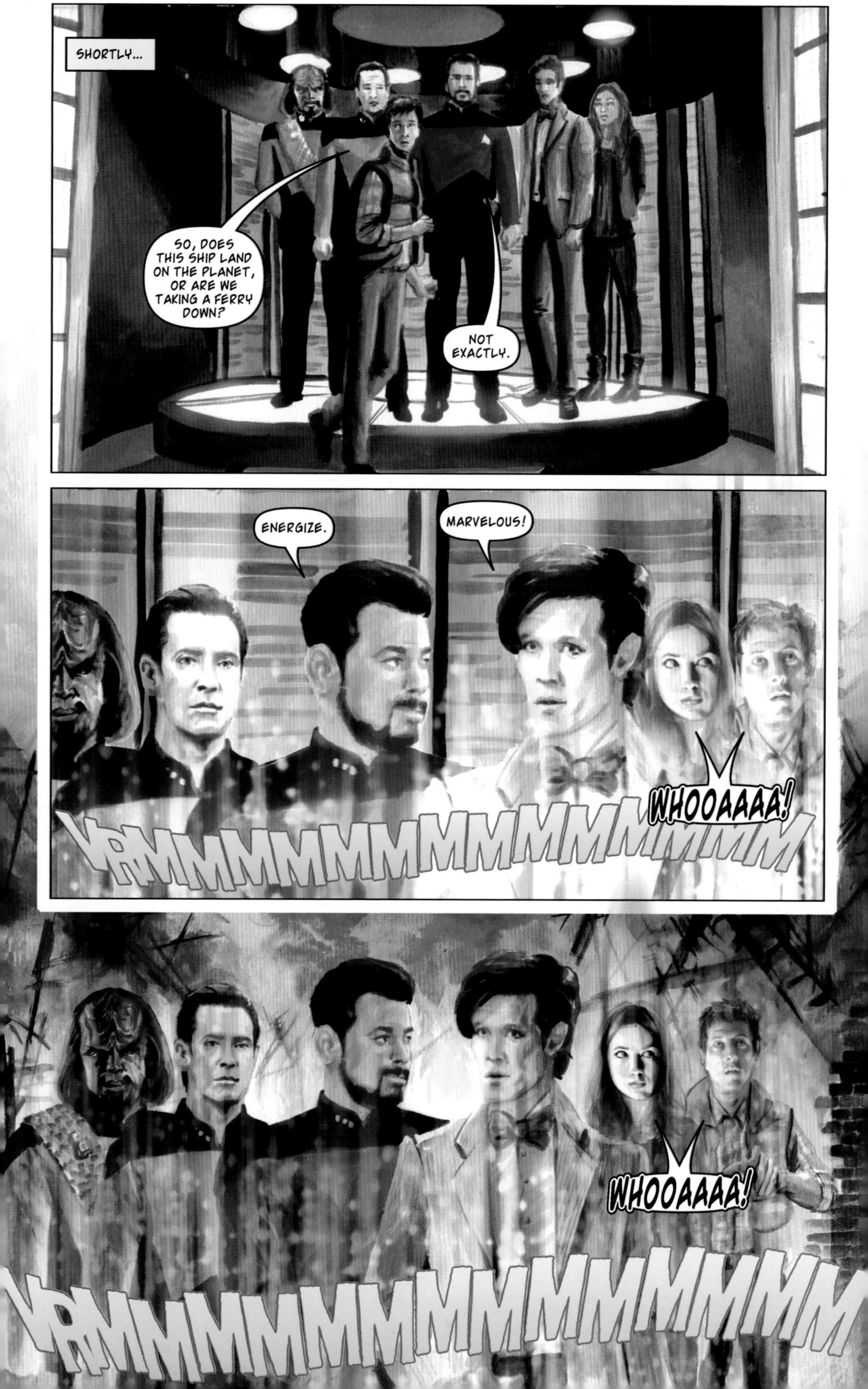
SHORTLY...
SO, DOES THIS SHIP LAND ON THE PLANET, OR ARE WE TAKING A FERRY DOWN?
NOT EXACTLY.
ENERGIZE.
MARVELOUS!
WHOOAAAA!
VRMMMMMMMMMMMMMMMM
WHOOAAAA!
VRMMMMMMMMMMMMMMMMM

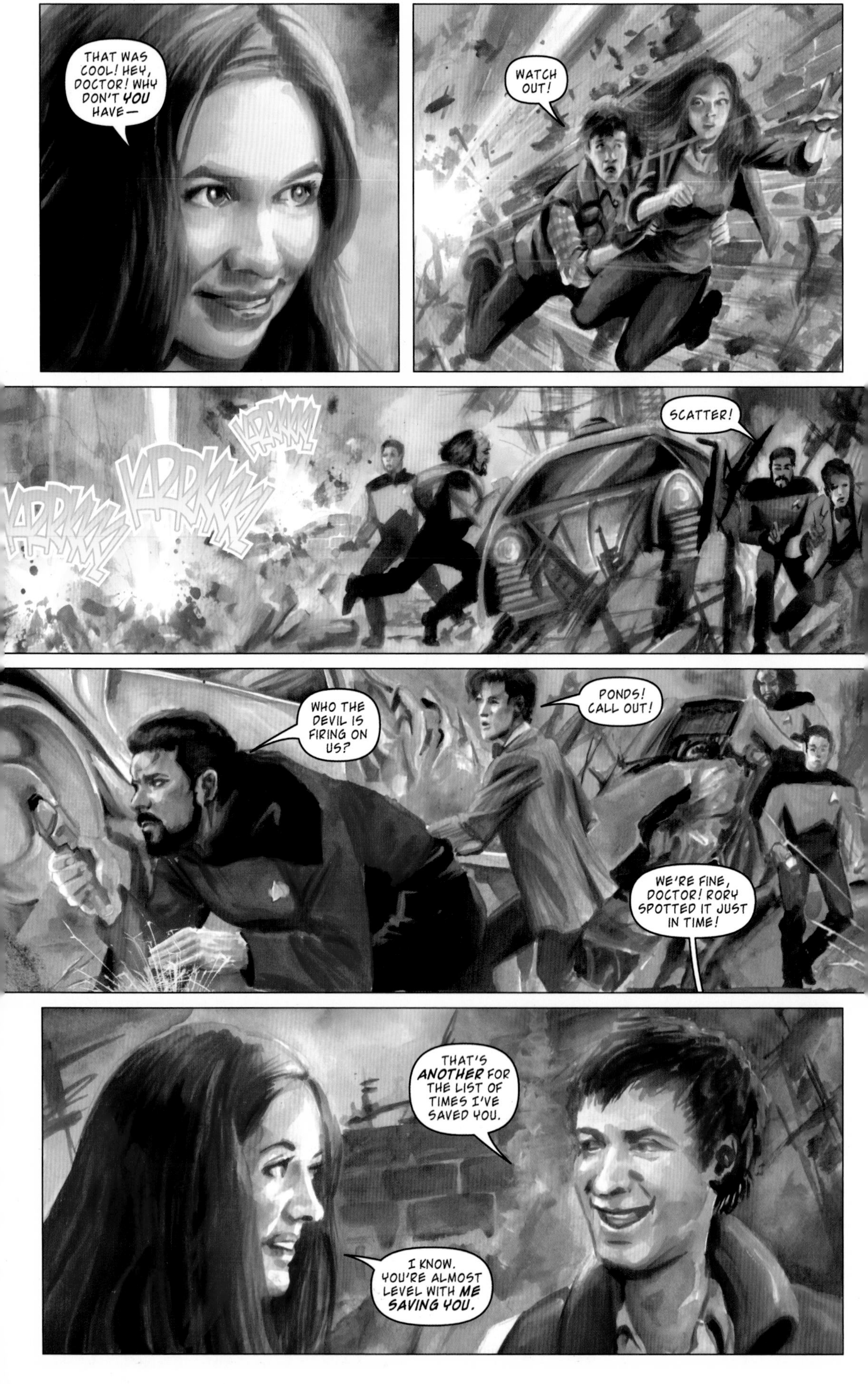
THAT WAS COOL! HEY, DOCTOR! WHY DON'T **YOU** HAVE—
WATCH OUT!
SCATTER!
WHO THE DEVIL IS FIRING ON US?
PONDS! CALL OUT!
WE'RE FINE, DOCTOR! RORY SPOTTED IT JUST IN TIME!
THAT'S **ANOTHER** FOR THE LIST OF TIMES I'VE SAVED YOU.
I KNOW. YOU'RE ALMOST LEVEL WITH **ME SAVING YOU**.

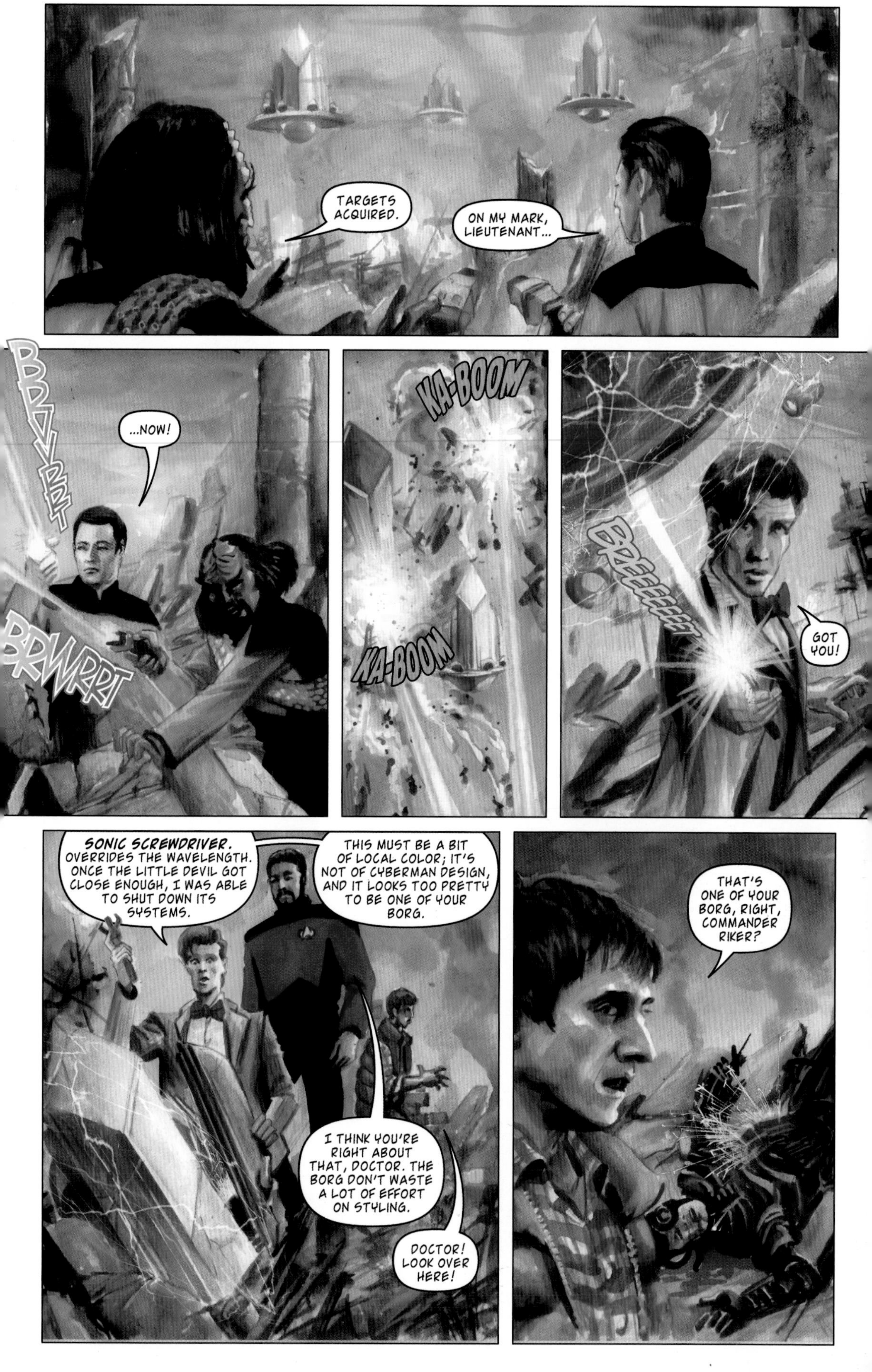
TARGETS ACQUIRED.
ON MY MARK, LIEUTENANT...
BRRVRRT
...NOW!
BRWRRT
KA-BOOM
KA-BOOM
BREEEEEEET
GOT YOU!
SONIC SCREWDRIVER. OVERRIDES THE WAVELENGTH. ONCE THE LITTLE DEVIL GOT CLOSE ENOUGH, I WAS ABLE TO SHUT DOWN ITS SYSTEMS.
THIS MUST BE A BIT OF LOCAL COLOR; IT'S NOT OF CYBERMAN DESIGN, AND IT LOOKS TOO PRETTY TO BE ONE OF YOUR BORG.
I THINK YOU'RE RIGHT ABOUT THAT, DOCTOR. THE BORG DON'T WASTE A LOT OF EFFORT ON STYLING.
DOCTOR! LOOK OVER HERE!
THAT'S ONE OF YOUR BORG, RIGHT, COMMANDER RIKER?

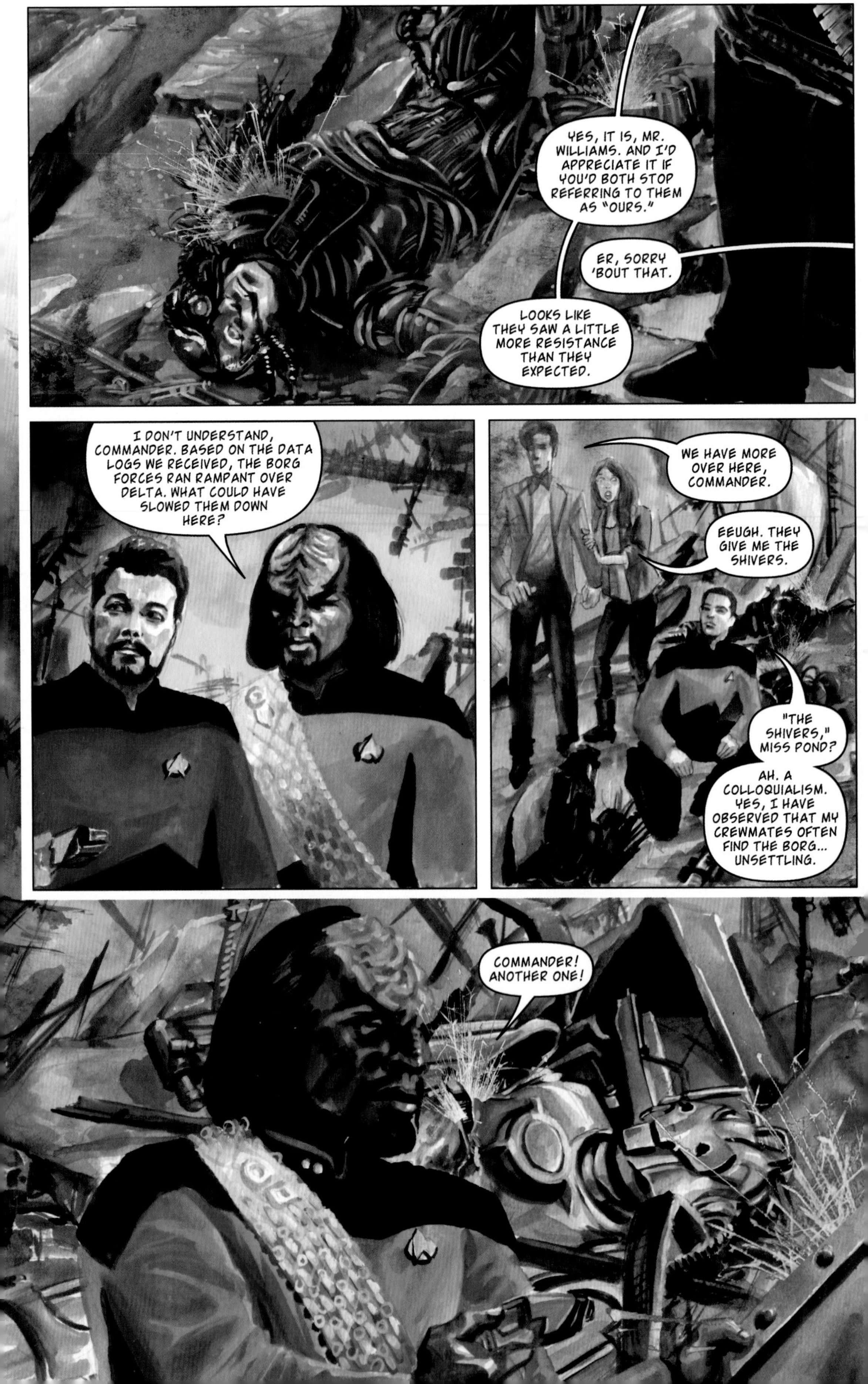
YES, IT IS, MR. WILLIAMS. AND I'D APPRECIATE IT IF YOU'D BOTH STOP REFERRING TO THEM AS "OURS."
ER, SORRY 'BOUT THAT.
LOOKS LIKE THEY SAW A LITTLE MORE RESISTANCE THAN THEY EXPECTED.
I DON'T UNDERSTAND, COMMANDER. BASED ON THE DATA LOGS WE RECEIVED, THE BORG FORCES RAN RAMPANT OVER DELTA. WHAT COULD HAVE SLOWED THEM DOWN HERE?
WE HAVE MORE OVER HERE, COMMANDER.
EEUGH. THEY GIVE ME THE SHIVERS.
"THE SHIVERS," MISS POND?
AH. A COLLOQUIALISM. YES, I HAVE OBSERVED THAT MY CREWMATES OFTEN FIND THE BORG... UNSETTLING.
COMMANDER! ANOTHER ONE!

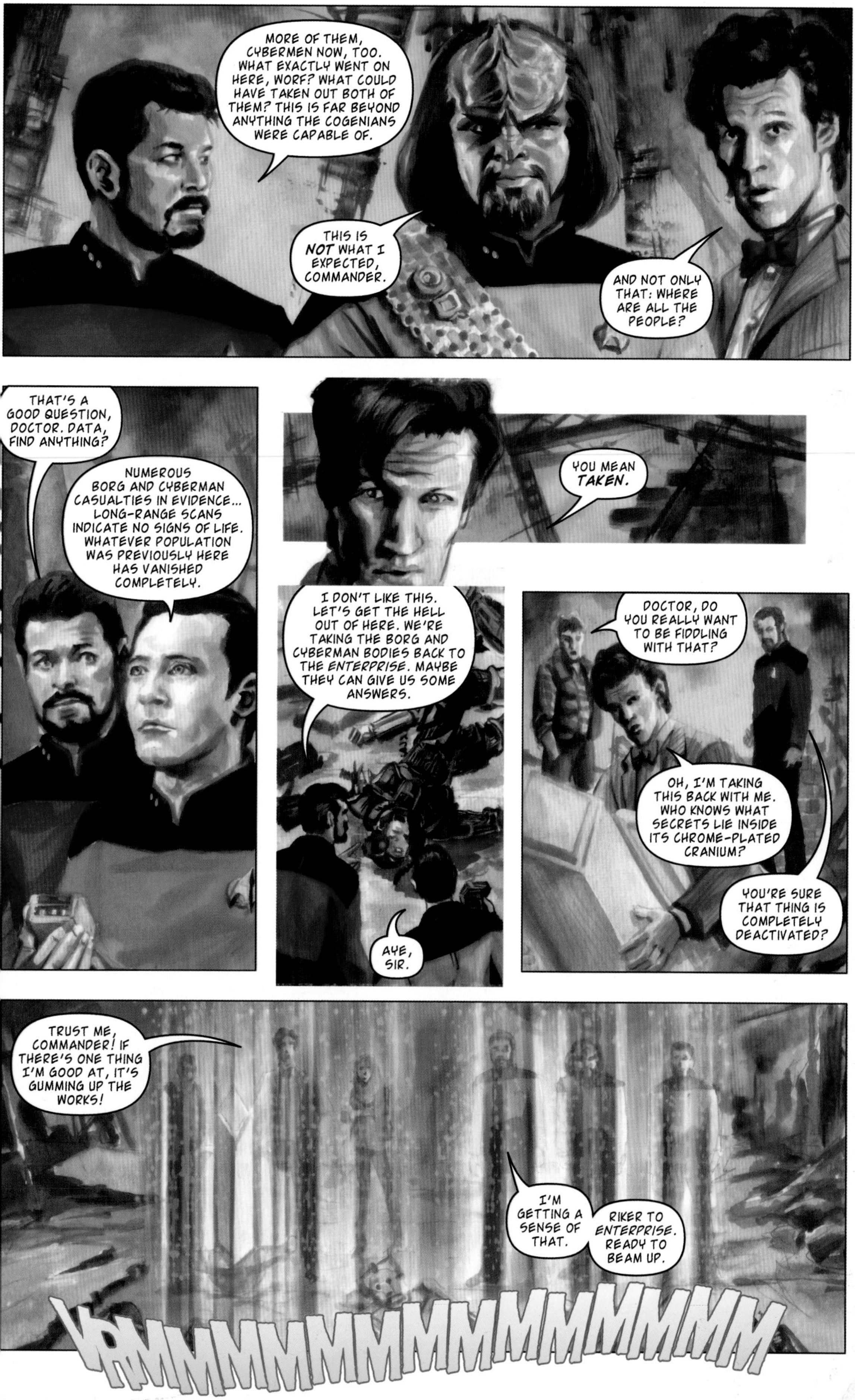

MORE OF THEM, CYBERMEN NOW, TOO. WHAT EXACTLY WENT ON HERE, WORF? WHAT COULD HAVE TAKEN OUT BOTH OF THEM? THIS IS FAR BEYOND ANYTHING THE COGENIANS WERE CAPABLE OF.
THIS IS *NOT* WHAT I EXPECTED, COMMANDER.
AND NOT ONLY THAT: WHERE ARE ALL THE PEOPLE?
THAT'S A GOOD QUESTION, DOCTOR. DATA, FIND ANYTHING?
NUMEROUS BORG AND CYBERMAN CASUALTIES IN EVIDENCE... LONG-RANGE SCANS INDICATE NO SIGNS OF LIFE. WHATEVER POPULATION WAS PREVIOUSLY HERE HAS VANISHED COMPLETELY.
YOU MEAN ***TAKEN.***
I DON'T LIKE THIS. LET'S GET THE HELL OUT OF HERE. WE'RE TAKING THE BORG AND CYBERMAN BODIES BACK TO THE *ENTERPRISE*. MAYBE THEY CAN GIVE US SOME ANSWERS.
AYE, SIR.
DOCTOR, DO YOU REALLY WANT TO BE FIDDLING WITH THAT?
OH, I'M TAKING THIS BACK WITH ME. WHO KNOWS WHAT SECRETS LIE INSIDE ITS CHROME-PLATED CRANIUM?
YOU'RE SURE THAT THING IS COMPLETELY DEACTIVATED?
TRUST ME, COMMANDER! IF THERE'S ONE THING I'M GOOD AT, IT'S GUMMING UP THE WORKS!
I'M GETTING A SENSE OF THAT.
RIKER TO *ENTERPRISE*. READY TO BEAM UP.
VRMMMMMMMMMMMMMMMMMM

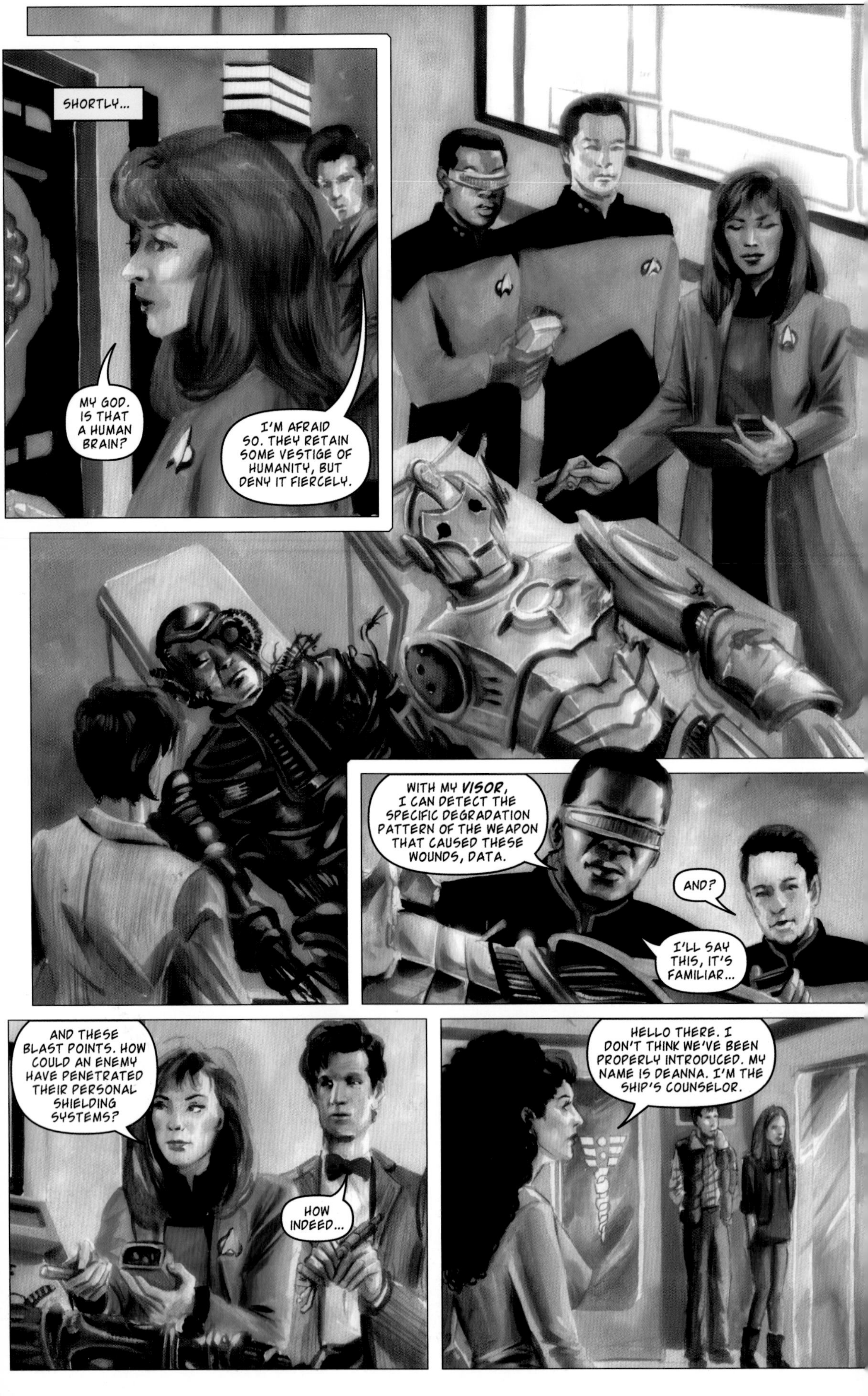
SHORTLY...
MY GOD. IS THAT A HUMAN BRAIN?
I'M AFRAID SO. THEY RETAIN SOME VESTIGE OF HUMANITY, BUT DENY IT FIERCELY.
WITH MY VISOR, I CAN DETECT THE SPECIFIC DEGRADATION PATTERN OF THE WEAPON THAT CAUSED THESE WOUNDS, DATA.
AND?
I'LL SAY THIS, IT'S FAMILIAR...
AND THESE BLAST POINTS. HOW COULD AN ENEMY HAVE PENETRATED THEIR PERSONAL SHIELDING SYSTEMS?
HOW INDEED...
HELLO THERE. I DON'T THINK WE'VE BEEN PROPERLY INTRODUCED. MY NAME IS DEANNA. I'M THE SHIP'S COUNSELOR.

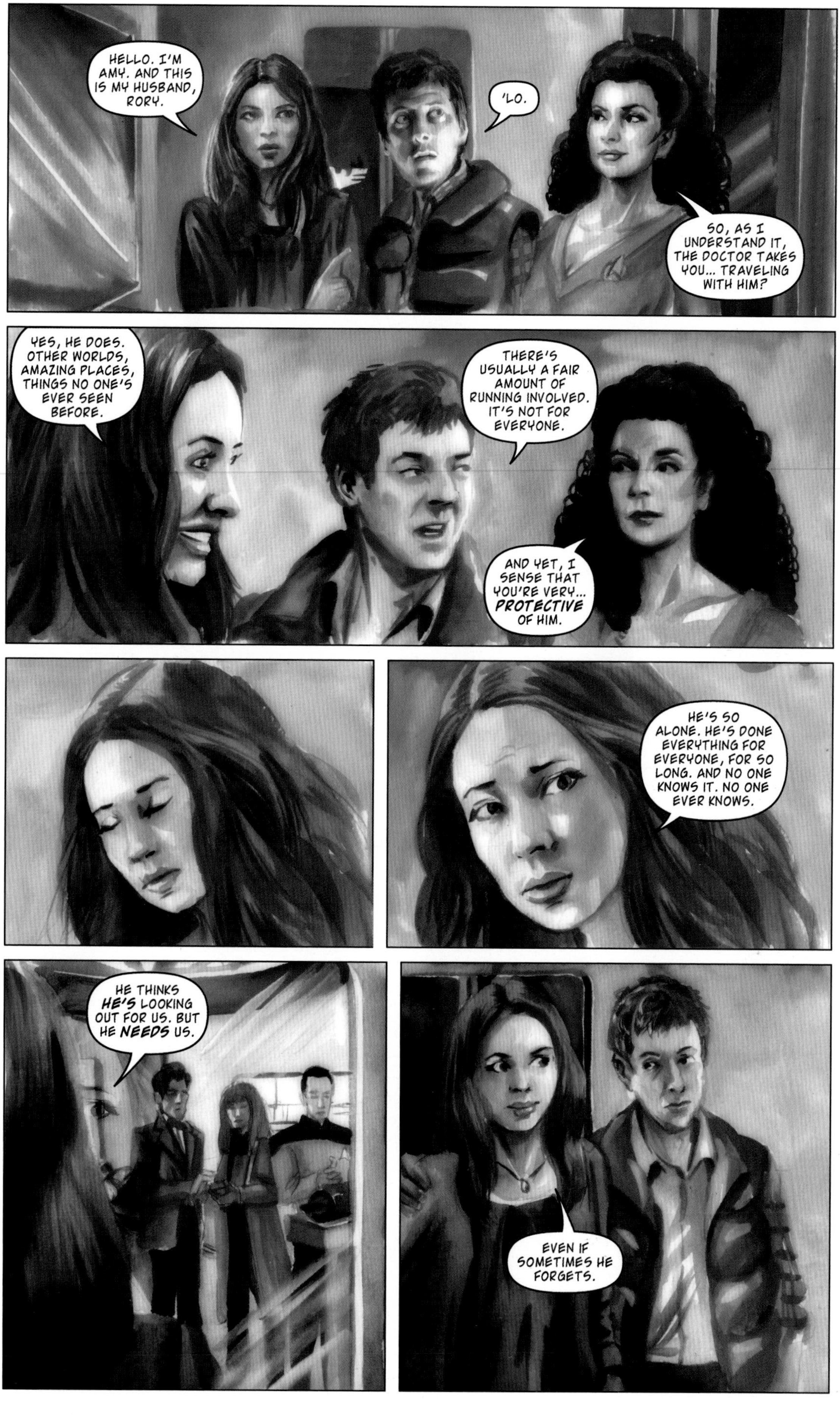
HELLO. I'M AMY. AND THIS IS MY HUSBAND, RORY.
'LO.
SO, AS I UNDERSTAND IT, THE DOCTOR TAKES YOU... TRAVELING WITH HIM?
YES, HE DOES. OTHER WORLDS, AMAZING PLACES, THINGS NO ONE'S EVER SEEN BEFORE.
THERE'S USUALLY A FAIR AMOUNT OF RUNNING INVOLVED. IT'S NOT FOR EVERYONE.
AND YET, I SENSE THAT YOU'RE VERY... ***PROTECTIVE*** OF HIM.
HE'S SO ALONE. HE'S DONE EVERYTHING FOR EVERYONE, FOR SO LONG. AND NO ONE KNOWS IT. NO ONE EVER KNOWS.
HE THINKS ***HE'S*** LOOKING OUT FOR US. BUT HE ***NEEDS*** US.
EVEN IF SOMETIMES HE FORGETS.

LATER...

THE EVIDENCE IS UNDENIABLE, CAPTAIN. THERE WAS NO ATTACK FROM A THIRD PARTY ON THE BORG AND CYBERMAN FORCES ON COGEN V.

I DON'T UNDERSTAND.

THE FRAGMENTATION AND DEGRADATION PATTERNS ON THE CYBERMAN'S WOUNDS MATCH PRECISELY THOSE OF BORG CUTTING BEAMS. AND HOW ELSE COULD ENERGY WEAPONS HAVE GOTTEN PAST THE BORG SHIELDING UNLESS THAT TECHNOLOGY HAD BEEN SHARED?

THE BORG AND THE CYBERMEN WERE KILLING EACH OTHER.

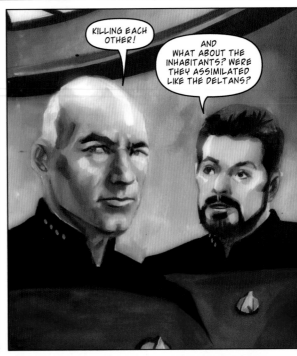

KILLING EACH OTHER!

AND WHAT ABOUT THE INHABITANTS? WERE THEY ASSIMILATED LIKE THE DELTANS?

I'M AFRAID I MAY HAVE SOME ANSWERS FOR YOU, COMMANDER. I MANAGED TO PICK MY WAY THROUGH THE ELECTRONIC BRAIN OF THIS SENTRY DRONE FROM THE PLANET, AND SECURED SOME VIDEO FROM ITS MEMORY. WITH YOUR PERMISSION, DOCTOR?

OF COURSE.

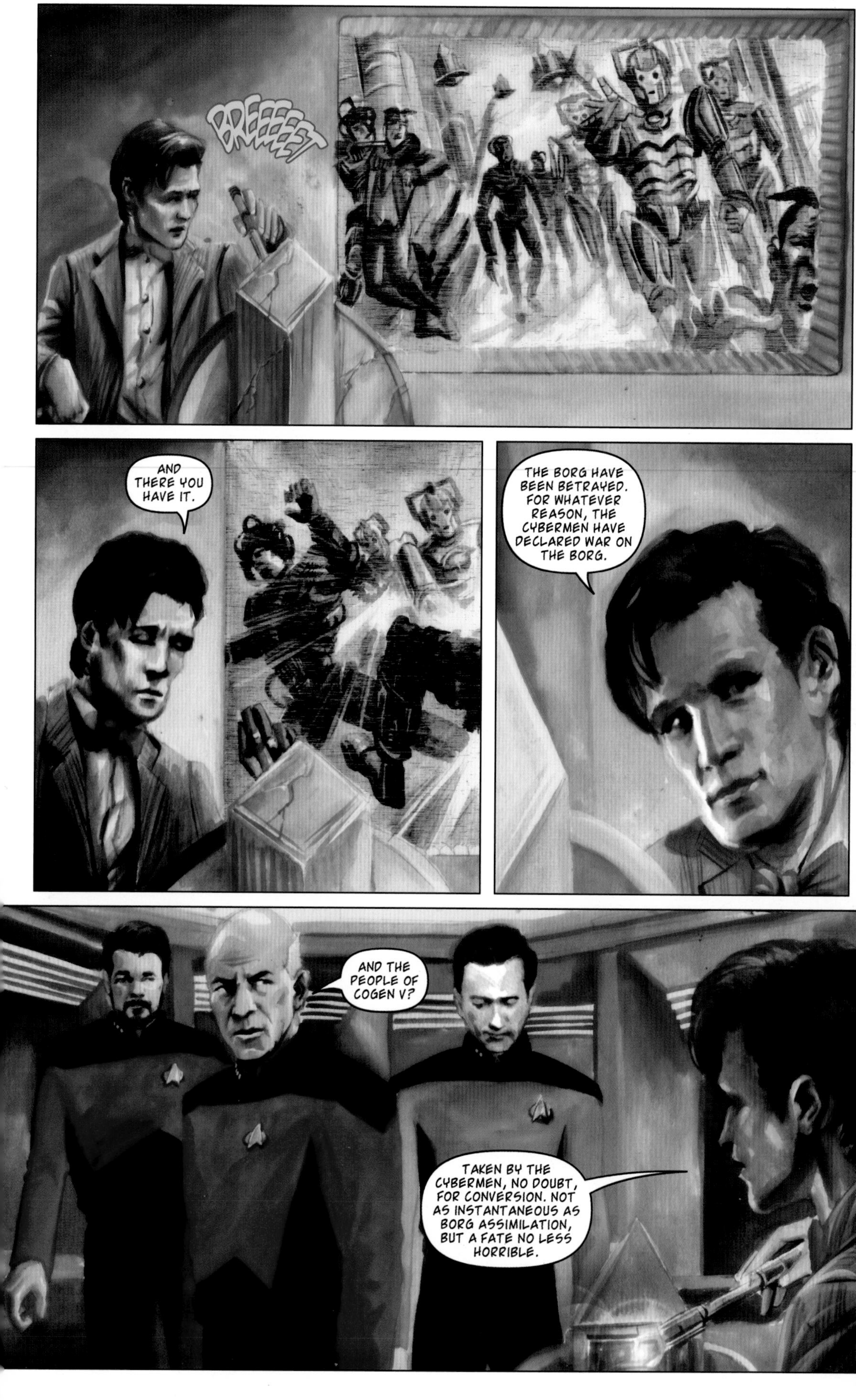
BREEEEEET
AND THERE YOU HAVE IT.
THE BORG HAVE BEEN BETRAYED. FOR WHATEVER REASON, THE CYBERMEN HAVE DECLARED WAR ON THE BORG.
AND THE PEOPLE OF COGEN V?
TAKEN BY THE CYBERMEN, NO DOUBT, FOR CONVERSION. NOT AS INSTANTANEOUS AS BORG ASSIMILATION, BUT A FATE NO LESS HORRIBLE.

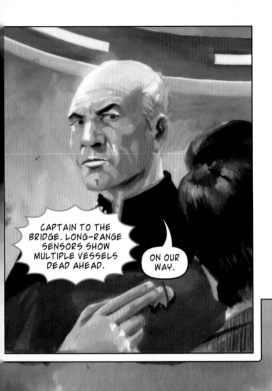

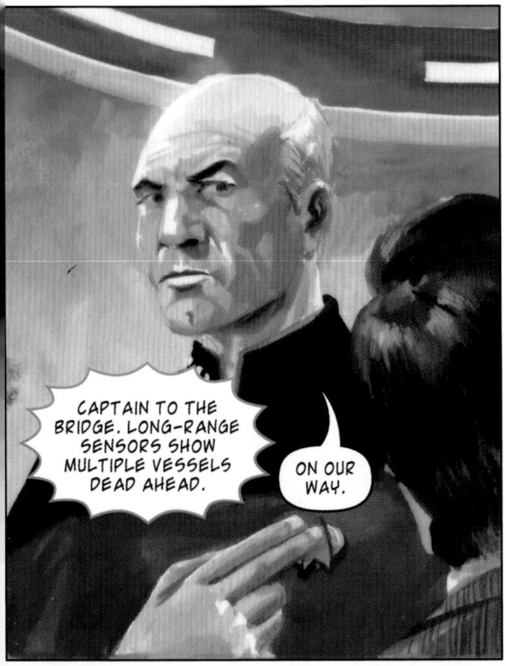
CAPTAIN TO THE BRIDGE. LONG-RANGE SENSORS SHOW MULTIPLE VESSELS DEAD AHEAD.
ON OUR WAY.

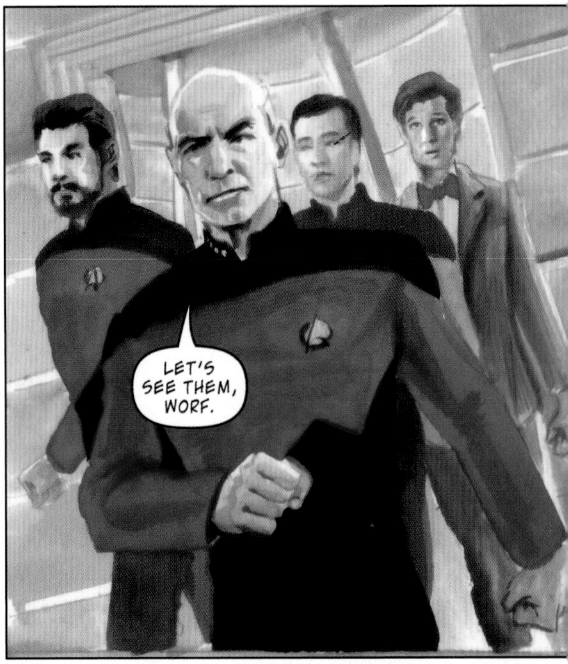
LET'S SEE THEM, WORF.

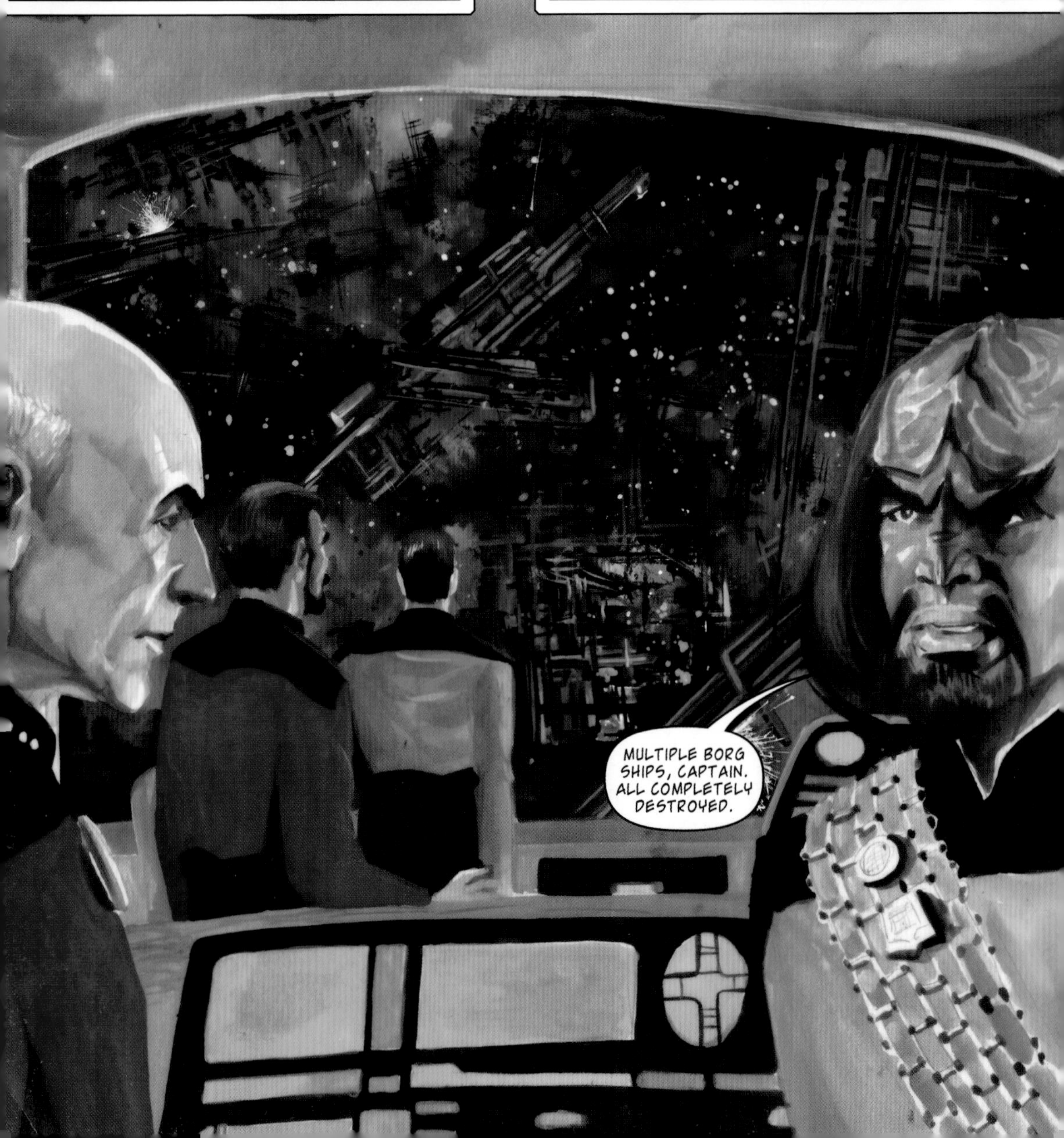
MULTIPLE BORG SHIPS, CAPTAIN. ALL COMPLETELY DESTROYED.

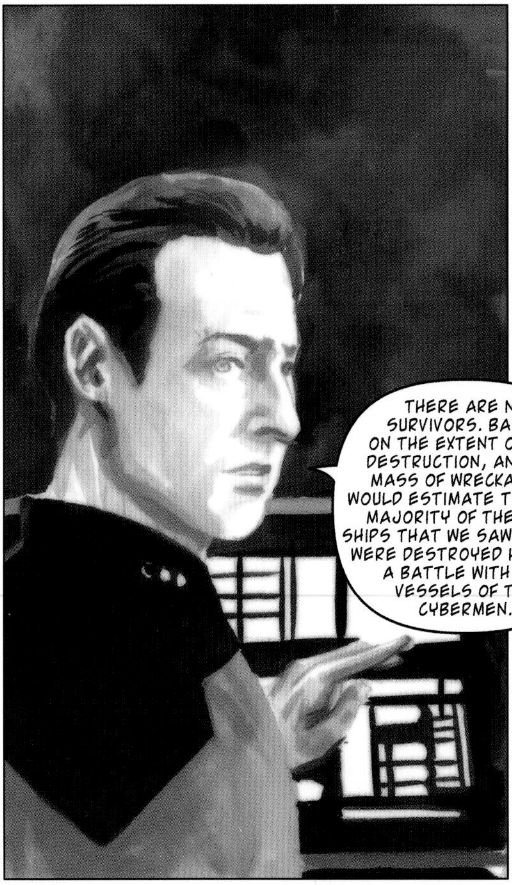
THERE ARE NO SURVIVORS. BASED ON THE EXTENT OF THE DESTRUCTION, AND THE MASS OF WRECKAGE, I WOULD ESTIMATE THAT THE MAJORITY OF THE BORG SHIPS THAT WE SAW EARLIER WERE DESTROYED HERE, IN A BATTLE WITH THE VESSELS OF THE CYBERMEN.

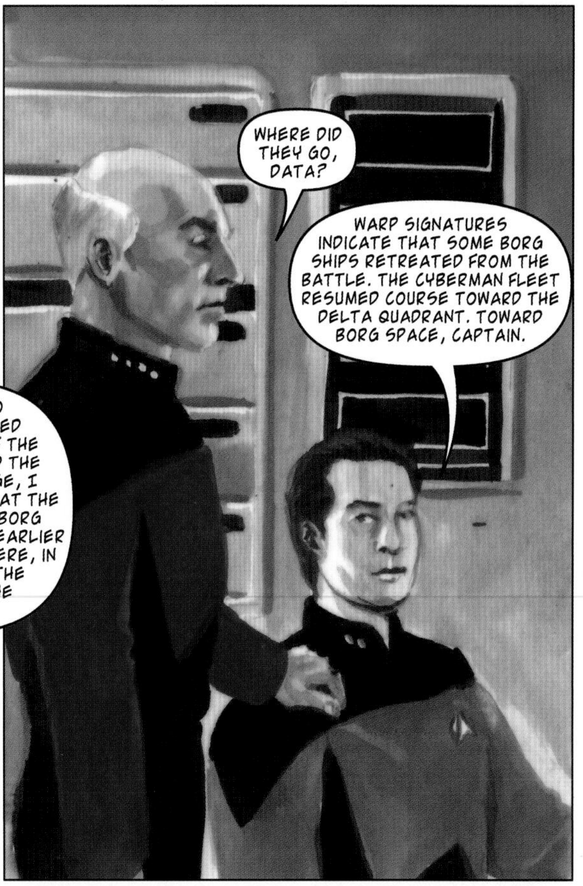
WHERE DID THEY GO, DATA?
WARP SIGNATURES INDICATE THAT SOME BORG SHIPS RETREATED FROM THE BATTLE. THE CYBERMAN FLEET RESUMED COURSE TOWARD THE DELTA QUADRANT. TOWARD BORG SPACE, CAPTAIN.

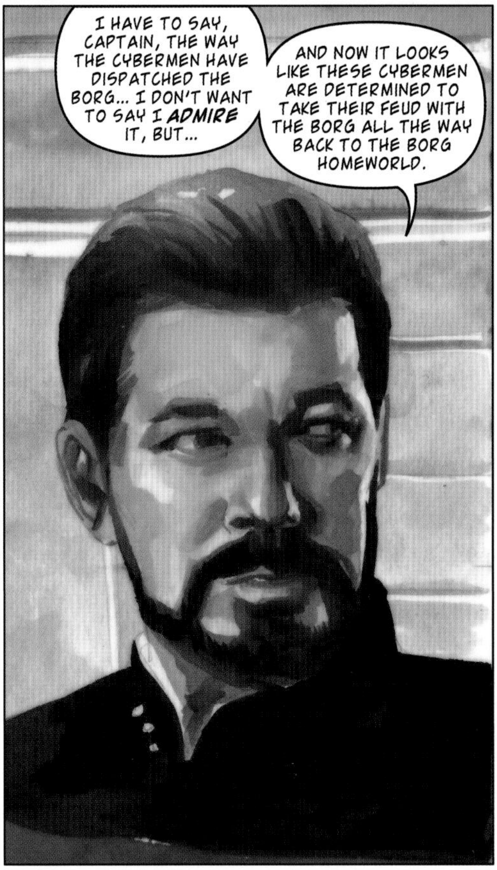
I HAVE TO SAY, CAPTAIN, THE WAY THE CYBERMEN HAVE DISPATCHED THE BORG... I DON'T WANT TO SAY I ADMIRE IT, BUT...
AND NOW IT LOOKS LIKE THESE CYBERMEN ARE DETERMINED TO TAKE THEIR FEUD WITH THE BORG ALL THE WAY BACK TO THE BORG HOMEWORLD.

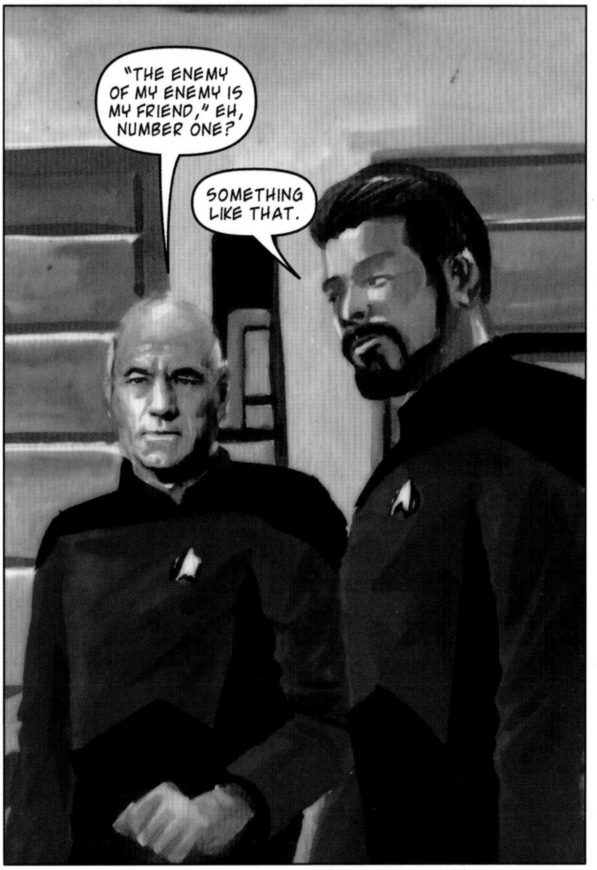
"THE ENEMY OF MY ENEMY IS MY FRIEND," EH, NUMBER ONE?
SOMETHING LIKE THAT.

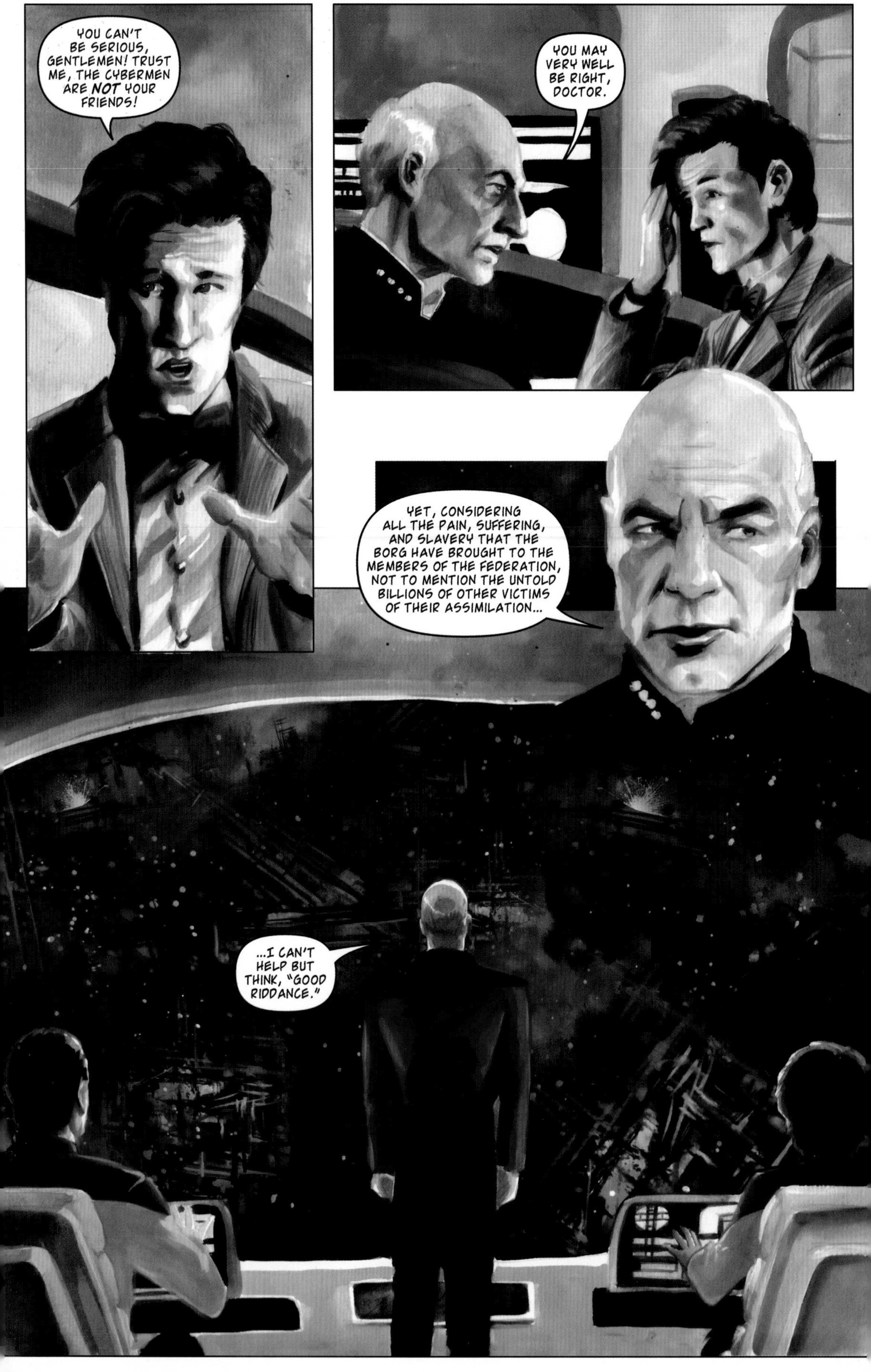
YOU CAN'T BE SERIOUS, GENTLEMEN! TRUST ME, THE CYBERMEN ARE NOT YOUR FRIENDS!
YOU MAY VERY WELL BE RIGHT, DOCTOR.
YET, CONSIDERING ALL THE PAIN, SUFFERING, AND SLAVERY THAT THE BORG HAVE BROUGHT TO THE MEMBERS OF THE FEDERATION, NOT TO MENTION THE UNTOLD BILLIONS OF OTHER VICTIMS OF THEIR ASSIMILATION...
...I CAN'T HELP BUT THINK, "GOOD RIDDANCE."

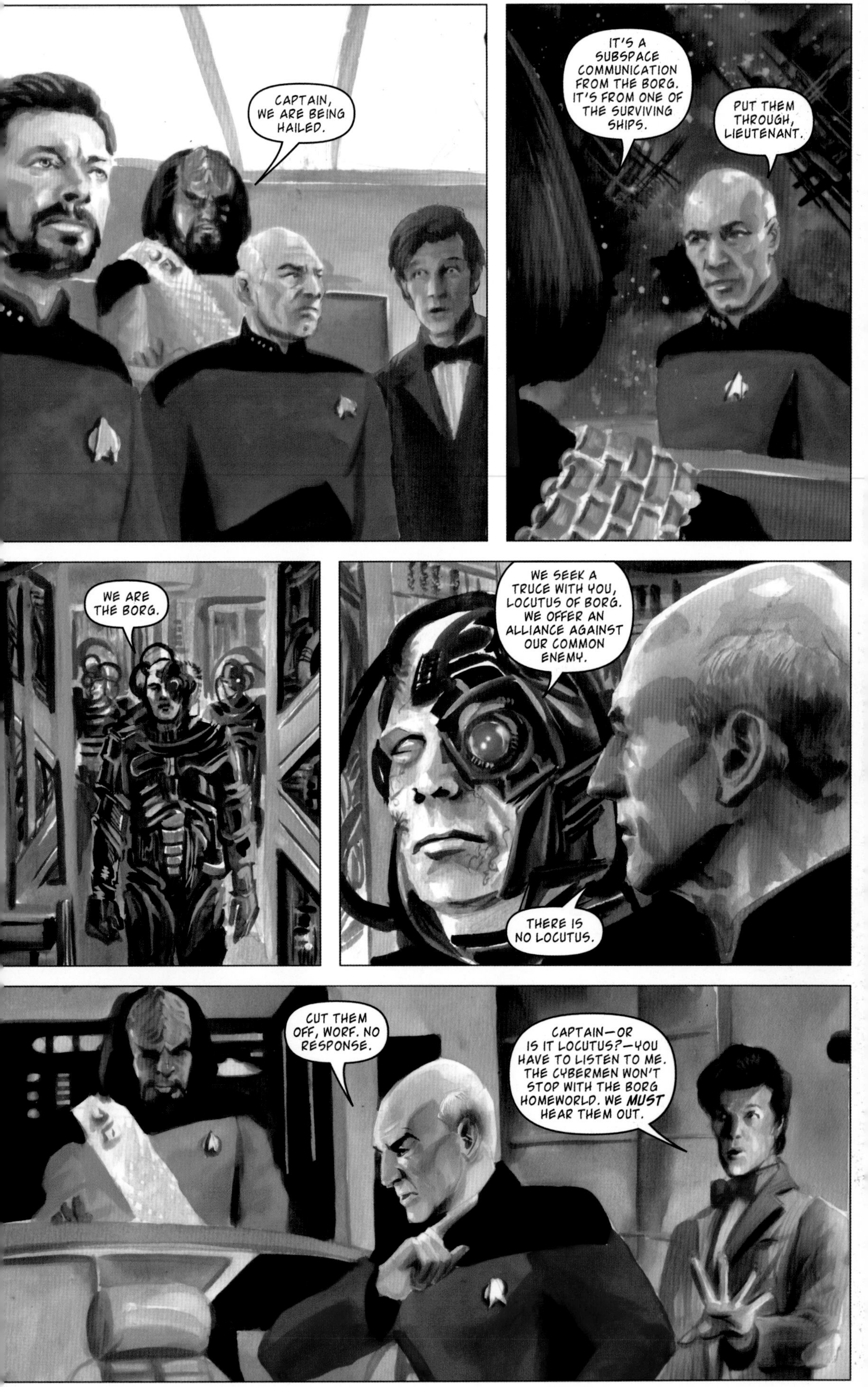
CAPTAIN, WE ARE BEING HAILED.
IT'S A SUBSPACE COMMUNICATION FROM THE BORG. IT'S FROM ONE OF THE SURVIVING SHIPS.
PUT THEM THROUGH, LIEUTENANT.
WE ARE THE BORG.
WE SEEK A TRUCE WITH YOU, LOCUTUS OF BORG. WE OFFER AN ALLIANCE AGAINST OUR COMMON ENEMY.
THERE IS NO LOCUTUS.
CUT THEM OFF, WORF. NO RESPONSE.
CAPTAIN—OR IS IT LOCUTUS?—YOU HAVE TO LISTEN TO ME. THE CYBERMEN WON'T STOP WITH THE BORG HOMEWORLD. WE *MUST* HEAR THEM OUT.

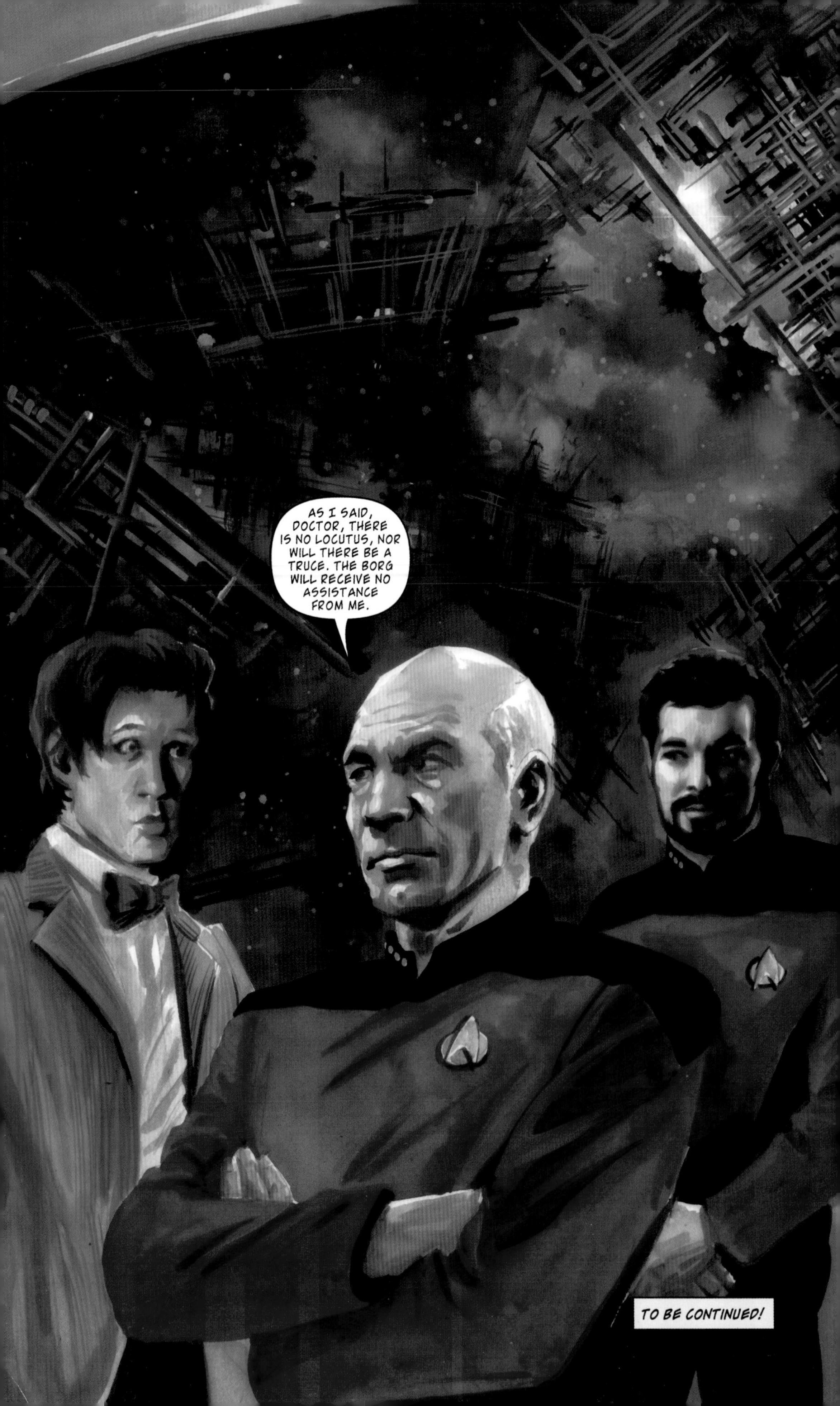

AS I SAID, DOCTOR, THERE IS NO LOCUTUS, NOR WILL THERE BE A TRUCE. THE BORG WILL RECEIVE NO ASSISTANCE FROM ME.
TO BE CONTINUED!

ART
GALLERY

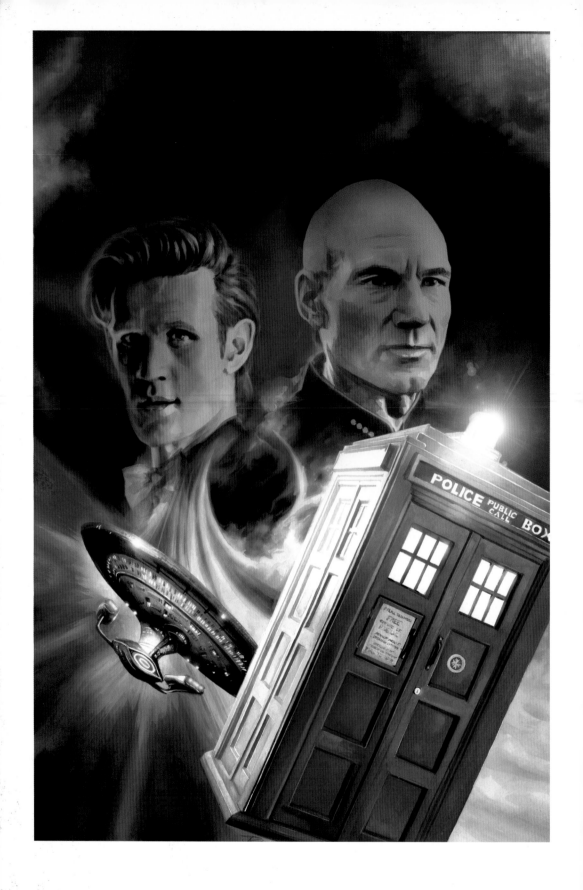

this page and opposite page: art by J.K. Woodward

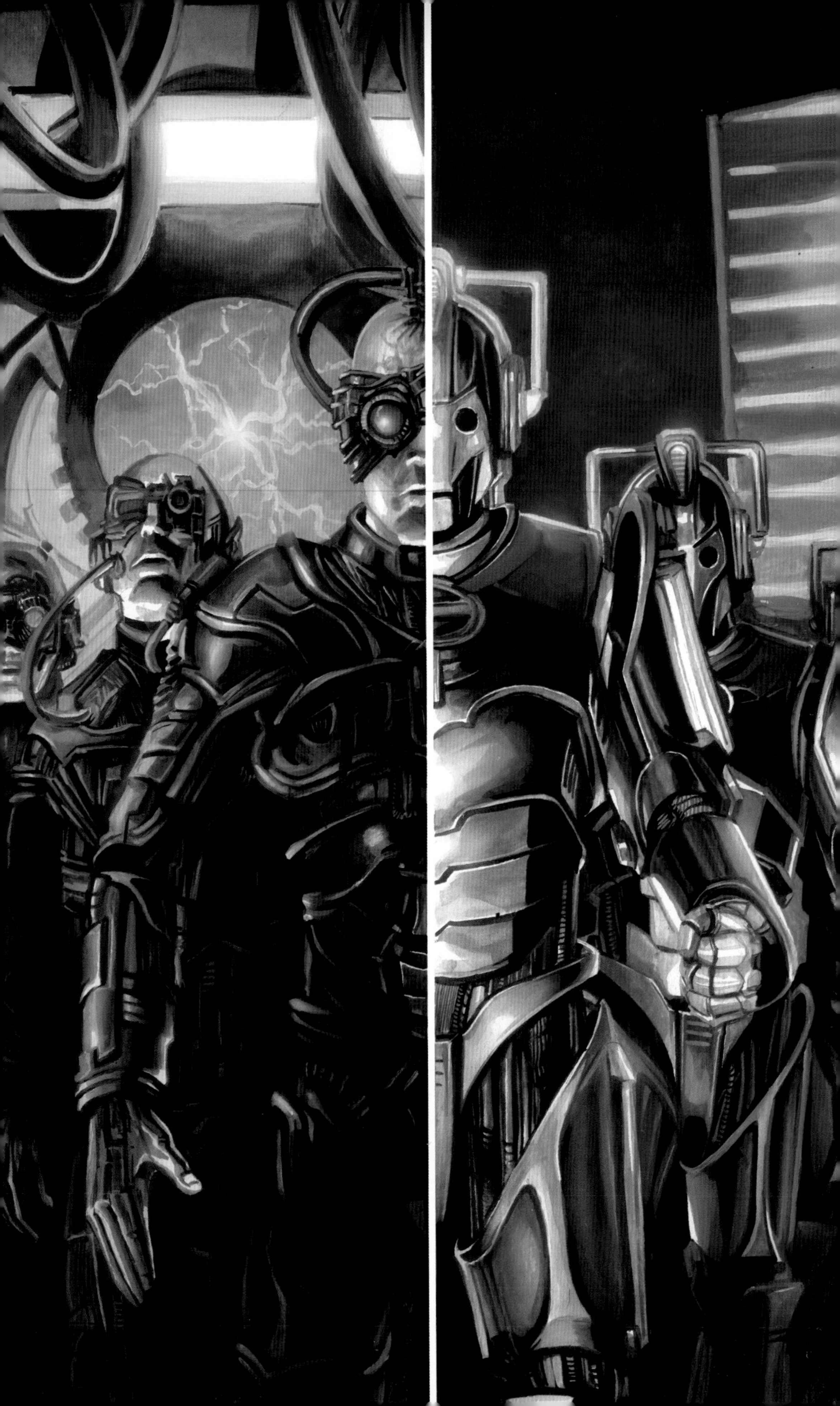

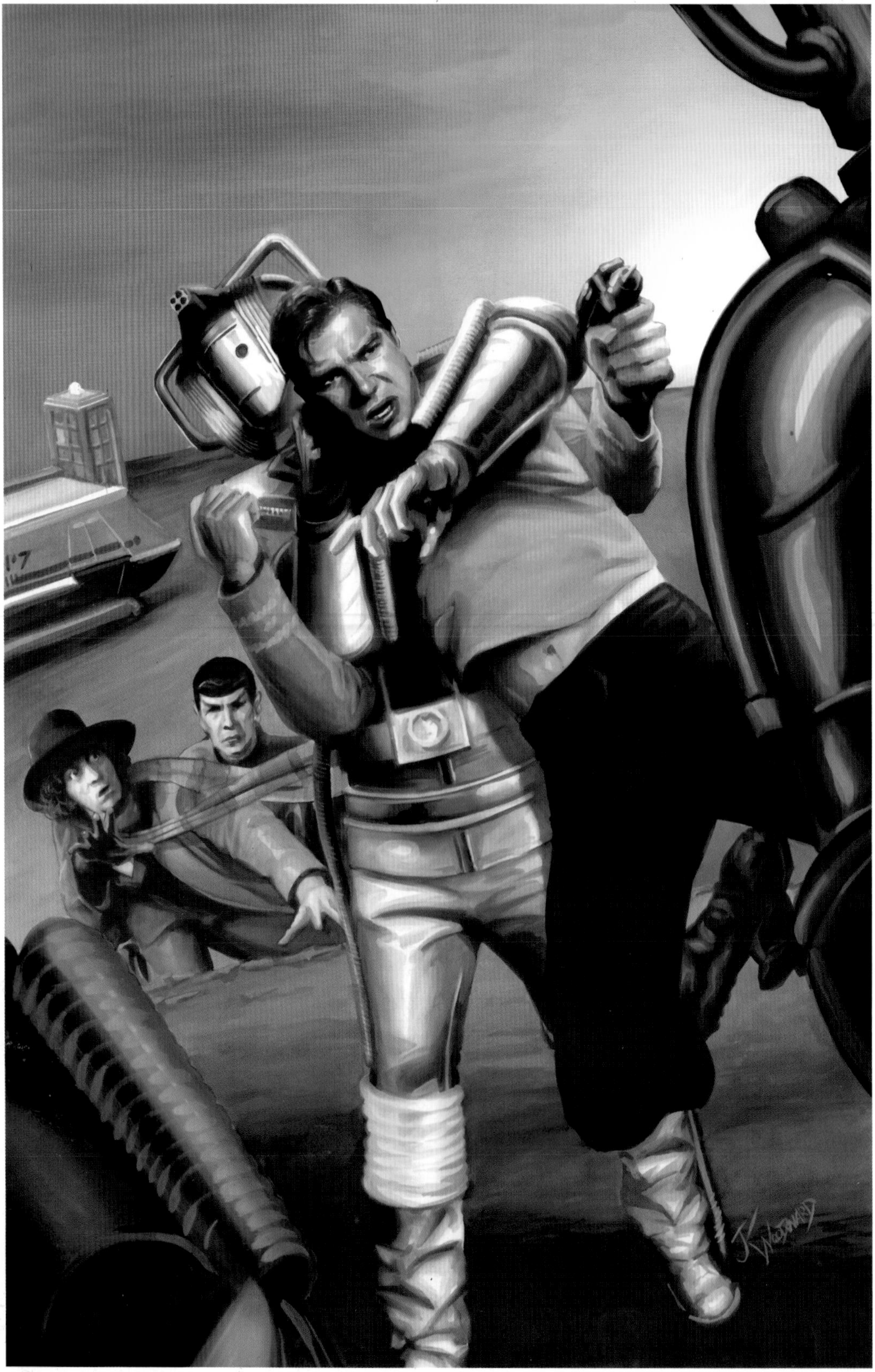

this page and opposite page: art by J.K. Woodward

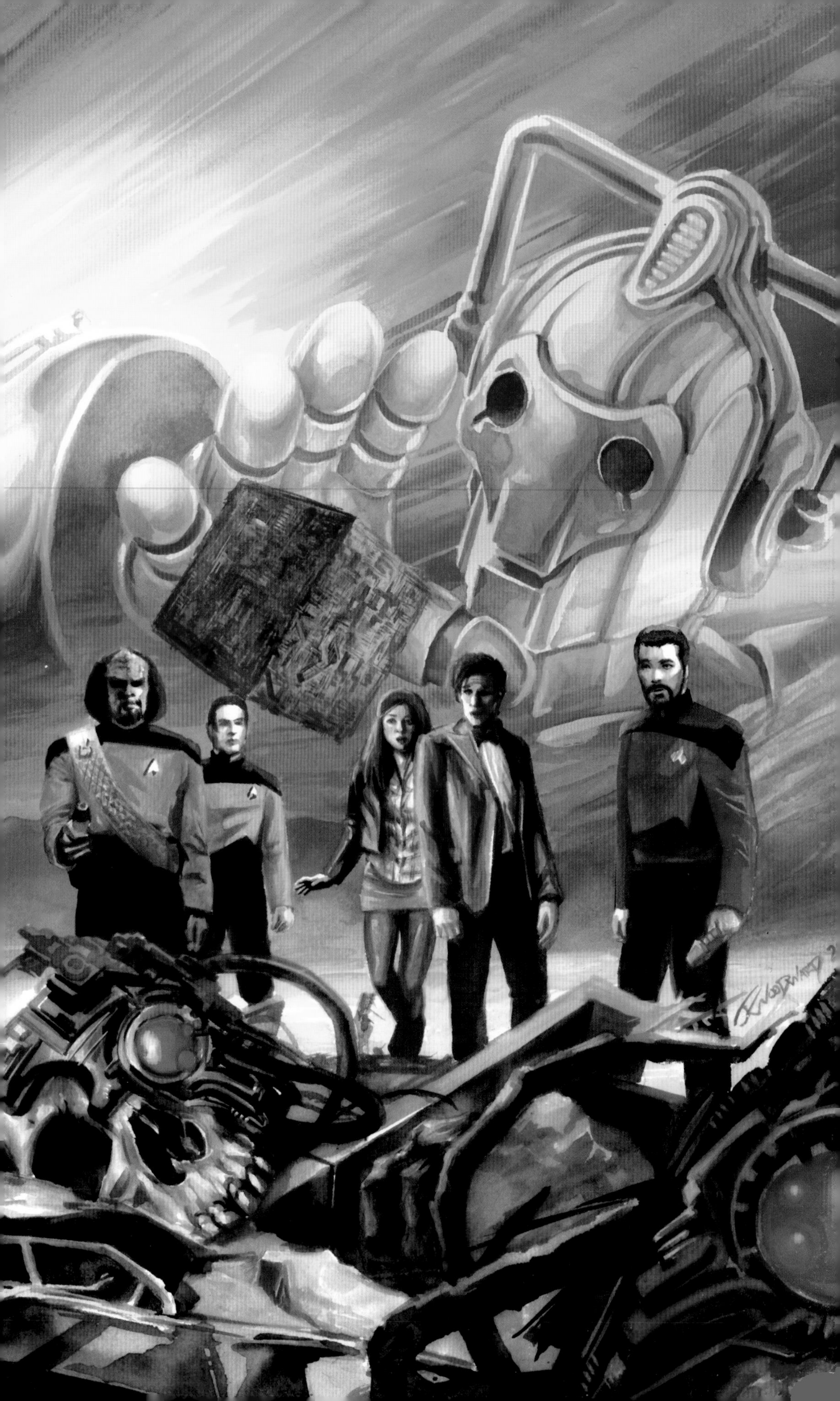

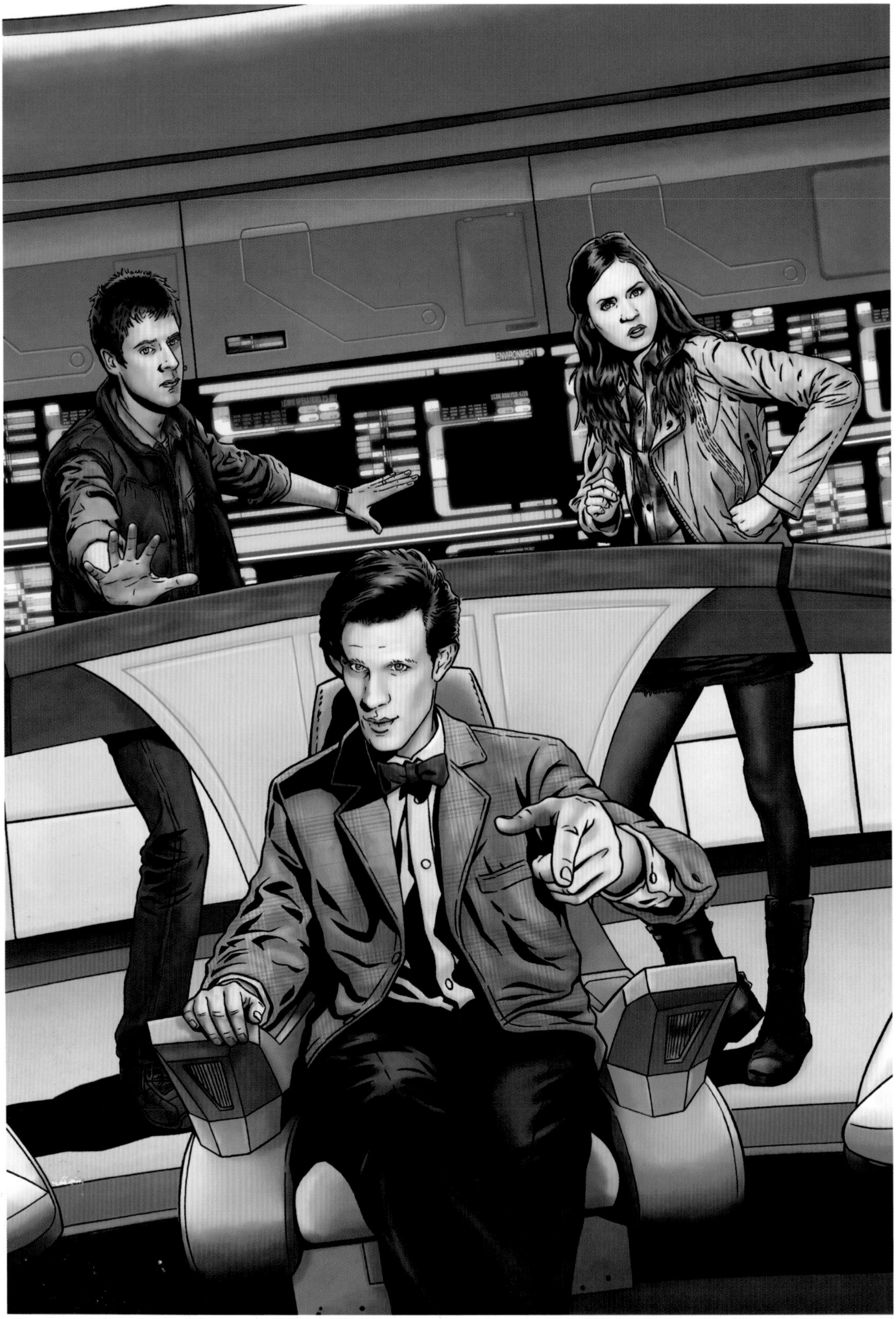
ENVIRONMENT

this page and opposite page: art by Joe Corroney

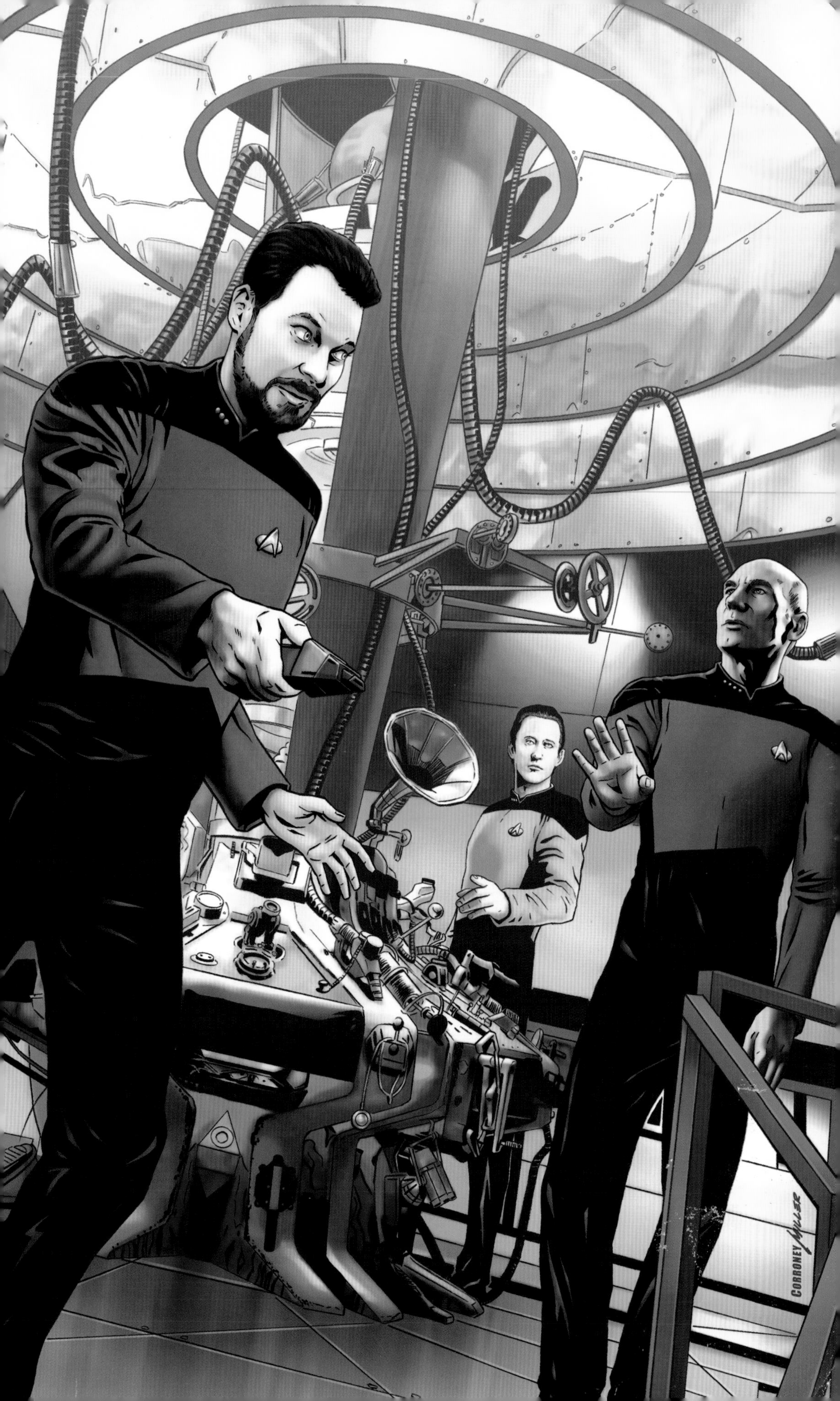
CORRONEY MILLER

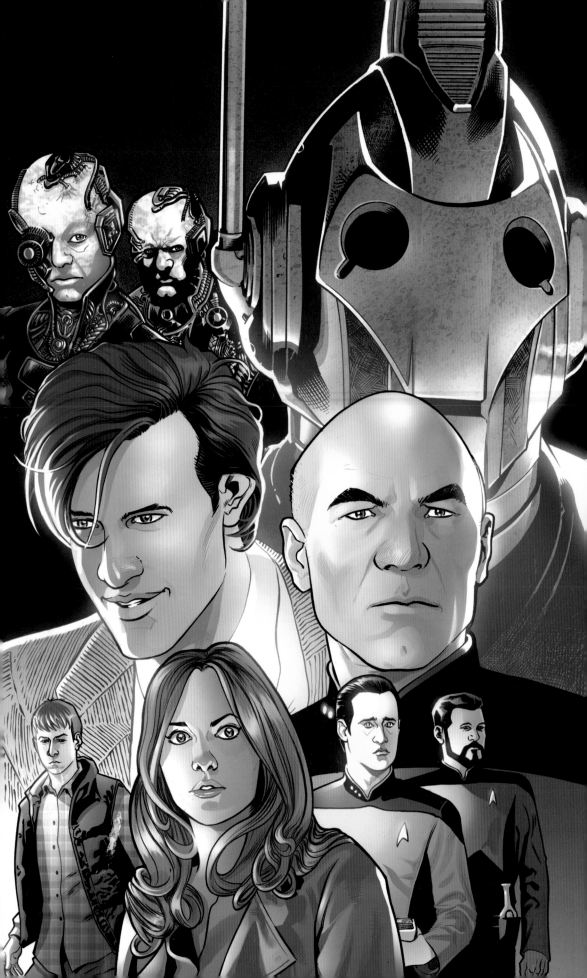

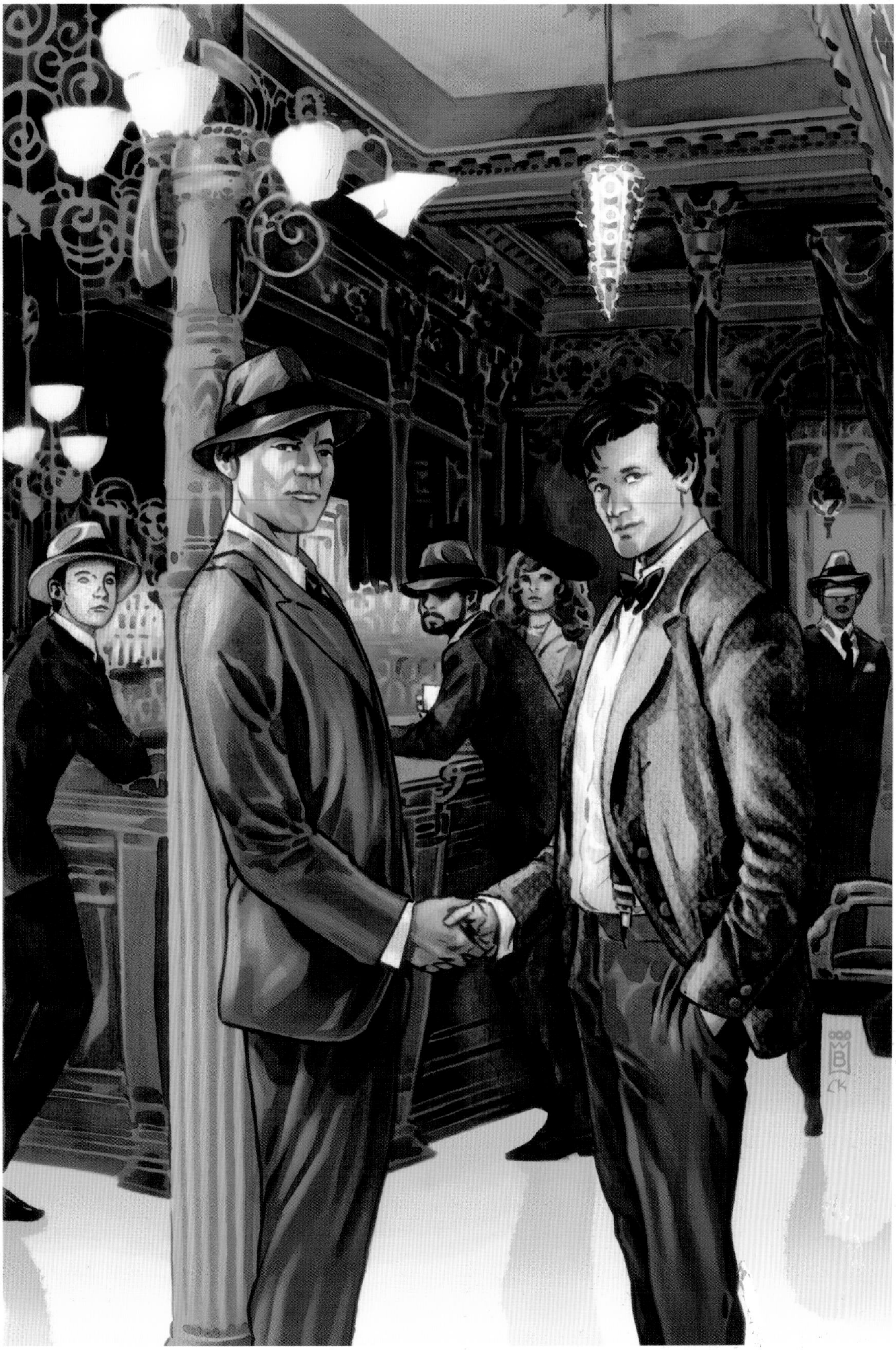

art by Mark Buckingham, Colors by Charlie Kirchoff

opposite page: art by David Messina, Colors by Giovanna Niro

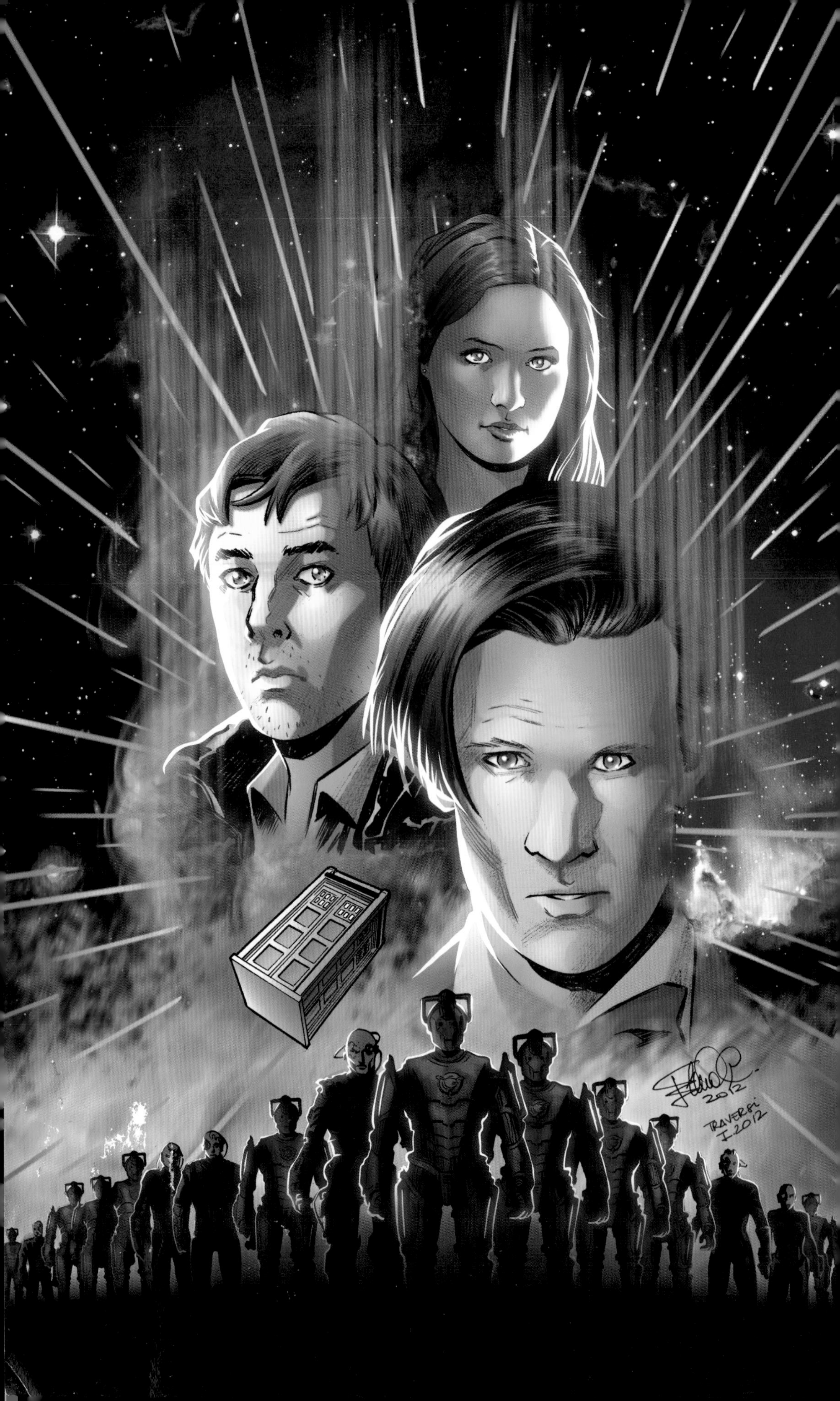
2012
TRAVERSI
I.2012

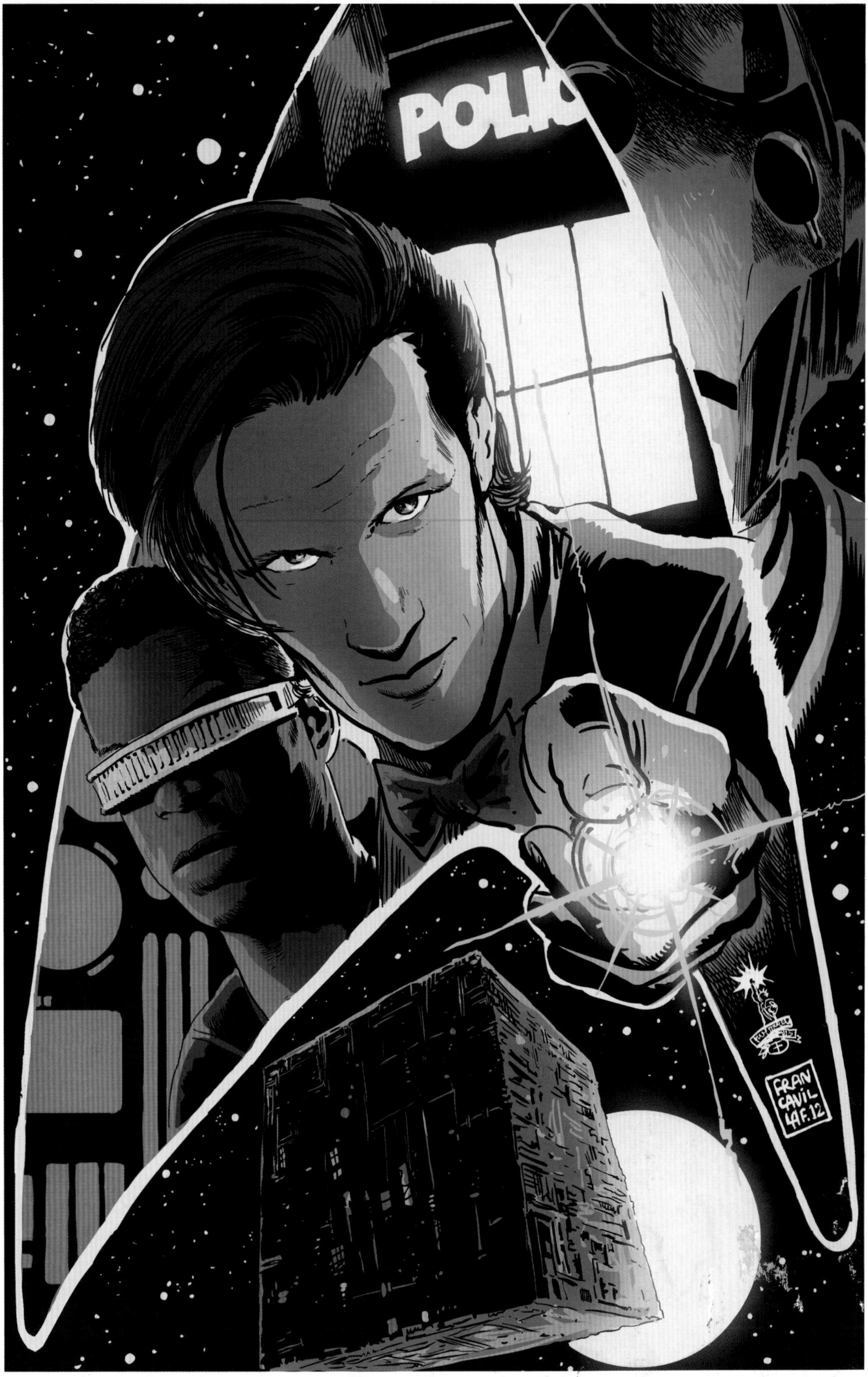
POLIC
FRAN CAVIL LAF. 12

art by Francesco Francavilla

opposite page: art Elena Casagrande, Colors by Ilaria Traversi

More Star Trek and Doctor Who titles from

STAR TREK
VOLUME 1

Star Trek, Vol. 1
ISBN: 978-1-61377-150-1

Doctor Who
Series 2, Vol. 1
ISBN: 978-1-60010-974-

STAR TREK
THE NEXT GENERATION
INTELLIGENCE GATHERING

Star Trek:
The Next Generation:
Intelligence Gathering
ISBN: 978-1-60010-199-1

DOCTOR WHO
A Fairytale Life

Doctor Who:
A Fairytale Life
ISBN: 978-1-61377-022-1

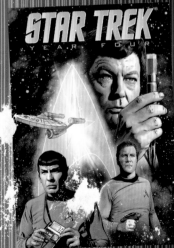

STAR TREK
YEAR FOUR

Star Trek: Year Four
ISBN: 978-1-60010-161-8

"BEAUTIFULLY DONE." — DAVID TENNANT
DOCTOR · WHO
THE · FORGOTTEN
TONY LEE · PIA GUERRA
WITH KELLY YATES · STEFANO MARTINO · NICK ROCHE

Doctor Who:
The Forgotten
ISBN: 978-1-60010-396-4